INSPECTING
A HOUSE

INSPECTING A HOUSE

REX CAULDWELL

The Taunton Press

Publisher: JIM CHILDS
Acquisitions Editor: STEVE CULPEPPER
Editor: PETER CHAPMAN
Copy Editor: CANDACE LEVY
Indexer: HARRIET HODGES
Cover Designer: STEVE HUGHES
Layout Artist: SUZIE YANNES
Cover Photographer: SCOTT PHILLIPS
Interior Photographer: REX CAULDWELL (EXCEPT WHERE NOTED)
Illustrator: RON CARBONI

The Taunton Press
Inspiration for hands-on living™

Printed in the United States of America
10 9 8 7 6 5 4 3 2

For Pros / By Pros® is a trademark of The Taunton Press, Inc., registered in the U.S.
Patent and Trademark Office.

The Taunton Press, Inc., 63 South Main Street,
PO Box 5506, Newtown, CT 06470-5506
e-mail: tp@taunton.com

Distributed by Publishers Group West

Library of Congress Cataloging-in-Publication Data
Cauldwell, Rex.
    Inspecting a house / Rex Cauldwell.
        p. cm.
    Includes index.
    ISBN 1-56158-462-2
     1. Dwellings—Inspection. I. Title.

TH4817.5 .C39 2001
643'.12—dc21   00-048408

To my granddaughters, Katy and Elizabeth, and all grandchildren everywhere

Acknowledgments

As always, it is impossible to thank and acknowledge all those people who have helped me put this book together. If I have omitted anyone, it was not intentional; just let me know and I'll be sure to bring you in on the next edition.

I'd like to thank the American Society of Home Inspectors; Peter and Chris Bartel; Katherine Cabaniss; Chris Burton and David Ratchford of Stucco Pro; Wayne Cook and all the great guys at CMC Supply; Sylvia Blankenship; Orkin Pest Control; all the nice ladies at Professional Equipment Supply; the wonderful people at Bacharach in both the United States and Ireland; Dan Redler of Siemens Electrical; Square D; James Handie Building Products; Raynor Garage Door; Tramex; Mirjam Pohl of the Geothermal Heat Pump Consortium, Inc.; Phil Rawlings; my friend at Faro Inspections; Charles Hayes; Tammy Sizemore; and all the people who let me photograph their houses on service calls, during inspections, and just because I thought there was something interesting to shoot.

Qué tus inspecciones sean agradables, tu vida feliz, y tus vaccaciones interminables.

CONTENTS

INTRODUCTION

This may sound like an exaggeration, but I believe the home inspector is responsible for saving more lives and property than any other tradesperson. Houses degrade from the day they are completed. And with human nature the way it is, many people won't fix a problem with their home unless they are forced to. Until the home inspection service came into being, houses were typically bought and sold in "as is" condition. This process continued from buyer to buyer until the house virtually fell apart or a disaster occurred.

The electrical system is a typical example. Owners of older houses have added extra receptacles and appliance loads to the point that you can almost see the smoke rising from the old ungrounded wiring and outdated, overloaded fuse panels. Many owners simply live with the problem. Only when the house is put up for sale does the electrical system get upgraded. In recommending the upgrade, the inspector can honestly say that he or she has possibly saved the house from burning down and perhaps taking some lives with it. Many times things look so bad it amazes even the most hardened of us. The inspector looks around the basement or crawl space, shudders, and then slowly backs out hoping nothing happens until he or she gets out of there.

Sometimes the plumbing isn't much better. The inspector often finds that drain lines are held together with duct tape and that water lines look like a sprinkler system. I know one homeowner couple who allowed a leaky pipe to drip onto the water heater for years, until it eventually ruined the heater. When they finally installed a new water heater, rather than fixing they leak, they moved the heater a foot over to the side and left the leak alone. I'm sorry to say that such illogic is commonplace when it comes to utilities.

Occasionally, houses are fixed up before they are sold, but these are the exceptions, not the rule. Owners who decide to sell a house rarely want to invest time and money in it because they usually won't get their money back. And when they decide the problem must be fixed, they do it themselves (although they may not quite understand the problem or how to fix it) or hire a not-quite-qualified nonprofessional to do it, which creates other problems. This process isn't new: The old saying "let the buyer beware" is just as appropriate now as it was when the Romans coined it.

A typical example would be homeowners who just found out that the hardboard composite siding on their house was rotting away. Or perhaps the siding is synthetic stucco and not only the siding but all the exterior walls are deteriorating. Rather than fix the problem themselves and be out many thousands of dollars, they would rather keep it quiet, sell the house, and let the new owners take care of it. But with the advent of the home inspection trade, many houses now get repaired before they're put on the market, because the owners know the house will be inspected and don't want the problems to hold up a sale. This gives the house a longer life expectancy and the new buyers a safer house. All in all, the home inspection profession has increased the quality of homes nationwide and made them safer for us all.

Who needs this book? Every home inspector who wants to be consistent and accurate in his or her inspection. But I didn't write it just for inspectors. It's also for every home seller who wants to know specifically what the inspector is going to be looking for, for every home buyer who wants to know specifically what to look for in the house he or she is buying, and for every Realtor who wants to judge the quality and resalability of the house he or she is getting ready to list.

Chapter 1

THE INSPECTION PROCESS

PROFESSIONAL COURTESY

THE RULES OF
THE PROFESSION

CREATING A SYSTEM
OF INSPECTION

TOOLS OF THE TRADE

The home inspector's job is to provide a general, overall inspection of the home—it's that simple. The inspector is someone who has a working knowledge of many trades and can give an "overview" of the condition of the home. An overview means that the inspector will be listing "areas of concern"; if these areas of concern are considered significant, the owner or buyer will be advised to contact a specialist in that area for expert evaluation. For example, if an inspector suspects that a house sided with synthetic stucco has moisture problems, he or she will recommend that someone certified to evaluate this material be consulted.

An analogy would be a general medical practitioner finding something wrong with a patient and then sending him or her to a specialist. The specialist in our case would be a structural engineer, licensed electrician or plumber, pest-control expert, well driller, HVAC technician, or similar professional. Inspectors are the general practitioners—they do not compete with the specialists, they work with them.

Anyone who wants a home inspected has two choices: Spend a lot of money and bring in experts in all the trades or spend significantly less money and bring in one person who has a general knowledge of all. Most homeowners can ill afford to bring in all those individual professional services. For a certified structural engineer, master electrician, master plumber, and so on to inspect a house would cost the homeowner well over $1,000 (a typical home inspection costs about $300). And think of the headaches of trying to get that many people to a house in a short period of time. It was from this need to have a single person with a general knowledge of all the trades that the home inspection profession was born.

Professional Courtesy

Cooperation with other trades is the hallmark of a good inspector. Home inspectors should always cooperate with other professionals and recommend specific trades (not specific companies or people) when they think there is need. This way, you, as the inspector, will develop a good relationship with other tradespeople because you'll generate work for them rather than taking work away from them.

It's important for the home inspector to be congenial and polite—not just to the customer but to the other trades as well. (It's also advisable for the inspector to have a close and amicable relationship with as many Realtors as possible.) If you see something wrong, don't condemn it. For some, it's human nature to look at something and then proudly proclaim that it is the worst piece of construction they've ever seen, but try to keep your opinions to yourself.

The home inspector cannot "fail" a house—no one can do that, except perhaps a structural engineer along with a state inspector. The work of the home inspector is simply to list areas of concern— to look for and list possible problems, to observe and report. Something may fail a specific test done by the home inspector, but it still just an area of concern for the owner and buyer. Many times the problems *should* be fixed, but sometimes there is no legal reason the owner has to fix them—other times legalities are involved.

The homeowner and buyer will have to agree on what is to be repaired and what isn't. It's possible the sellers won't fix anything—they may simply tell the buyer, "If you want the house, fix

You'll need a trained eye to detect some problems; but others will be alarmingly obvious, as is the case with this combination brick-and-wood front-porch column, which is dangerously close to collapsing.

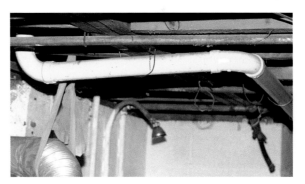

The inspector's job is to list "areas of concern" (observe and report), not to offer advice on how they should be fixed. One area of concern in this basement is a kitchen drain line that runs uphill.

it yourself." On the other hand, it's possible that the sellers are so desperate to sell the house that they'll fix anything just to do so. When neither party can agree on who is to pay for the repairs, I've even seen the Realtor pay just to allow the sale to go through.

Professional Organizations

It is recommended that all professional home inspectors join one of the following national organizations so they can stay current with what is happening in the field as well as share and obtain knowledge with others. It's also worth finding out if there's a local organization in your area. Many home inspectors belong to several organizations. The inspector should also take as many of the trade magazines as possible to keep current with the home inspection business.

> National Association of Home Inspectors
> 4248 Park Glen Rd.
> Minneapolis, MN 55416
> (800) 448-3942
> (612) 928-4641
> www.nahi.org
>
> American Society of Home Inspectors
> 932 Lee St., Suite 101
> Des Plaines, IL 60016-6546
> (800) 743-2744
> (312) 372-7090
> www.ashi.com

The inspector will need to remove the cover of the main service panel; but for the most part, you should not disassemble appliances to evaluate them. (Photo by Scott Phillips.)

The Rules of the Profession

Professional organizations such as the National Association of Home Inspectors (NAHI) and the American Society of Home Inspectors (ASHI) have a Code of Ethics and Standards of Practice that the home inspector should adhere to. In addition, local organizations (such as the California Real Estate Inspectors) provide professional local guidance to inspectors in their communities.

Both NAHI and ASHI are very specific about what home inspectors should and should not do. For example, the inspector should not disassemble any appliance or equipment within the dwelling or even take the cover off a receptacle or switch plate. The inspector's job is to visually inspect—not technically evaluate to the point of disassembling the appliance. One exception to the do-not-disassemble rule is the cover of a main electrical service panel or subpanel. The cover will have to be removed to inspect the breakers (or fuses) and wiring within. And if the furnace has a burner cover, it may also have to be removed.

Similarly, the inspector should not report on the life expectancy of a component or system. Homebuyers sometimes assume that just because it went through an inspection it cannot fail the next day and everything comes with a warranty to last forever. It's up to the inspector to make sure the buyer does not make those assumptions.

What follows is a general list of what an inspector should *not* do, a combined adaptation from the Standards of Practice of NAHI and ASHI and my own system. Any deviation from NAHI and ASHI is of my creation and should not be thought of as NAHI and ASHI policy. If you are a member of either organization, you must follow their guidelines, which sometimes go into much greater detail than those listed below and may even differ. In addition, each locale will have its own list that applies to specific problems that may exist in that area.

1. **Do not attempt to predict how long something will last.** If you can do that, you can add fortune telling to your list of skills. This includes offering warranties or guarantees. However, certain products—such as roof shingles, siding, and water heaters—do have projected life expectancies, and you can pass that information along to the homeowners, assuming they don't misinterpret it as a guarantee. When people ask me the life expectancy of a water heater with a five-year warranty, I tell them five years and one day.

2. **Do not explain why something doesn't work or how much it will cost to repair.** If it does not work, just say so; don't speculate on the reason why or what it will cost to repair. I know that many inspectors do this, but you risk making enemies of other tradespeople if you underestimate the cost of the job. You are not the expert on repair; they are—be kind, be quiet.

3. **Do not offer advice on the material that it takes to fix something.** Again, this should be left to the professional in that specific area. If the floor joists are rotten, just say they're rotten. Don't start giving the buyer a list of required materials to repair them.

4. **Do not comment on the suitability of anything for any specific use or the adequacy or efficiency of anything.** Keep your opinions to yourself. If, in your opinion, the overhead paddle fan is too small to adequately circulate air, keep it to yourself. By criticizing, all you are doing is creating problems. You don't want to get into a debate of opinions. And you don't

want to be overruled by an expert—even if you are right.

5. **Do not say that something is a code violation unless you are certified in that field.** What is a code violation one year may not be the next. Codes are constantly changing, and there's no way anyone, except an expert in his or her specific field, can keep up with them. A specific test is either an area of concern or not, depending on what your company wants to call it.

6. **Do not comment on market value or marketability.** There's nothing wrong with saying how nice a house is—this is being polite and is in the realm of general conversation. But never comment on market value or money or even marketability. If a sale gets lost because you don't think the price of the house is right, the Realtor will never use you again.

7. **Do not comment on the advisability or inadvisability of purchase of the property.** Memorize the following: "I am not a real estate expert." This is what you recite when asked to comment on the property.

8. **Do not comment on any component or system that was not available to be observed.** For example, a house either has water pressure or it doesn't. You have no idea why. It's possible that the pump isn't working properly or that there is not enough water in the well. Similarly, do not comment on underground items such as buried storage tanks. If you cannot see it, you cannot comment on it—period. In my opinion, this rule applies to septic tanks as well.

9. **Do not give verbal or written assurance of the presence or absence of pests, such as wood organisms, rodents, or insects (beyond the obvious, such as termite tracks).** You can and should point out and log obvious damage. However, a professional in that field will have to give a complete examination if the owner wants a written guarantee. You may say, "It appears that there is no damage" or "I don't see anything." The accent here is on the word *see*. There may be insects and damage you cannot see.

10. **Do not propose or do any work against any law or code—or do any work requiring an occupational license that you do not have.** Normally, the inspector inspects and the tradespeople fix. In most places, it is considered a conflict of interest to have the inspector do both.

11. **Do not project the operating costs of components.** You do not comment on how much it costs to operate anything—in particular, the annual cost of utilities.

12. **Do not do anything within the house or property that may be dangerous to you, other persons, or the house and property.** Always be wary when you fire up and operate any system or component that is shut down or otherwise inoperable. It may be turned off for a reason. It would be nice to say that you should never start any system that has been shut down, but many times the breakers are thrown in the building you're inspecting and it will be up you to turn the breakers back on again. Be especially wary in crawl spaces and flooded basements. Some inspection organizations have height restrictions below which you shouldn't go into a crawl space (for example, 3 ft.). If it doesn't look safe, it probably isn't, so stay out.

13. **Do not operate any system or component that does not respond to normal operating controls.** You are not to troubleshoot the system or fix it to make it operate.

14. **Do not disassemble switches and receptacles or any other electrical or electronic component to determine why they do not work.** Just write it up that they do not work.

15. **Do not report on the quality of interior wall and floor finishes, such as carpeting, paint, wallpaper, varnish, and other finish treatments.**

As you walk around the outside of the house, check for any potential problems with the grade and note the condition of the siding, doors, and windows.

Creating a System of Inspection

The single most important thing a home inspector can do upon entering the trade is to create a methodical system of inspection. Experienced inspectors already have their own system—one they have developed from years of working in the trade, a set pattern that they have either created or just fallen into. This set pattern has a purpose other than the outgrowth of habit. A set pattern ensures that the inspector won't forget part of the inspection or be wasting time by constantly going from the outside to the inside or from basement to attic. Only a set, established procedure will ensure the inspector of a smooth, fast inspection that covers all the bases.

I normally inspect the outside first, and I start looking the minute I pull up to the driveway. As I approach the house, I normally take in the grade surrounding the house to see if there's any obvious problem. The utility is another check my eyes take in at about the same time. I immediately check off whether the service entrance is aerial or buried, and then monitor the grade as I

Roofs that are in poor condition are obvious from the ground. Note the plants growing in the gutter, a sure sign that this gutter is blocked.

A System of Inspection

walk the utility power line from house to pole. At the house, I inspect the grounding system, service entrance, and meter base. With this done, I walk around the house, again checking the grade as well as the driveway and sidewalk, but paying particular attention to the siding and roof. After that comes the inspection of the structural system (the foundation), deck, columns, and crawl space. If there's a garage, I'll inspect that before I go inside the house.

Once the exterior inspection is done, I move inside to check the service panel and the water supply. After that, it's on to the heating and cooling system. This will most likely take me into the basement, which entails a lot of plumbing and electrical checks if the basement is unfinished. Following that, I go to the kitchen and bath and then the appliances. As I walk through the house, I make a quick inspection of all the rooms, hallways, and staircases, checking for electrical outlets; lighting; and the condition of doors, windows, walls, floors, and ceilings. The final check is the attic.

I'm not suggesting that this is the only way to inspect a house, but it's the system that works for me. Bear in mind that a home inspection is not

The Inspection Form

As you inspect a house, you need to record your findings on a preprinted form. The easiest and cheapest way to get the form is to generate your own and make multiple copies—after all, only you know exactly what you'll be inspecting. Standard preprinted forms are also available from various sources; one of the best I have seen was developed by Charles Hayes of Faro Systems (4300 Montgomery Ave., Suite 104, Bethesda, MD 20814; 301-657-8420). You'll need to make at least two copies (one for the buyer and one for your records); the Realtor may also request a copy.

What is listed on the form depends on the type of houses in your area. Every item you might possibly inspect should be listed so that all you have to do is check the relevant box. It will take too long to write down what you've inspected as well as what condition the item is in as you are making the inspection. How far you want to subdivide your findings depends on how detailed a report you intend to produce. For example, in reference to the water source, a simple inspection form might list just three categories:

Water source
- ☐ City water
- ☐ Spring
- ☐ Well

However, a more discriminating inspector might further subdivide the above into:

Water source
- ☐ City water
- ☐ Spring
    - ☐ Gravity feed
        - ☐ With pump
        - ☐ Without pump
- ☐ Well
    - ☐ Hand dug
    - ☐ Drilled metal casing
    - ☐ Drilled plastic casing

Type of pump (if any)
- ☐ Submersible pump
    - ☐ 2-wire
    - ☐ 3-wire
    - ☐ Low-yield water cutoff device
- ☐ Jet pump
    - ☐ Deep-well pump
    - ☐ Shallow-well pump

Type of tank (if any)
- ☐ Galvanized tank
- ☐ Bladder tank
- ☐ Other

necessarily a strictly linear process; it's unlikely, for example, that you'll inspect all the siding, all the roof surfaces, and all the grading in separate steps. There's a good deal of overlap from one to another as you walk around the house, and you never know what you'll find that will pull you away from your usual order of inspection.

For the purposes of this book, I have grouped related subjects that logically go together in the same chapter—even though they may not be inspected sequentially. For example, the chapter on the electrical service inspection includes the service entrance (one of the first things I check) and the service panel (something I typically don't check until I go inside). Similarly, all the information on inspecting doors and windows is grouped together, even though I check the exterior of doors and windows at a different time from when I inspect the interior.

Tools of the Trade

Knowledge and tools go hand in hand. If you're going to be a home inspector, it's important to act like one and invest in the proper tools. That said, you really don't need a lot of tools to get started. I've seen sets of inspection tools advertised for the beginning inspector, but I don't recommend you rush out and buy one. Included in the sets are some tools you'll probably never use (because inspection procedures and the tools required are not always exactly the same in all parts of the country), whereas other tools that you need will be missing.

Basic tools

The basic tools you need to inspect a house are the same tools you'd find in any carpenter's toolbox: screwdrivers, pliers, nail pullers, utility knives, tape measures, and levels. You'll need a variety of tools just to be able to get into some areas of inspection. For example, you'll typically need a few different types of prying tools to get into scuttle holes and access panels to inspect the attic, crawl space, or dirt basement. You never know if the access panels are going to be nailed

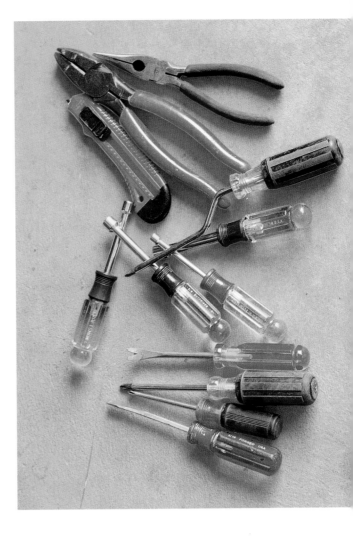

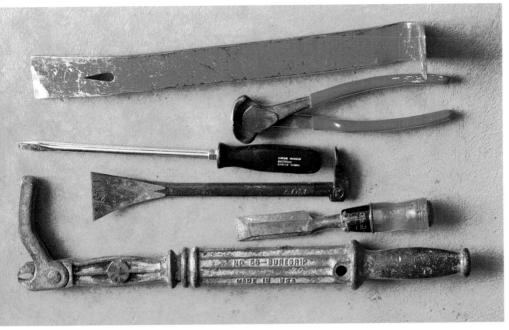

The author keeps a variety of screwdrivers, pliers, nail pullers, and other prying tools on hand for removing access panels for attics and crawl spaces.

shut, screwed tight, glued, or open to the public. As in the Scouts, it pays to be prepared.

Some tools you can make yourself. For example, I fashioned a sharp-pointed awl from an old screwdriver whose head was worn down. (You'll need an awl to check for wood rot in siding, trim, and floor joists.) I've also rigged up a water-pressure gauge for testing water pressure at an outside hose bib (see p. 234) and a thermostat bypass for checking a furnace in summertime (see p. 184).

Inspecting a house can be dangerous work. Of paramount importance, take care of your eyes. Sometimes you'll be looking directly overhead and debris will fall directly into your face as an access panel breaks free. Another danger zone is when you open a service panel or subpanel. You never know what is going to happen when you pull the lid off. If a spark hits your eye, you could be blinded for life. The bottom line: Wear safety glasses. Inspecting a house can also be dirty work, so make sure you have a pair of coveralls on hand for when you're scurrying around a crawl space or dirt basement.

You'll need an awl to probe for rotted wood. It's easy to make one by grinding the blade of an old long-handled screwdriver to a point.

If you're serious about turning darkness into day, consider using diving lights. The larger light shown here takes six D-cell batteries, whereas the smaller one takes four C-cells.

Never lean a ladder against a house unless the ladder is nonconductive. These ladders are fiberglass.

Because a good deal of the inspector's work is in basements, attics, and other dark and dreary spaces, it's important to have a reliable source of lighting. Some inspectors carry a trouble light and extension cord with them throughout the house, but that can be a real inconvenience. It's much easier to use battery-operated lights. A common method is to use a flashlight (attached to a metal ring on your belt to keep it by your side). Another popular choice is a headlamp, which straps to your forehead and frees up both hands as you do the inspection. Low-cost headlamps are available at hardware stores but look for high-quality lamps in specialty inspection catalogs, diving stores, and stores that sell cave lights. My favorite form of lighting for inspections is a high-intensity diving light. Although diving lights are relatively expensive (about $80 for the larger light shown in the photo above), once you start using them, nothing else will do.

Some people use ladders to inspect the roof, others prefer binoculars. Always check with your insurance company before using long extension ladders—some companies may prohibit you from using them. To save money on ladders, you may be tempted to use metal ones—they are light and less expensive than other types, and perhaps you already own one. But don't use them for outside inspections! Using metal ladders outside is dangerous: You never know when a bare wire or a hot siding nail is going to brush against a ladder. When outside, always use nonconductive ladders, such as fiberglass or wood.

Extension ladders have a tendency to "kick out," which means that the bottom of the ladder slips away from the building. To prevent this,

For safety, rotate the swivel feet up to the position shown and step down hard on the bottom rung to sink the feet into the ground. This prevents the bottom of the ladder from kicking out when you are climbing.

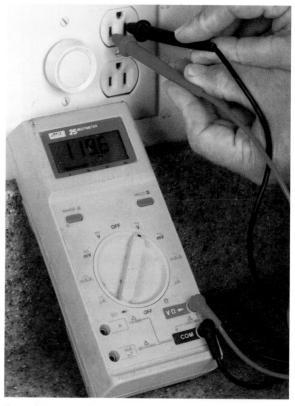

One of the uses for a multimeter is to check the voltage at electrical receptacles. If the voltage is less than 110 volts, make note of it.

make sure your ladder has swivel feet that can be stuck into the ground for better stability. At the other end, consider using a stabilizer bar and wrap some toweling or other protective padding over the ends to prevent the ladder from marring the wall or roof.

Whether or not your insurance agency allows you to climb ladders to get to the roof, you'll need a pair of binoculars to inspect the shingles, flashing, and chimney. I recommend you buy a pair with at least 10 × 50 magnification (they should cost about $50).

Electrical testing tools

Inspecting the electrical system is a critical part of the home inspector's job, and it's important that you have the right tools for this work. You'll need

a high-quality multimeter to make continuity, current, and voltage checks. I carry two models with me: Fluke model 25 and Fluke model 30.

Model 25 (see photo above) is autoranging, which means that you don't have to know the voltage before you measure it and you don't have to switch the meter to the right scale. Simply put the probes on the testing points. It has a continuity tester built in to test light bulbs and water-heater elements around your own home. On inspection jobs, I use this multimeter to verify the voltage amount, to verify that there is no voltage from the panel to either the ground or the neutral bus in the main panel, and to check that metal water lines and ductwork are not electrically hot before I handle them.

Model 30 (see the photo at right) is a clamp-on meter that measures how much current is flowing in a wire so you don't have to touch the wire. Just hook the fingerlike probes around the wire, and the meter will measure the electromagnetic flux that emanates from the wire. I use this tool to verify that there is no current on the ground wires.

You'll need a plug-in circuit analyzer to check if a receptacle is wired properly and to test ground-fault circuit interrupters (GFCIs). Some inspectors use a simple three-bulb tester; but, although these are good for a general check, they are not adequate for a detailed inspection. My tool of choice is a SureTest branch circuit analyzer (see the photos below). Besides standard wire checks and GFCI testing, the SureTest looks for a "bootleg" ground, where the installer has jumped

A clamp-on meter is used to verify that the current flowing through a ground wire is zero.

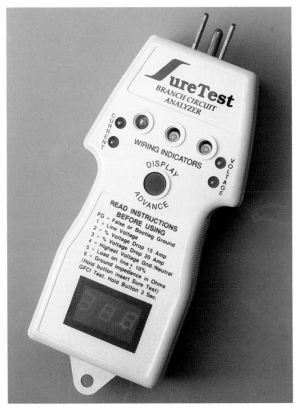

Professional inspectors use a SureTest plug-in tester rather than a three-bulb tester for checking electrical circuits.

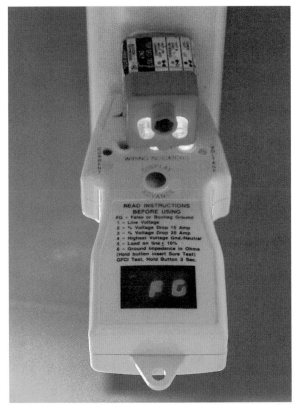

Both testers are shown plugged into a receptacle with a bootleg ground; the three-bulb tester indicates that everything is okay, whereas the SureTest picks up the "false ground."

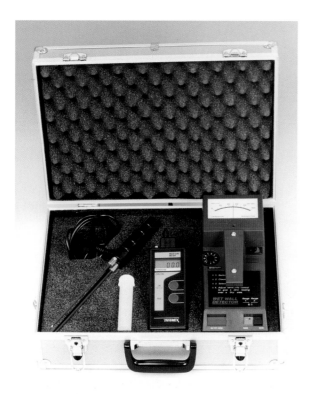

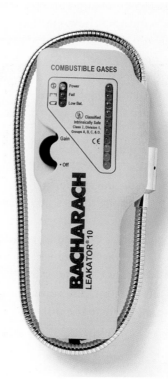

Specialty tools like these moisture meters are used by professional home inspectors who specialize in synthetic stucco. The handheld wet wall detector on the right will verify the presence of moisture under synthetic stucco without having to drill holes. (Photo courtesy of Tramex.)

If the house under inspection has gas appliances, you'll need some way to test for leaks. The best tool to use is a handheld "sniffing" device, which uses a probe to detect for leaks along pipe and fittings and sounds an alarm if gas is present. (Photo courtesy of Bacharach.)

a wire from the neutral to the ground in an attempt to fool the tester into thinking the receptacle is grounded (the three-bulb tester does not pick this up, but the SureTest indicates "false ground"). The SureTest can also be used to test for high or low voltage in a circuit and voltage drops in 15- and 20-amp circuits.

Specialty tools

Aside from the basic tools and electrical testing tools, home inspectors may also need some specialty tools. The type of tools you'll need depend on the type of construction where you work. For example, if there's a lot of synthetic stucco siding in your area, you may want to invest in a "wet wall detector" (you may also need to get trained and certified for specific

inspections). This tool is expensive—as are other specialty tools like the carbon monoxide sniffer and gas sniffer that you will need to test for gas leaks (see chapter 9), but this is what separates the pros from the amateurs. Another specialty tool, the draft checker (made by draft-rite), has a probe that inserts into a hole in a furnace flue and can measure the furnace draft, including downdrafts.

An enterprising inspector will identify areas of inspection that others haven't found or recognized yet, acquire the right tool and/or knowledge, and make a significant amount of money before the rest of the pack catches up. But there are risks involved with this approach: Sometimes things don't turn out quite the way you predicted—asbestos testing in home inspection is one example that comes to mind.

Chapter 2

THE SERVICE INSPECTION

THE SERVICE ENTRANCE

THE SERVICE PANEL

A new business was getting ready for the utility crew to arrive and install their service-entrance cable (SEC). The owners had done their own service-entrance work, and the meter base and service panel had passed inspection months ago. I was there to inspect the grounding system to see if it was up to par for some new lightning-suppression equipment that was to be installed.

The inspection took me into the meter base. My eyes did a double-take the second I took off the meter base lid. I saw that the utility conduit came in the bottom and the power to the building was leaving via a conduit out of the top. All that looked okay. But the top cable was connected to the top lugs of the meter base. The bottom lugs were empty awaiting the new utility cable. Can you see the problem with this? Everything was nice and neat, and the conduit and cables looked as though they belonged there, but the owners had reversed the connections.

No matter whether the service is aerial or buried, the utility *always* connects to the top lugs and the building's SEC *always* connects to the bottom. There is no exception. The way buried utilities are designed is that if it looks right, it's wrong—the system is illogical, but you get used to it. The top cable enters the meter base and circles around to connect to the bottom lugs; the utility cable comes in the bottom and then circles around to connect to the top two lugs.

This old three-wire service drop with three individual conductors covered with what used to be cloth insulation is an accident waiting to happen. Anyone who touches the lines will be electrocuted.

I gave the owner the bad news. For the building's SEC to reach the bottom lugs of the meter base they needed 12 in. to 18 in. of additional cable, and the cables weren't going to stretch. All the cables for the 600-amp service had to be pulled the next day and longer ones installed—at great expense and just a few hours before the utility crew arrived to hook up the new service. Not all the violations you'll encounter at the service entrance or service panel will be of this magnitude, but this story highlights just how important the service inspection can be.

The Service Entrance

The service entrance is generally considered to be the large power entrance cables that originate at the utility pole transformer and terminate at the main service panel at or within the house. It's common to inspect the service entrance first, because it's what you see as you drive up to the house. It will be either buried or aerial. If it's the former, there is normally nothing to inspect.

Simply note on the inspection form that it's a buried entrance. If it's aerial, there are several things to check. Even though the installation and maintenance of the utility cable are the responsibility of the utility, the cable should be included in the inspection because it affects the house.

The utility service cable

The first thing I look for when I inspect a house is the location of the utility transformer. Is it near the house or a dozen poles away? In rural areas, utility companies like to save money by keeping the transformer on the pole in the main power line along the road. If the house is several thousand feet away from the main line, the utility service cable (also known as the service drop) will be several thousand feet long. Such a long run can lose a significant amount of power before it gets to the house: For example, the voltage might drop from 125 volts at the pole to 105 volts at the house.

I use four poles, or three spans (a span is the distance between poles), as my reference; this is

A Glossary of Electrical Terms

Service entrance

The large power cables that originate at the utility transformer and terminate at the main service-entrance panel at or within the house.

Utility or power service drop

The power cables that swing from the transformer pole to the house attachment point at the masthead or siding, where they splice into the service-entrance cable that runs down the side of the house.

Service-entrance cable (SEC)

The cable that splices into the power service drop and runs down the side of the house and connects into the utility meter base. The SEC also connects the meter base to the main service panel.

Meter base

The box where the utility meter plugs into the SEC to measure the power coming into the house. Also known as the *utility meter base*.

Telephone drop

The small telephone cable that pulls out of the larger main cable and swings to the house.

Grounding electrode conductor

Typically called the ground wire, the large-diameter wire that starts at the main service panel grounding/neutral bus and terminates at the ground rod.

Service panel

The box where the SEC terminates and from where all the individual house circuits branch out. Circuit breakers and fuses are located in the service panel to protect all the individual circuits. Also known as the main service panel or main panel.

The main

The single large circuit breaker, located in the main service panel, that turns off all power going into the panel and thus to the house.

Overcurrent protection

The fuse or circuit breaker that will open the circuit if a direct short or an overload (excessive current drawn by the load) occurs.

Water pipe bond

The large-diameter bare or insulated ground wire that goes from the service panel to the metal water pipes to keep them at zero volts.

Panel bond

The electrical connection between the bus ground and the metal frame of the panel.

Equipment grounding conductor

The bare or green wire that starts at the main service panel and travels through the house cables, terminating at the receptacle grounding slot or, for hard-wired appliances, on the appliance frame itself.

Ground fault

A hot wire touching anything that is grounded.

Subpanel

Any panel downstream from the first panel closest to the meter base.

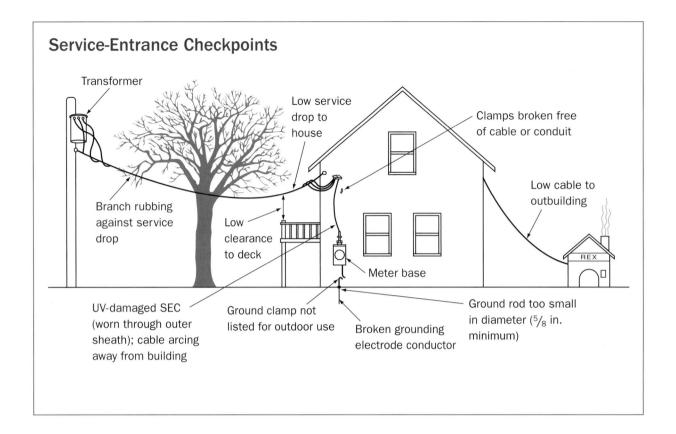

Service-Entrance Checkpoints

Transformer

Low service drop to house

Clamps broken free of cable or conduit

Low cable to outbuilding

Branch rubbing against service drop

Low clearance to deck

REX

Meter base

UV-damaged SEC (worn through outer sheath); cable arcing away from building

Ground clamp not listed for outdoor use

Broken grounding electrode conductor

Ground rod too small in diameter ($^5/_8$ in. minimum)

normally around 1,000 ft. If the distance from transformer to house exceeds three spans, I write it up as a possible low-voltage problem and note that the voltage should be checked under load at the service panel. (The voltage at the panel, which is checked with a multimeter, should never be below about 10 percent of the nominal voltage; for example, if the nominal voltage is 120 volts, write up any reading below approximately 110 volts.)

Proper height The basic height rule from the service drop to the ground is 12 ft. (10 ft. at the drip loop); if the cable crosses a public road, it must maintain a height of 18 ft. You don't have to measure the height exactly (even though there is a telescoping fiberglass pole made for that purpose), just use common sense. If you can reach up and grab the cable or hit it with a stepladder, it's too low.

Usually, the service drop is installed at the proper height, but the line can be pulled down by

ice storms or a fallen tree. I've seen some drops so low to the ground that they could have been used as clothes lines. Similarly, if a deck is added or the grade is built up under an existing service drop, the effective ground level is raised, which can cause clearance problems.

Just as a service drop shouldn't be too low to the ground, it shouldn't be too low to the roof either. Except where they are attached to a masthead across a corner of the house, the utility cables are not supposed to swing low across the roof. Having the cables close to the roof presents a danger to roofers when they put on new shingles as well as to anyone else who may need to walk on the roof. Another problem is fire. If the house catches fire and the utility cables are low to the roof, the fire will burn through the cables. No firefighter will want to go on the roof with the utility cables so low. An additional problem comes with the constant rubbing of the cables across the rough roof, especially at the

Utility cables are allowed to cross a roof as long as they are high enough (normally construed to be 8 ft. on low-pitched roofs and 3 ft. on high-pitched roofs) so that they won't present a hazard to those who have to work on and maintain the roof. This one is only a few inches above the peak.

peak. Eventually, the rubbing wears through the insulation and exposes the hot conductor. If someone on the roof grabs the cable to move it out of the way, he or she could be electrocuted.

Proper height also applies to the aerial telephone drop, the small telephone cable that runs from the larger main cable to the house. As with the service drop, the telephone drop should maintain a height of 18 ft. across roads and 12 ft. across the property. Although overlooked by most inspectors, this is an important check—a small child sitting on top of a hay wagon was killed in Charlottesville, Virginia, when a low telephone cable caught him by the neck as the wagon drove under the cable.

Also be on the lookout for telephone drops lying on the utility line. If the drop ever wears into the hot power conductor, it can burn up the homeowner's telephone as well as the switch gear in the telephone company's main office. On one inspection I performed, the telephone drop had worn down and was shorting into the bare neutral of the utility cable. The homeowner had lost several thousand dollars worth of appliances to fire.

The telephone drop (service to house) is lying on top of the power utility service drop and pulling down on it. If the telephone drop wears down and shorts into the bare neutral of the utility cable, the homeowner may hear static on the telephone line and electronic appliances could start to burn up in the house.

Proper clearance A service drop that runs through trees or shrubbery can present a real problem. The constant swaying of a tree will cause branches to rub through the insulation of the service drop. A child climbing the tree could get electrocuted. And there's considerable danger to the house. If one of the hot legs shorts into the

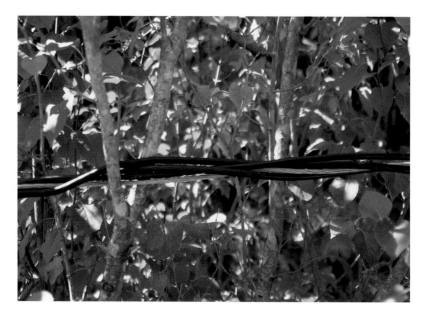

A service drop rubbing against tree limbs is often ignored, but it poses a real threat to the house. The swaying tree limbs will eventually rub a bare spot on the hot wire insulation.

tree (the tree sap acts as a semiconductor), you will lose electricity on that one leg. If the neutral breaks or burns in half, some of the appliances inside the house will start to go up in smoke.

Bare service drop Check that the utility drop's insulation is intact all the way to the house. If the service-entrance system is the old-style three-wire conductor, the conductor cloth insulation may be shredded and falling apart, exposing the bare metal (see the photo on p. 18). This is common in old installations that have never been converted to the new triplex system that uses thermoplastic insulation around the conductors. Anyone reaching up and touching the bare conductor or bumping it with a metal ladder will be electrocuted.

Service drops to outbuildings Although they are not part of the utility entrance, I normally check the clearance of any power lines from the house to barns and other outbuildings at the same time I check the main utility drop clearance. (The clearance specs are the same whether a cable is running to a house or to an outbuilding.) Well houses present the worst problem, because

they are so low to the ground—the power cable sometimes swings down to 3 ft. to 4 ft. off the ground where it terminates at a 2x4 sticking up from the well house.

Besides height, the most common problem with power lines to outbuildings is the use of the wrong type of cable. Most do-it-yourselfers will run indoor nonmetallic (NM) cable, which is usually white, instead of underground feeder (UF) outdoor cable, which is typically gray. Unlike NM cable, UF cable is ultraviolet (UV) light protected and has solid thermoplastic insulation. If you can, try to verify the UF printing on the sheath.

Another potential problem on lines to out-buildings is bare conductors at the splice at the house where the line comes out of the wall. I've also seen bare cloth-insulated wires recycled for use in feeding the outbuildings. If someone carries a metal ladder around the building and hits the wire, he or she will be electrocuted.

The service-entrance cable

The service drop attaches to the siding of the house or to a service mast. At this point, there is a

Service Drop Checklist

- [ ] Type of service entrance:
  - [ ] Aerial
  - [ ] Buried
- [ ] Excessive length of service drop (possible low voltage)
- [ ] Service drop at proper height:
  - [ ] Above ground
  - [ ] Above road
  - [ ] Above roof
- [ ] Telephone drop at proper height
- [ ] Service drop not rubbing against trees
- [ ] Service drop has insulation intact all the way to house
- [ ] Utilities to outbuildings at proper height and of correct cable
- [ ] Service drop attached to house securely

splice and the cable changes names. What was the utility service drop (also sometimes called a triplex for its three cables) is now the service-entrance cable (SEC). The SEC can be an all-in-one cable clamped to the house or individual conductors within conduit. The splice is also the location where installation responsibility changes—it is the electrician's responsibility from the splice down.

Service drop attachment to the house If the service drop attaches directly to the siding, the inspector needs to verify that the attachment is secure. Over time, ice, splits in the siding, or old age can pull the service drop off the house. The service drop might have pulled away from the house completely or it might be hanging on by the screw threads of the porcelain insulators. If the cable has pulled loose from the house but

The service drop attachment to the siding should be secure, not pulling away from the house as in these two examples.

The service mast can bend if the span from the utility pole to the mast is too long, there is a heavy buildup of ice on the service drop, the pipe is too small in diameter, or the mast sticks high above the roof. This is a dangerous situation.

hasn't fallen to the ground, the only thing that might be holding the SEC onto the building is the cable clamps on the siding.

The National Electrical Code (NEC) does not require a gooseneck cover (weatherhead) where the SEC splits out of its sheath and makes its bend at the top of the house. However, some local codes do, so you will have to know what your community's codes require and write up any infraction accordingly.

To obtain proper clearance across a lawn or road, the utility cable may have to swing to a masthead that extends above the roof. If a heavy utility service drop places too much tension on the steel masthead, the masthead can bend. This is a common occurrence in cold areas where ice buildup on the power lines can add a lot of weight or a fallen tree limb can hit the lines. If the mast bends far enough, it can pinch the cables inside and short them out.

Another reason the mast typically bends is because the pipe isn't strong enough. Code requires only a small-diameter mast when it has to house only small-diameter cable, but the pressure on the mast comes from the service drop not from the cable in the pipe. Sometimes you will see the problem addressed with a down-guy

attached from the masthead to the roof to counter the pressure of the utility cable, but on all my service entrances I prefer to use a heavier-duty 2-in.-diameter mast.

SEC attachment to the house Another problem in this area is when the conduit leading up to the mast hasn't been securely attached to the wall. The only thing that keeps it from being pulled off the house is the soffit and roof. In this case, the pipe at the bottom will start to pull away from the house and the SEC will pull out of the meter base—a very dangerous situation.

I was once called in to do a plumbing inspection for a man who knew he had problems with his house, even though the plumbing drain-line work had just past the county inspection. The plumbing problems were no big deal—it was the service entrance that caught my attention. It was an aerial mast system with about 15 ft. of steel conduit going up from the meter base through the soffit with about 3 ft. of mast above the roof. The conduit didn't have the first clamp to hold it against the building (clamps should be placed every 3 ft. or 4 ft.), and as a result, the pressure of the utility drop was pulling the conduit and mast right off the building. As it pulled

On this house, the installer used polyvinyl chloride (PVC) instead of steel for the mast. And to make matters worse, the mast isn't fastened to anything. The pressure of the tilting mast is pulling the SEC out of the top of the meter base. The utility company should have refused to connect to the house even if it did pass inspection.

The SEC going down to the meter base should be clamped onto the siding. The siding on this house was replaced, but no attempt was made to resecure the cable to the building.

away from the house, it was ripping the plastic soffit and crushing the shingles on one side—leaving a large gap on the other. If it were not for the thin roof sheathing, the entire assembly would have come toppling down.

If the SEC is not run in conduit, it must be clamped against the house. On some old houses, the clamps have long pulled free, but you'll also find loose SECs on houses where new vinyl or metal siding has been installed. The siding installers remove the old clamps to install the siding; when they later reinstall the clamps, they

typically fail to use a longer attachment screw, which is needed to grab into the old wood siding under the new plastic siding. The screws pop loose, letting the clamps fall to the ground and the SEC to swing away.

Condition of the SEC Check that the SEC is in good condition. On some houses, the cable is so old that the outer jacket is gone, and you can see the braided conductor. UV light has taken its toll. The cable will need to be replaced if the weathering is so severe that it has eaten away

If the SEC looks this bad and you can see through the stranded neutral, it's time to replace the cable. Write it up on your inspection report.

some of the braided strands. Otherwise, it just needs to be taped over with some approved covering. This is an electrician's call; as an inspector, all you need to do is note the worn covering. Be wary if a house has a small weathered SEC outside and a large, brand-new service panel on the inside. Chances are the work was done without a permit and the new box has more capacity than the old SEC. If a permit is obtained, inspectors normally force the installer to replace an undersize, worn SEC when the service is upgraded.

I was once called to do an inspection on a house where the SEC went straight through an open window to get into the house. I'm not exaggerating. The cable lay on the ground for 40 ft. and then entered the house through an open window (the meter base was on a pole in the side yard). And that wasn't the worst part: The owner's dogs had been chewing on the cable. It's one of the few jobs that I've walked away from.

It's not unusual to take the SEC around a corner of the house, but if it is being cut by a sharp, angled edge or the cable's insulation is being worn through, there's a problem. A similar

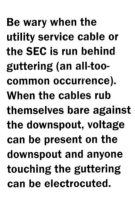

Be wary when the utility service cable or the SEC is run behind guttering (an all-too-common occurrence). When the cables rub themselves bare against the downspout, voltage can be present on the downspout and anyone touching the guttering can be electrocuted.

SEC Checklist

☐ Masthead not bent

☐ Conduit attached securely to house

☐ SEC clamped to house

☐ SEC in good condition

This old 60-amp meter base has broken free of the building.

problem occurs where the utility cable is stuffed behind the guttering and a sharp edge cuts into a hot conductor. I've seen many houses where the utility cables were bent so tightly around the house guttering that it had finally worn into the cable to the extent that you got a shock every time you touched the downspouts. The same thing can happen when worn cables rub against metal siding.

The meter base

Check to make sure that the meter base is securely bolted to the siding. A floating meter base is extremely dangerous; if the screws used to attach the meter to the siding come loose inside the base, they can easily short out to the metal housing—and there are no circuit breakers to trip (none in the house anyway). If this happens, it will be "melt-down" time, with sparks and molten metal flying everywhere.

Also note any problems with the meter base itself and any cables going into or out of the base that aren't protected. The most common (and most obvious) problem, and the one that has caused more meter-base failures than any other, is a bad seal on top of the base. The rubber seal at the top of the meter base is alleged to be a watertight connection, but I've seen many connections that have failed. Many building inspectors won't pass the service entrance during the construction phase unless there is an additional seal of silicon or putty around this connection. When water comes in, it will eat away and destroy the meter base. If the homeowner is unlucky enough to have a cutoff box below the meter base, he or she will lose that too.

The hub connection at the top of this meter base has been sealed with silicon to stop a water leak, but the damage has already been done. The meter base has corroded to the point where one leg is giving problems.

Always look for the obvious. Here, the installer brought the SEC out of the side of the utility meter base without the protection of any type of electrical connector. Don't ask me how it passed inspection. It didn't pass mine.

What's wrong with this picture? The top cable going into the meter base is the utility feeder. It's good for around 60 amps (the same as the meter base). However, there are two cables coming out the bottom of the meter base, each going to a separate service panel. One goes to the original 60-amp panel inside the basement. The other SEC goes to a new 100-amp panel on the porch, which the owner has added without getting a permit. The house now pulls 160 amps through a meter base and utility cable rated for only 60 amps.

There are a couple of other things to watch out for at the meter base. First, note if any cables leave the meter base without any connector to protect them against the sharp metal edges of the box. Second, be on the lookout for an illegal tap off the meter base. This is where an installer has clipped the seal, pulled the meter, attached a second service cable that runs to a new panel, and then put the meter back in. The illegal tap overloads the utility drop and meter base.

Grounding system

Many houses have grounding problems, which often get ignored. The inspector should verify that a ground rod exists, even though it is possible (and legal) that the house could be using the rebar in the footing as a grounding medium. If you can't find a ground rod, make note of it—an electrician can decide whether the building is properly grounded.

Once you've found the rod, verify that the ground wire (the big copper wire that goes to the service panel) is connected to the rod and not just hanging loose. Many times the ground wire, also known as the grounding electrode conductor, has been cut free from the rod by a lawn mower or the clamp has fallen away. The most common problem I come across with the grounding system

An aluminum alloy pipe clamp should not be used on a ground. If you look closely, you can see the corrosion where the screw is in contact with the ground wire. Also, the screws on these clamps have a habit of working loose.

This is what a ground rod connection should look like: The ground wire is attached to a $\frac{5}{8}$-in.-diameter (or larger) ground rod with an acorn connector.

is the connector itself. Instead of using an approved clamp (normally an acorn clamp or some other clamp rated for direct burial), the installer has used a clamp approved only for indoors or has used a hose clamp. The most common ground rod is a $\frac{5}{8}$-in.-diameter (as a minimum) galvanized or copper-clad rod. Old galvanized pipes driven in the ground are allowed as ground rods, but they invariably have an old rusted connector that makes a poor connection to the ground wire. Metal plumbing pipe cannot be used as the sole grounding connection.

The Right Meter Base for the Job

The meter base should match the fuse or circuit-breaker panel. Many times you can tell what amperage the service-entrance panel should be simply by looking at the utility meter base. For example, a small circular meter base normally feeds an old-style 60-amp fuse box. Once you get inside, if there's a large circuit-breaker box (150 amp or higher)—I write it. Someone has probably upgraded the electrical system illegally: That is, they changed the old fuse panel to a new, higher-amperage circuit-breaker panel and didn't upgrade the SEC or meter base.

People do this to avoid getting a permit. A small square meter base normally indicates a 100-amp service; a large rectangular or square meter base, a 200-amp service; and a giant one, 400 amp. If you suspect that an illegal upgrade has been made, make note for an electrician to check it.

Meter Base and Grounding System Checklist

- ☐ Meter base secure
- ☐ Cables into meter base sealed and attached properly
- ☐ Proper ground rod and connector
- ☐ Ground wire attached to ground rod

The Service Panel

The service-entrance panel is the heart of the electrical system. This is where all circuits start and the panel must be in good operating condition for the rest of the house's electrical system to work properly. If a problem starts here, it is like a virus—eventually it will infect the entire system. Not surprisingly, the service panel is one of the most important inspections in the house.

Although most of the service-panel problems will be apparent to the eye, don't be afraid to let your other senses work as well. Touch the outside of the panel to see if it is overheating, something that can happen before the panel fails. And use your nose, too. Many times I've been able to smell a problem, such as overheating, before I could see it.

Panel location

The first thing to note is whether the service panel is inside (the most common location) or outside. If the panel is outside (that is, in an area where it can be rained on), it must be rated for outside use. A rainproof box can be recognized by a solid front panel, normally hinged at the top, that lifts to expose the circuit breakers. The standard inside panel has a side-hinged door.

There's some confusion about whether a panel on an open porch needs to be watertight. Normally, a watertight box is not required as long as

there is a roof overhead. But, although the panel wouldn't get hit directly by vertical rain, it would certainly get wet if wind blew the rain in from the open sides and front of the porch. So whether a panel on a porch should be rated for outside use depends on how strict the local authority is in its interpretation of the code. Either way, always take a close look for corrosion in panels that are exposed to the elements (discussed on pp. 32 and 34).

Minimum clearance around the panel

The area around the service panel must be kept clear to allow easy access to the panel. "Minimum

Service Panel Safety

Don't inspect the main panel unless you know what you are doing. Working in the service panel is dangerous. There are hot wires everywhere. Even with the main off, the feed to the main breaker is still hot.

Don't do too much prying around in the box—I've been "bitten" a couple of times by a bare hot wire that I didn't even know was there (in one case, a wire that looked as though it had good insulation had a slit down its back side). I'm still alive because I follow my rule of threes: *Always have three layers of protection when you work around hot wires.* For example: rubber gloves, insulated tools, and rubber-soled shoes; insulated tools, rubber mat, and rubber-soled shoes; and insulated tools, rubber mat, and wooden platform.

It's also advisable to wear safety glasses whenever you open a service panel. You never know what you might be getting into when you pull the cover off. If a spark hits you in the eye, you could be blinded for life.

Clearances around a Service Panel" shows the required distances. In many houses, the area around the panel is used for storage. Typical problems are shelves, bookcases, boxes, and workbenches.

If there's a workbench or a countertop in front of the service panel, I write it up. A person who is short won't be able to reach over the counter and shut off the breaker in an emergency. If a shelf won't allow the panel door to open at least 90 degrees, write it up. I worked on one house that had a hot-tub pump system mounted in front of the panel; the inspector failed it (rightly so) and the entire system had to be moved. Another inspector failed a panel because a sewer line ran immediately overhead. I was the electrician called in to move the entire panel and all the circuits and to lengthen the SEC. But the most illogical panel location I've ever seen was a panel mounted in a kitchen wall in a corner behind the stove. To get to the panel, you had to hop up onto the counter and crawl over the burners on your knees.

Opening the panel

Proceed with caution as you open the service panel—you never know what might happen when you pull the cover off. One panel I opened had a screw literally doing a balancing act between ground and the hot feeder cable. Only about ⅛ in. separated the two. The bottom line: Always wear safety glasses to protect your eyes from sparks when you're inspecting the panel.

The screws that hold the cover of the panel on should be special screws with blunt ends. I pulled a cover off one time and in the upper-right-hand corner of the panel was the blackest, burned, arc-welded area I've ever seen in a box. The owner had attached the lid with a long pointed sheet-metal screw. As the screw turned, it drove itself right into one leg of the SEC. Because this part of the cable has no overcurrent device (except the cutout at the utility pole), the screw exploded as

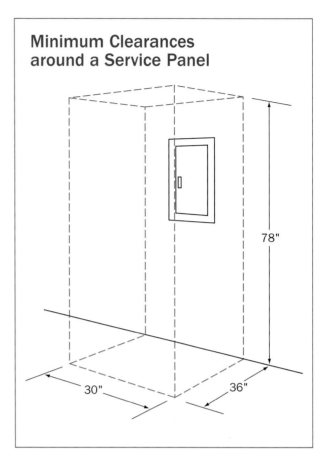

Minimum Clearances around a Service Panel

78"

30"

36"

There are a couple of problems here. The cable on the right enters the panel without the benefit of an NM connector. The cable on the left has a connector, but the three individual conductors do not have a jacket, allowing the sharp edges of the connector to cut through the wires' insulation.

excessive current ran through it. I can only imagine what happened to the owner's nerves.

Also check for any cables that enter the service panel without an NM connector. Cables need the connector to protect them from the sharp edges of the panel and to prevent the wires from being yanked out. A missing connector is one of the most common violations in the business.

Fuse box or circuit-breaker panel

The new owners of a house will want to know whether they have an old-style fuse box or a circuit-breaker panel, so note which type is present. If the new owners are with you when you do the inspection, now's the time to discuss the panel. Tell them how big the panel is (in terms of number of circuits and amount of current) and how many extra circuits are available if they want to add anything.

The most overlooked problem is no violation at all—a 100 percent full panel. It's not that someone has made a mistake, even though most times the installer put in too small a panel, but the prospective buyer needs to know that nothing can be added to the panel without some work being done or perhaps a major upgrade.

Panel amperage

The amperage of the panel, which is the maximum current that can flow through it, needs to be noted on the inspection form. The highest is likely to be 400 amps, which consists of two 200-amp panels. The lowest permissible in most areas is 100 amps. You do get 300-amp panels, which is a 200-amp panel and a 100-amp panel, but they are rare. The most common is a 200-amp panel (the minimum size I'd recommend), followed by 150-amp panels. The size number should be stamped on the main breaker and/or listed on the paperwork glued to the lid.

All circuit breakers or fuses need to have the circuits they control listed; if they are not listed, write it up. You'll have no way of knowing if the

existing marking is right or wrong, but some will be obviously incorrect—for example, if the panel listing has single-pole breakers listed where there are double poles.

Water damage

Look closely for water problems in panels that are in basements or outside on porches. Moisture can destroy a panel. Panels on porches are exposed to windblown water. Panels in basements are exposed to airborne moisture (especially if a clothes dryer vents into the basement) and water that follows the SEC down into the box. Sometimes the water flows down the stranded neutral (within the cable) like a river into the basement panel. Look for stains inside the panel when you take the cover off (normally brown iron stains or white from corrosion).

Look closely for signs of water damage in the service panel, especially if the panel is in the basement or on a porch. One of the most obvious signs of moisture damage is white corrosion on the breakers and hot tabs (as shown here).

Manufacturer Problems

Over the years, I've worked on a lot of service panels manufactured by Federal Pacific (a company no longer in business). These panels are renowned for problems with the breakers.

Be very careful when you remove the lid from a Federal Pacific panel—it's common for the breakers to pop right out of the bus as the lid is removed, because it is the pressure of the lid that keeps them in place. In addition, there's a frame ring that will want to fall down onto the hot circuits—you'll have to hold onto this at the same time as you hold the lid to keep it from falling. (When you reinstall the lid, press the circuit breakers firmly back into place with your thumb so the stab lock doesn't pull up off the bus.)

Another problem to watch out for is that on Federal Pacific breakers the buses aren't staggered down the center of the panel as you'll find on all other makes (bus A, bus B, bus A, etc.). Therefore, it's very easy for a Federal Pacific double-pole breaker to be installed incorrectly. I see it all the time. In other words, the installer inserted the breaker where it looked as though it should go—right between two plastic tabs on the bus. Powered this way, a 240-volt appliance will not work. To get 240 volts on a Federal Pacific panel, you have to straddle the plastic tab, which doesn't look like the right thing to do.

I've experienced several instances in which a Federal Pacific breaker did not trip when it was supposed to. One do-it-yourselfer wired in his own three-way switch into a direct short. The breaker did not trip, and the whole branch circuit caught fire. So look around the panel to see if there are any obvious burned and arced areas that have shorted out.

Another panel I've had problems with is the Homeline series made by Square D. If the house under inspection has such a panel, watch out for bent tabs and breakers that cover the neutral bus. Their ground-fault circuit interrupter (GFCI) and other full-size breakers can cover the screws of the ground/neutral bus so you can't tell if the screws are loose or tight.

If the panel under inspection has breakers that look like these (manufactured by Federal Pacific), be very careful. They have a habit of popping out of the bus when you take the lid off.

Federal Pacific breakers have a very thin housing that is easily broken. Sometimes they crack open from heat; other times they're damaged just from being handled.

Sometimes the water damage comes from an unusual source. The worst case I've seen is when an ice-maker water line was leaking immediately above the main panel. I was called in when one leg of a 240-volt feed corroded through and power was lost. By this point, a river had been flowing through the panel for months, and the box had algae growing inside it.

As we all know, water and electricity don't mix. If you find water pooled around the floor below the panel, it's not advisable to touch the panel, let alone remove the cover. As a professional electrician I sometimes have to. Sometimes I've pulled the utility meter, other times I've turned the main off with a long wooden pole.

Overloaded panel

An overloaded panel will be obvious—there will be several wires under one breaker screw. Typically, you are allowed only one wire under one breaker screw, although there is an exception to the rule: Square D, type-QO, size 15-, 20-, and 30-amp breakers are listed for two wires up to

With most breakers, including this one, only one wire is allowed under one breaker screw.

10 gauge. Almost every inspector will flag this as a violation, but it is not.

Another thing to look for is a tap off the main circuit breaker's lugs. This wire is an illegal feeder to another panel—probably one right next to the main panel. The wire is totally unprotected with any type of overcurrent device. Do not confuse an illegal tap with surge-protection wiring. Sometimes two small wires feed into the main lugs and go to a small lightning-surge arrester mounted on the panel.

Unprotected taps (wires with no overcurrent protection) are also something to watch for in fuse panels. They can be off the main, just as in a circuit breaker panel, but more often you will see them off the plug fuse, which is protecting two circuits instead of the one it is designed for. Most times you'll see them tapping a 120-volt circuit off half of the 240-volt water-heater circuit.

Be careful when you take the cover off an overloaded panel. It will probably have too many cables within and look like the proverbial bird's nest—which means you may have trouble getting the cover back on. And when you do put it back on, be very careful not to pinch any wires between the cover and the box.

Excessive overcurrent protection

It is possible to have excessive overcurrent protection in circuit breakers (and in fuse boxes). This problem, which occurs when undersize wire is used with oversize breakers, is most common with a 14-gauge wire that's connected to a 20- or 30-amp breaker or a 12-gauge wire connected to a 30-amp breaker or fuse. All new houses must have 12-gauge wire to the kitchen and utility room receptacles. The newest codes require 12 gauge for the bath receptacles as well, but you would see this in only new construction. However, the kitchen and bath may be impossible to write up in older houses, because you don't know what can be grandfathered in. If in doubt about the gauge number, try to read it off the cable sheath.

Square D, type-QO breakers (15, 20, and 30 amps) are an exception to the rule of one wire per breaker screw. These breakers are UL listed for two wires up to 10 gauge. Note that the wires do not go into a hole to be held down with screw threads. The screw pushes a plate down that has two slots for two wires.

A common violation is an illegal tap to a second panel off the lugs of the main. This is normally done when the first panel runs out of room. The problem here is that the small leads to the second panel have no overcurrent protection. In addition, the main leads coming in from the meter base now have a lot more current on them than they were designed for.

This panel didn't pass inspection because the hot bus is exposed. The holes above the circuit breakers should be covered with filler plates (or some extra breakers).

If you see a single-pole breaker with a white wire, write it up.

Service Panel Checklist

- ☐ Location of panel:
  - ☐ Inside
  - ☐ Outside
- ☐ Minimum clearance area around panel observed
- ☐ Cables into panel have NM connectors
- ☐ Type of panel:
  - ☐ Circuit breaker
  - ☐ Fuse box
- ☐ Panel amperage:
  - ☐ 400 amps
  - ☐ 200 amps
  - ☐ 150 amps
  - ☐ 100 amps
  - ☐ Other
- ☐ Circuits listed
- ☐ Signs of water damage
- ☐ Overloaded panel
- ☐ Excessive overcurrent protection
- ☐ Panel has solid front with no finger holes

Panel with filler plates missing

Filler plates are the little metal knockouts that are removed from the panel front when breakers are installed in the panel. If a breaker is missing from that spot, someone can reach through the front cover and touch the hot bus, so write it up as a violation. Electricians have little push-in plugs to cover the holes; make sure the plugs are in place where necessary.

Breaker problems

It's important for the inspector to check that the right circuit breakers are used in the panel, that they are wired correctly, and that they are not damaged. "Know Your Breakers" will help you understand the different types of breakers that are available.

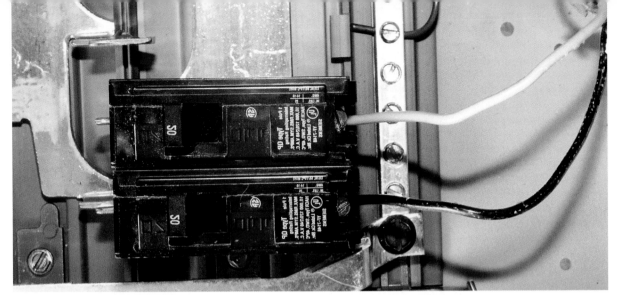

A double-pole breaker with its attachment arm missing. Although it looks like two single-pole breakers, it's really one integral breaker. Technically, there should be a piece of black tape on the white wire to indicate that it's a hot conductor. However, because this is rarely done and even more rarely enforced, I ignore it.

Know Your Breakers

Single-pole breaker

A breaker that connects to one pole or hot bus of the main service panel. It provides power to 120-volt appliances.

Double-pole breaker

A breaker, twice the size of a single pole, that attaches to both poles or hot buses in the main service panel. It provides power to 240-volt appliances.

Quad breaker

Four breakers in one, used when space is at a premium. It is the same size as a standard double-pole breaker and can be used in special panels with slotted buses. Used illegally in standard panels that don't have slotted buses.

Two-in-one breaker

Two half-size single-pole breakers in the same physical space as one. Can be illegally modified like the quad.

Half-size breaker

A very thin breaker (half of a two-in-one) that tends to be hard to work with. It has the same limitations as the quad and two-in-one breakers.

A common problem is the use of a white insulated wire on a single-pole breaker. This problem is overlooked on double-pole breakers, even though the white wire is supposed to have a black piece of tape on it to act as an indicator that it is really a hot wire. However, if I see a white wire on a single-pole breaker, I write it up. I also write up old houses that are wired totally backward—white wires are hot and black wires are neutral.

Another thing to watch for is the wrong use of breakers. Two single-pole breakers should not be used as a double-pole breaker. This problem typically occurs when the installer runs out of double poles and doesn't want to go and get the correct breaker. I typically see this at the same time I see the white wire on one of the breakers. I trace both wires, and if they go to the same cable, I know it's a 240-volt circuit using two single-pole breakers as a double. Similarly, double-pole breakers should not be used as single-pole breakers.

Check for quad double-pole breakers that are being used without the attachment bar. The

A double-pole breaker being used as two single-pole breakers. This is not allowed.

Two double-pole breakers. The double-pole breaker on the left is intact; the one on the right has its lever broken and the connector handle is missing. If you see this in the panel, write it up.

attachment bar falls off easily; when this happens, it's possible for only half the breaker to trip, leaving the other half hot. You can't buy these bars anywhere—they come only with the breaker. When the bar is lost, installers hate to throw the breaker away so they'll often stick it in when nobody's looking. Be sure the circuit is actually being used as a double pole before you write it up. You can have the exact same arrangement with single poles on both ends. So you'll have to look at the wiring. If there's a white wire on the breaker, odds are its being used as a double pole.

The right tab for the right breaker There are two types of tabs for common breakers: full and slotted. A large panel such as a 40/40 panel can take 40 full-size breakers. If the panel is labeled 20/40, this means the panel can take 40 breakers but 20 of them have to be the half-size breakers that fit only onto a slotted bus on that panel. These panels are physically smaller than 40/40 panels and, therefore, will turn into what electricians not so fondly call a "bird's nest"—a complete tangle of wires.

Problems arise when two-in-one breakers or quad breakers are installed in panels designed only for full-size breakers. To get them in, the clip has to be broken out of the back of the breaker—which, of course, is not allowed. By doing this,

you could actually get 80 breakers in a panel. Each panel has a maximum number of allowed breakers (listed on the panel door). Look at the bus tab. If it has a slot cut out of it, it is designed for half-size and quad breakers. If not, someone has illegally modified the breaker to fit the panel. This is done by pulling out the metal plates in the back of the breaker. An inspector friend of mine knew, even before he opened the panel door, that he was going to fail a new panel in a house under construction: On the floor in front of the panel were a dozen small stainless-steel clips that had been removed from the two-in-one breakers to allow them to fit onto the bus tabs.

Breaker damage A problem you come across more than you might think is a broken breaker. The damage is usually obvious—typically, a broken handle. I've seen this on both single- and double-pole breakers, but I've no idea how it happens. It's as though someone had hit the breaker with a hammer.

The Right Tab for the Breaker

The inspector must verify that dual and quad breakers are not being installed on full-tab buses instead of slotted buses.

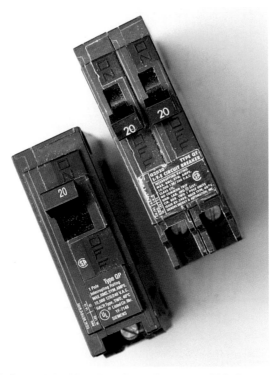

Full-size and dual breakers have the same width, but they are not always interchangeable within the panel.

Rear view; note the vertical slots. The dual breaker has a stainless-steel clip (inside the breaker) covering the top half of the slot.

When inserted, the two-in-one breaker cannot fit onto a full tab because of the internal stainless-steel clip. This is why some installers open up the back of the breaker to remove the clip; this is what the inspector must check for. Dual and quad breakers are not allowed on a full bus.

This is a slotted bus—the only bus that dual and quad breakers can fit on. The metal clip slides into the slot, allowing the breaker to fit into the panel.

Burned-Out Breakers

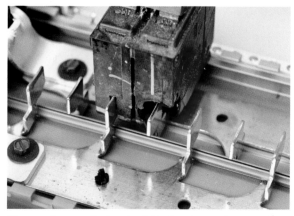

Always observe the back of the breakers when possible. The bottom right corner of this double-pole breaker has burned off.

The top tab of this main service panel used to have breakers on it until it was destroyed by arcing caused by water flowing in the panel. The other tabs are very corroded and should not be used.

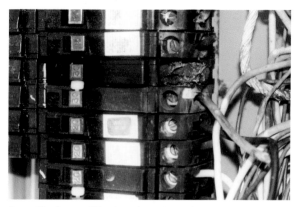

Scan the tops of the breakers to make sure none are burned or destroyed. Four breakers in this panel were destroyed by lightning and never repaired.

Circuit Breaker Checklist

- ☐ No white insulated wire on a single-pole breaker
- ☐ Two single-pole breakers being used as a double-pole breaker
- ☐ Quad breaker without attachment bar
- ☐ Right tabs for right breakers
- ☐ Broken breakers
- ☐ Burned tabs

When a breaker fails, an excessive load can burn the wiring, destroy the breaker, and arc onto the tab. The cause of breaker failure is typically water or lightning damage. Once burned, nothing can be used again. If a new circuit breaker is installed on a burned tab, as might occur if the panel is nearing full capacity, the circuit may or may not work. At best, it will work for a short while. Most of the time it will give either a partial voltage or none whatsoever. It's a dangerous hookup, because the burned tab is giving a semiconductor circuit, which may heat up and cause even further damage or a fire.

Sometimes the first clue that there's something wrong with the breaker, is discoloration on the wire that's connected to it. If the connection has become overheated, normally because of a loose connection, there'll be discoloration or burned insulation close to the breaker screw.

Wiring problems within the service panel

Wires inside the panel are supposed to stay within the gutter area along the outside edges, as designated by the four gutter posts; they are not supposed to go across the face of the panel. If wires do cross the panel, it is not only messy but also extremely dangerous. The worst case I've seen

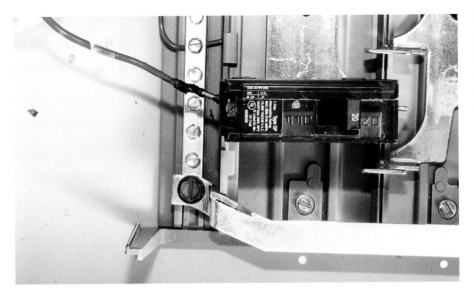

The insulation on this hot conductor has been over-heated and destroyed where it connects to the circuit breaker—probably because of a loose connection.

is a box in which the installer had run all the bare ground wires left to right about ¼ in. above both bare busses. Running insulated wires directly across the busses where the circuit breakers go is bad enough, but running bare ones is unforgivable.

Watch for cable strands that have been trimmed or bent out of the way. You'll run into this problem when the installer couldn't get all the conductor into the breaker or lug, and so he or she cut off or bent some of the strands. In the trade, it's called giving the cable a haircut. I normally ignore one or two missing strands but write it up if it's excessive (admittedly a subjective call). You normally see this at the main and when a large cable (such as a stranded neutral) has been forced into an opening that's too small. The problem is that if you reduce the number of strands within the conductor, you reduce the amount of amperage the conductor can take.

Another thing to look out for is exposed hot conductors. This happens when the installer strips out too much insulation from the hot conductor to fit under a terminal. Anyone working in the panel could easily touch the hot wire and get electrocuted. Although you may find this

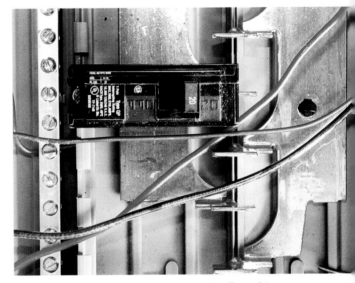

Whether insulated or bare, wires are not allowed to cross the hot bus. This happens when the wires are too short to reach the breaker and the installer takes a shortcut across the middle of the panel.

Panel Wiring Checklist

- ☐ Wires crossing panel face
- ☐ Excessive trimming of cable strands
- ☐ Exposed hot conductors
- ☐ Single-strand aluminum wiring
- ☐ Aluminum/copper splices

anywhere in the panel, it's most common at the main breaker. Also watch out for hot wires that have their insulation slit.

Aluminum wiring Single-strand aluminum wiring has caused problems nationwide when it has been used to wire receptacles and switches that are not designed for aluminum wiring. Simply put, if you see single-strand aluminum wiring going into 15- and 20-amp breakers, write it up as an area of concern. Chances are the installer did not use receptacles, switches, and

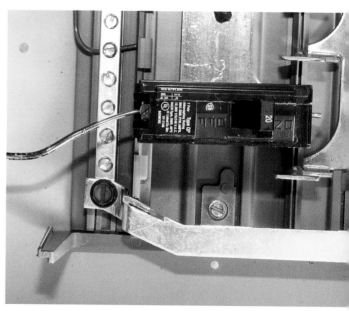

Check for excessive bare conductor showing where the wire attaches to the breaker. Anyone working in the panel could easily touch the hot wire.

Look for individual strands cut off or bent to the side where the main feed enters the main breaker attachment post. This happens when installers can't get the cable inside the post—they either cut a few strands or bend a few off to the side in an effort to shrink the cable's diameter.

splicing material acceptable for aluminum or aluminum to copper splicing. A certified electrician will need to verify whether there is a problem. Large-diameter aluminum wiring, such as used for the service entrance and for large appliances, typically has no significant problems. However, some local authorities have banned its use, so the inspector needs to be aware what is allowed in his or her jurisdiction.

In the main panel, you'll sometimes see splices where a copper ground wire has been inserted under a lug or screw with an aluminum neutral or ground wire; this is not allowed. It typically happens when the service-entrance box is too small and the installer was pressed for room on the neutral/grounding bar. Many installers think that if the notice on the lid or metal lug itself says you can use copper or aluminum you are allowed to put them together. You are not. By doing so you are putting copper *and* aluminum together, not copper *or* aluminum. Either can go on the bus, but they cannot be laid on top of each other.

Aluminum to copper (single-strand) splices are sometimes found under wire nuts. This is a very controversial issue. Where you'll find it is in a house that has some aluminum wiring and some copper wiring. The only way you are allowed to splice copper to aluminum is with an approved method. One method is to use the purple wire nuts that Ideal has listed for such use. But take a close look at the splice and wire nut. Check for any sign of overheating or burning and write it up if you see it. Another approved method has been developed by AMP Inc.: The splice is crimped by a special tool and can be installed only by a certified AMP-trained technician.

Panel grounding

Every main panel needs a grounding electrode conductor (ground wire) from the neutral/grounding bus to a grounding electrode (normally a ground rod). If the house has metal water pipes, there must also be a ground wire connecting the pipes to the neutral/grounding bus. The water pipes may not be used as the sole grounding electrode. Water pipes are something to be grounded, not something to be grounded to. If the house has a ground wire going from the service panel to the metal pipes that go outside and there is no other ground wire, write it up.

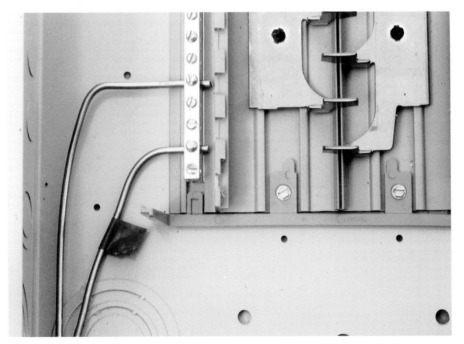

This panel has two large-diameter grounding wires. The top one goes to the copper water line; the bottom one (with the green tape) goes to the ground rod. If the house has metal water lines, the inspector must verify the presence of both ground wires. If you can't find the ground wire that goes to the copper pipe and there's a subpanel, look in there.

A bonding strap, also called a panel bond, is required in every main service panel to connect the neutral/grounding bar to the panel frame.

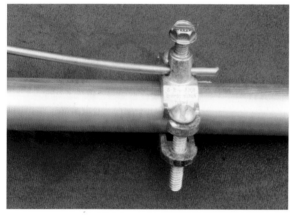

The copper pipe bonding connection. If the house has metal water lines, this bond, which connects to the main panel, is required. The connector must be easily accessible.

For additional protection, there must also be a bonding strap (or panel bond) connecting the neutral/grounding bus to the metal frame of the main panel. Its purpose is to add the frame to the grounding system so the metal can never become a conductor if a hot wire touches it. You may not always be able to inspect the bonding strap.

Sometimes it is obvious, but other times it will be hidden so well that only an electrician will be able to find it.

While I have the panel open, I use a clamp-around amp probe to measure current on the ground wire. The purpose of the wire is to bleed stray voltages to ground in an attempt to keep all nonconductors at zero voltage No current of any magnitude is supposed to flow continuously in this wire. If there is a measurable current, there's a problem and you should write it up.

The second ground wire is the water pipe bond. If the water lines are metal, a large grounding wire must originate in the main service panel and connect to the metal pipes. If this ground wire is missing and you touch the water pipe with one hand and earth ground with the other, you're in trouble. I've measured 120 volts to ground on some copper pipes. The connection at the water pipe must be accessible, which means you must be able to see it and get your hands on it. If the connection is not obvious, mark it up.

If the water pipes are metal, there must also be a bonding jumper around the water heater. This allows the ground connection to be unbroken if

Using a Multimeter to Check for "Hot" Pipes

To verify that a metal water line is not electrically hot before you handle it, use a multimeter to measure from a ground or neutral to the water line. Put one probe on the grounding/neutral bus in the main panel and the other on the metal water pipe. In case the pipe is too far away, I carry a long single wire with alligator clips on it to bridge the gap. One side clips on the grounding/neutral bus or even to the grounding electrode conductor (ground wire) that goes to the ground rod, if it's closer. The other end clips onto one probe lead—it makes no difference which one. With the opposite probe lead, touch the copper or galvanized water line.

Warning: Never touch the metal water lines while your body or feet are in contact with moisture in the earth or concrete until you've made this test. If the water line is electrically hot, you want to know it before you start moving around in a crawl space—not after.

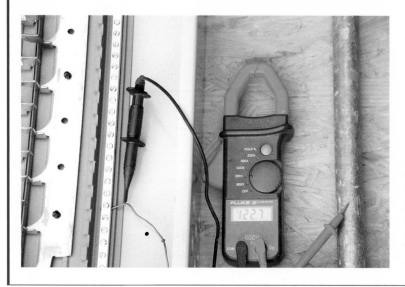

It's important to make a voltage check between the metal water lines and the neutral/grounding bus in the panel. If you have a reading such as indicated here (or anything much above zero), the water line is electrically hot— a dangerous situation.

the water heater is replaced or a nonmetal water heater is installed (for more on the bonding jumper, see chapter 7).

I always make a voltage check from the metal water pipe to the neutral/grounding bus in the panel using a multimeter (see "Using a Multimeter to Check for 'Hot' Pipes"). You should get close to zero volts and good resistance continuity. These are two different tests. If I get line voltage on the water pipes, I forego the continuity test. If the panel is too far away, I measure to the ground lug of the closest receptacle.

In a main panel, don't worry if you see white wires in the same bus as the ground wires. Only in the subpanel must the neutral and ground wires be separated. However, if there is a cutoff switch outside next to the meter base, the main panel becomes a subpanel and the wires must be separated. The neutral must float, and the ground must be connected to the panel itself.

Subpanels

A subpanel is typically used to minimize the number of wires needed to reach across the entire length of a house. If the house needs 20 circuits

The Subpanel

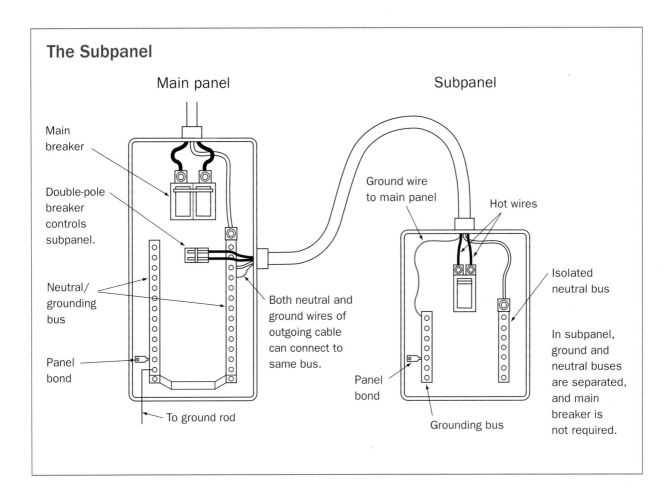

Main panel

Subpanel

Main breaker

Double-pole breaker controls subpanel.

Neutral/ grounding bus

Panel bond

To ground rod

Both neutral and ground wires of outgoing cable can connect to same bus.

Ground wire to main panel

Hot wires

Panel bond

Grounding bus

Isolated neutral bus

In subpanel, ground and neutral buses are separated, and main breaker is not required.

Panel Grounding Checklist

☐ Ground wires present

☐ Bonding strap present

☐ Bonding jumper around water heater

☐ Subpanel grounds isolated from neutrals

far away from the main panel, it's sometimes better to run a wire from the main to a subpanel. The disadvantage of using a subpanel is that it is easy to install it incorrectly.

The most common violation is that the neutrals are not isolated from the grounds. The neutrals and the grounds must be separated on different busses. What often happens is that the

installer uses a standard service panel that does not come with isolated buses, and thus grounds and neutrals get mixed together. If the neutrals get wired in with the ground wires, you have parallel current paths from the subpanel back to the main panel. In other words there will be neutral current on the ground wires.

Fuse boxes

Old-style fuse boxes worked very well for their time—even when abused and overload. However, the common four-plug, 60-amp fuse box is not adequate for today's homes; 100-amp service is the smallest service allowed to come on line nowadays. If the house under inspection has a 60-amp box, make note of it and add that it is inadequate.

Take a close look at how the fuse box is wired. The wire coming into the fuse block on the upper right is supposed to be the stove wire—a large gray cable. But sometimes a smaller wire is installed here, and it is overfused by the 40-amp cartridge fuses that are there to protect the large stove cable.

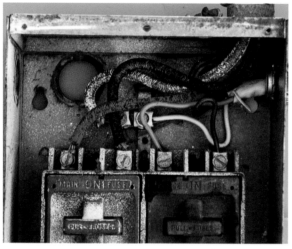

A no-win situation. This old fuse panel had a dryer working off its range circuit (upper right). The 10-gauge wire is still fused with the range's 40-amp cartridge fuses.

The most common problem in old fuse boxes is that someone has played musical chairs with the fuses. Once a homeowner starts replacing things, there is no telling what size fuse is protecting what size wire. But once the music stops, the overcurrent protection rarely matches the fuse. In other words, 30-amp plug fuses have been installed, allegedly protecting 14- and 12-gauge cable; but 14 gauge must be protected with 15-amp fuses and 12 gauge, with 20-amp fuses. (If the panel has been converted to S-type fuses, this cannot happen—each different amperage fuse has a different thread size.) What probably prompted the fuse replacement was the owner getting tired of changing the fuses on the overloaded circuits; he or she kept upping the fuses till they no longer blew. In this situation, more current can be pulled on the wire than the wire is allowed to conduct, the insulation starts to melt, and a fire can occur. Another common problem to watch for is doubling up on one circuit—just as with circuit-breaker boxes. This happens when one plug circuit fails and the homeowner doubles up the load on another circuit.

Fuse-box wiring has lots of potential problems. The empty circuit on the far right has gone bad within the box, and the homeowner doubled up on the second from right circuit (problem #1). This started blowing the fuse on the doubled-up circuit, so the homeowner increased the fuse till it held—and that was at 30 amps (problem #2). The next circuit is a Fusestat, or type S circuit; note that there's a circular device screwed into the fuse holder's threads (fuse removed) to make the hole slightly smaller. This device will allow only a 20-amp fuse to be installed. The circuit on the left has a 12-gauge wire and is fused at 30 amps instead of the required 20 (problem #3).

Chapter 3

SIDING, DOORS, AND WINDOWS

SIDING

DOORS

WINDOWS

S iding, doors, and windows are key parts of the exterior inspection. Because these three elements are highly visible, their condition is a big factor in the salability of the house. But the inspector is less concerned with how they look than with how they perform. Siding, doors, and windows are designed to protect the house from rain, snow, wind, cold, and/or heat. When they cannot keep the elements out, energy bills sky-rocket and the house structure is exposed to decay. This is where inspector comes in: to deter-mine whether the siding, doors, and windows are sound before a new owner buys the house.

Siding

However much a salesperson or contractor will try to persuade you otherwise, there's no such thing as the perfect siding. All have advantages and disadvantages, and they all deteriorate—some just faster than others. It's up to the home inspector to determine whether the deterioration is significant enough to note to the buyer. For example, minor hairline cracks a few inches long are typically ignored, but large cracks that allow water to get behind the siding should be written up because they can lead to rapid decay within the walls.

As you make your initial walk-about inspection of the exterior, note the type of siding on your

You probably won't see much worse siding than this in the course of your inspections. The thin outer layer of the painted plywood has pulled away, and the paint is peeling and blistering.

form (the most common types appear in the checklist at right). You'll be looking for different things with each type of siding; but, regardless of material, always look for the obvious first. For example, is the siding falling off the house? Are there large holes or areas of the siding that are ripped open?

You never know what you'll find. One inspection took me to a summer home deep in the woods that had been vacant for two years. The owner told me that the house was in prime condition the last time he'd seen it, but it was anything but when I arrived. There were holes and splinters all over the surface of the siding—it looked as though someone had drilled holes in it with a spade bit and then used a prybar to rip it apart even more. The damage was particularly bad around the doors and windows, and my initial thought was that someone had tried to break into the house. But then I spied the true culprit: a pileated woodpecker lurking in the woods. These birds get to be very large and can destroy almost anything made out of wood. Seems they have a taste for uninhabited houses.

Type of Siding Checklist

- [ ] Painted wood
- [ ] Cedar boards (horizontal or vertical)
- [ ] Cedar shingles
- [ ] Board and batten
- [ ] Exterior plywood
- [ ] Hardboard composite
- [ ] Asbestos cement
- [ ] Fiber cement
- [ ] Vinyl
- [ ] Aluminum
- [ ] Block
- [ ] Brick
- [ ] Stucco
- [ ] Other

Inspector Beware

As you inspect the exterior of the house, you'll be looking for signs of insect damage (see p. 58), but you must also be on the watch for insects that can do damage to you. Don't be so engrossed in what you are doing that you walk straight into a hornet's, yellowjacket's, or bee's nest. Nests of stinging insects may be underground, in the insulation within the crawl space, under the house soffits and eaves, or in trees close to the building.

Watch for insects that repeatedly fly in and out of one particular spot (invariably the nest) and pay attention to buzzing sounds around you. Obviously, you don't want to disturb a nest if you find one, but sometimes this can happen before you're aware of it. For this reason, it's wise to have on hand insect spray, a sting kit, a first-aid kit, and some antiseptic wash. And if you are allergic to insect stings, make sure the appropriate medication is readily available in your car or truck.

Be on the lookout for stinging insects as you do your exterior walkabout. A hornet's next like this one (new or old) tucked under the eaves is not something you want to disturb.

Whether the siding has been damaged by fowl, old age, insects, or bad construction, it's the one thing the owner will try to make look good in an attempt to sell the house fast. A new coat of paint can cover a lot of defects and can also distract you from the underlying problems. That's why it's important to carry an awl to probe the siding and trim. You'll be checking for the obvious—such as rot, disintegration, and delamination; peeling and blistering paint; cracks; and missing sections of siding—but don't overlook the not so obvious. Check where the siding butts up against the trim or against anything else that protrudes from the

wall, such as a brick, block, or stone chimney. Be especially vigilant where the siding has been drilled through for plumbing, electrical, phone, or other projections. Water will get into the cut edge and begin the process of rot.

Painted wood

The reason we paint wood siding is to place a weatherproof covering over the wood grain to prevent moisture from entering and destroying the wood. But even under the best of circumstances, the paint will eventually wear off, making

Here's a not-so-obvious problem waiting to happen. The hardboard siding has pulled away from the brick, leaving a gap for the water to penetrate the edge of the board. Somebody has tried caulking the gap, but the caulk has pulled away too.

Always check carefully around any projections through the siding. Although the plumber put a little sealant around the pipe, it has pulled loose and water is now entering the cut hole and rotting out the board.

When the paint has worn away from the siding to this extent, it can no longer keep out the weather; write it up.

painted wood a particularly high-maintenance siding. Although it isn't necessary to comment on the type of paint (oil or latex) or the quality of the paint job, you should note major defects such as blistering and peeling as well as areas where the paint has worn away.

When is the condition of the paint bad enough to write up? If only one or two boards are affected, I usually overlook it because significant moisture is probably not getting under the paint surface. But if the paint has cracked or separated from the wood siding over large areas of the house and bare wood is showing, I always make note of it on my report. Sometimes the problem is more serious than just a crack in the paint sur-

face, so check to make sure that the wood itself is not cracking, delaminating, swelling, or disintegrating. This is a particular problem with painted siding made of plywood, oriented strand board (OSB), or other types of flat-grained or pressed wood.

Also be on the lookout for mold, mildew, and blackening of the painted surface. Some new

Lead Paint

Lead-based paint is a significant problem in older houses and is one of the most common causes of lead poisoning in children. Lead was first used in residential paint in the United States in 1884, and its use continued until the government banned lead-based paint in 1978. Even though lead paint is no longer manufactured, it remains on the exterior and interior walls of many older houses. However, lead-based paint is not considered a significant problem unless it has been sanded or is cracking and chipping off the wall. (You can get lead into your body by breathing or swallowing dust or lead-impregnated paint chips.)

There are two methods of testing for the presence of lead-based paint. One is called x-ray fluorescence, which uses portable detectors to x-ray a painted surface. These detectors are available for inspectors to buy, but without manufacturer training and certification by the state or the Environmental Protection Agency (EPA), you cannot make an official test. The second method is laboratory testing. Do-it-yourself kits are available at hardware stores, but there's some concern about their accuracy and I do not recommend that you use them.

If a test for lead-based paint is required by the local jurisdiction, contact your local public health organization for information on trained, licensed professionals. I would also strongly suggest to the homeowners that they test not just the painted surfaces but also the soil around the house, which may be contaminated with lead-impregnated dust and paint chips. More often than not, however, the contract offered to a buyer on a suspected house will simply have a lead-paint exclusion clause and no testing will be necessary.

There are a number of local, state, and federal laws concerning what sellers must disclose to prospective buyers about houses with lead-based paint. Typical requirements are as follows:

- Sellers must give buyers an EPA/Department of Housing and Urban Development (HUD) pamphlet on lead paint.

- Sellers must disclose known lead-paint hazards.

- Sellers must provide available records or reports to buyers.

- Buyers must be given 10 days to do a lead-risk inspection.

- Contracts must contain specific disclosure language.

- Agents and sellers share joint responsibility for disclosure.

- Sellers and buyers can waive or amend the 10-day inspection.

---

exterior paints are prone to these problems after only a year of application, because they don't contain the mildewcides of older paints. When a side of the house never receives the direct rays of the sun and there is enough moisture, it's common for mold and mildew to cover the siding, especially if trees or bushes are growing close to the house. Sometimes it will be visible as a gradual blackening of the entire side of the house, other times as black spots. Left unchecked, mold and mildew can ruin the siding.

Cedar siding

For sheer beauty and longevity it's hard to beat cedar siding. Typical board types are beveled and pattern. Beveled cedar siding comes in many styles and is one of the most common types of

If the house is sided with a low-grade cedar siding, you'll see a lot of large knots over the surface. This knot is still intact, but make a note of any that have popped out, exposing the felt underneath.

horizontal siding you'll see on houses. Pattern cedar siding is solid, full-width boards that fit together with a tongue-and-groove or shiplap joint; it is usually installed vertically. Cedar siding comes in different grades, with the poorest having the largest knots (make a note of any knots that have popped out of the siding).

Cedar board siding will split like any other wood. The thinner the siding, the easier the wood will split. Some of the splits will appear as the wood weathers, but other splits are there from the start. The ends of the boards are most prone to splitting, and unscrupulous contractors will install cedar siding with splits at the end (rather than taking the time to trim them back to sound wood). Look for the worst split-end (and large-knot) boards to be installed on the back of the house. The best siding is invariably installed on the house front, the next best on the house sides, and the worst on the house back. For this reason, it's a good idea to begin your check of the siding at the back of the house.

Cedar siding is also available as shingles or shakes, which are thin, rectangular pieces of wood tapered at one end, typically 12 in. to 18 in. long and of random width. Because shingles are thin, they are very easily split or broken during installation or after they are installed. The problem is

Over time, shiplap cedar siding applied vertically tends to split off along the edges.

exacerbated with age, because the shingles sometimes start cupping and breaking apart as they dry. Look for missing pieces of shingles and split sections that look as though they might fall out or blow away.

Whether board or shingles, cedar siding can be painted, stained, or left to weather to a silver gray.

Cedar siding exposed to the weather may blacken with mold if left untreated or unpainted.

Darker coloring on cedar siding is a sign that the affected area is being drenched by splashing or dripping water, possibly from a leaking or missing downspout.

If left to weather without any surface treatment, cedar doesn't always turn the desired color. As it ages, a black mold can take over, turning the once beautiful red a dark and ugly creosote color. If left unchecked, the mold will ruin the siding. (A simple fix for the homeowner is to spray the siding with a chlorine solution to kill the mold.)

Also check for discoloration of the siding at the house corner. This typically occurs on a house where the downspouts are missing and the gutter water cascades down and splashes over the siding. Discoloration on the lower courses of siding can also be caused by splashback, where the rain hits the ground and splashes back onto the building. Whatever the cause, heavy weathering not only discolors the siding but also eventually tears away at its grain.

One final thing to check for is the wrong type of nail used to install cedar siding. If you see long rust streaks down the siding, you can assume that the installer used the wrong type of nail; stainless-steel nails are the preferred fasteners.

Board-and-batten siding

Board-and-batten siding is a vertical design created from wide boards spaced apart with narrower boards (battens) covering the joints. You don't see much of it used on new houses anymore, but it is still available. It seems to be more common on older homes in rural areas and is either painted or unpainted. The main things to look for are boards that have split and large, empty knotholes that allow water to get behind the siding. Almost any type of wood can be used for board-and-batten siding, although cedar was the traditional choice. Poplar is currently a favorite board for this type of siding, but it tends to split easily.

Exterior plywood siding

Exterior plywood (sometimes known as T-111 after a popular specific type made by Georgia-Pacific) looks like regular plywood, but its individual laminations are bonded together with (allegedly) waterproof glue so it can be used outside. This material is available with one finished side in a variety of groove patterns and face textures, making it suitable for use as siding. Exterior plywood siding comes in inexpensive, standard 4-ft. by 8-ft. sheets and installs easily, which are two reasons why contractors and do-it-yourselfers like it so much. You'll see a lot of it on low-cost, budget-priority buildings.

Along with increased popularity seems to have come increased failure of the product. The most common reason for exterior plywood failure is improper installation. Exterior plywood, like all plywoods, needs to have its grain impregnated with paint or some other finish to keep water from being absorbed into the wood. This means it must be painted or sealed every few years (which rarely happens). Left to the elements, the siding will start to delaminate, bow, and disintegrate all too quickly, no matter that it is impregnated with waterproof glue. If the entire wall is having problems, you'll see a continuous in and out bowing or waving of the upper and bottom edges from one side of the house to the other.

Another installation problem is the flashing. When two sheets of exterior plywood butt up against each other vertically, a metal Z-flashing needs to be used. The flashing is installed underneath the bottom edge of the upper sheet and then bends over the top edge of the bottom sheet. This keeps water flowing off the top sheet of plywood from hitting the end grain of the bottom sheet. I've seen plastic Z-flashing used on a few buildings, but it doesn't seem to do much

Cedar Siding Checklist

- [ ] Major cracks
- [ ] Broken and missing sections that have split off
- [ ] Split ends and empty knotholes
- [ ] Heavy weathered areas
- [ ] Black fungi and mildew
- [ ] Rust streaks from nails or screws

With board-and-batten siding, look for splits in the long vertical boards. Ignore small cracks, but write up anything that's as long as the one shown here.

If the exterior plywood siding is failing, you'll see from a distance the raised top and bottom edges of the siding bending out. This building is about 10 years old, but it's not unusual for the siding to fail in a matter of months.

Always check that flashing is installed between the ends of butting sheets of exterior plywood siding. This building is brand new; but without the flashing, the plywood is already starting to bow.

good. Even the metal Z-flashing doesn't always eliminate the problem of water saturating the upper edge of the siding. The problem is most significant on the hard-weather side of the building (the side that's exposed to the prevailing wind and driving rain), so make sure you inspect all sides.

Installation is not the only problem with exterior plywood. Delamination, bowing, and the grain pulling out in large splinters can happen even when the plywood was installed properly. Look for bowing so pronounced that it is pulling the nails right out of the wood. Many times you'll see a large group of nails at one spot where the installer tried to keep the plywood against the building. And don't forget to look down. The bottom edge is hit by water and dirt splashback

The cheap plastic Z-flashing is warping as much as the plywood. You can see the center raised sections of the siding cupping and pulling away from the backing.

It's common to see a bunch of nails where someone has tried to nail a cupped board back to the wall, but this simply accelerates the process of splintering and delaminating.

from the ground, which will quickly destroy the plywood.

Hardboard composite siding

Hardboard composite siding was developed as a low-cost alternative to solid-wood siding. Made from wood fiber, fillers, binders, and glue, the horizontal siding board could be called anything but solid wood. But like solid-wood siding, it also needs to be painted.

Hardboard composite siding is one of the two most controversial siding materials around (the other is synthetic stucco). It has failed in many areas of the country, and many class-action suits have been filed against various manufacturers. As a result, this type of siding has been taken off the market, but there are still thousands of houses sided with this material. The most common variety is a long horizontal board with a bead along the bottom edge.

When inspecting a house with hardboard composite siding, first stand back about 40 ft. and

Exterior Plywood Siding Checklist

- ☐ Overall waving in and out of the siding
- ☐ Overall disintegration
- ☐ Delamination, bowing, and splintering in individual boards
- ☐ Missing flashing
- ☐ Large groups of nails installed to secure bowing plywood
- ☐ Disintegration and bowing of the bottom edge next to the ground

Insect Damage

Most home inspectors are not licensed pest-control experts and, in my opinion, should not give verbal or written assurance of the presence or absence of insects in a building. However, you can and should point out any obvious damage. If insect damage is found, note it on your report and recommend that a professional pest-control expert be consulted. Each area of the country has its own local problems for the inspector to be aware of. One of the most common insect problems is termites.

Termites

There are 41 species of termites in North America, most of them concentrated in the southeastern United States. The only state that does not have termites is Alaska. The most common termite, the subterranean termite, builds its nest in the ground. These termites construct mud tubes, which are used to explore for food and connect their underground nest to that food source. They can enter a building without direct wood contact with the soil through these tubes. Subterranean termites can be attracted to a particular house by bad back-filling practices, such as throwing wood into the ditch area around the house.

Termite workers are about $\frac{1}{4}$ in. long and wingless. They will tunnel in all wood products, except pressure-treated, and can cause extensive structural damage. Termites will eat most cellulose fibers, which includes most of the house. Be on the lookout for hollow areas where they have eaten the wood, as well as for their mud tubes.

Look for termites entering the building and termite damage to floor joists and other wood building materials. (Photos courtesy of Orkin Pest Control.)

One of the most common signs of termite infestations is swarming, which is detectable as winged adults crawling all over the ground or house wall. Swarming occurs when a colony reaches a certain size and then migrates to establish new nests. This usually occurs three to eight years after the colony starts and at a specific time of year, depending on location. In North Carolina, for example, swarming begins in February or March and continues into the fall. If you see a swarm outside, it doesn't necessarily mean the house is in danger—all it means is that there is a colony around. Simply make note of the swarm and recommend that a professional exterminator service come in and take a look.

Do not automatically think you have found a termite because it has wings—termites fly in the spring, but so do ants. The way to tell the difference is by the antennae and waist. A winged ant has elbowed antennae, whereas a termite's are straight. A winged ant also has a narrow waist, whereas the termite has a thick waist.

Carpenter Ants

In my part of the country, carpenter ants are the insect enemy of choice. These giant ants don't eat the house, but they are the best little tunnel builders around. They'll normally tunnel parallel to the grain in long beams but will eat straight through thin cedar siding to nest inside the wall. Use an awl to poke around suspect areas (typically wood framing, siding, and trim that are water damaged) and observe the route the foraging workers take. Carpenter ants love to tunnel into foam insulation, so be particularly wary of any areas where the insulation is visible.

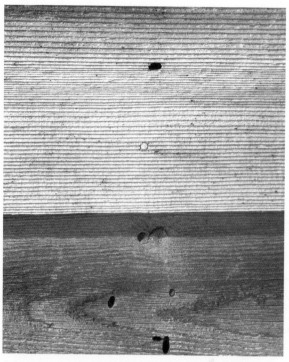

Carpenter ants don't eat wood but they will tunnel through almost anything to get to a nest—as they have in this cedar siding. Look for holes up to about ¼ in. in diameter. (Photo courtesy of Orkin Pest Control.)

Wood-Destroying Beetles

Wood-destroying beetles, also known as powderpost beetles, are common throughout the United States (especially in warm, humid climates), but they are not that easy to detect. They typically get into the house in the construction lumber itself or are carried in on firewood. If wood-destroying beetles are active in the house, you may notice a talcum power residue immediately below where they have been working. Once you see the powder, poke your pointed screwdriver or awl into the suspect wood and pull up—it should pull out like thin paper. Typically, the wood will look sound at first inspection and then cave in or pull out as you poke into it.

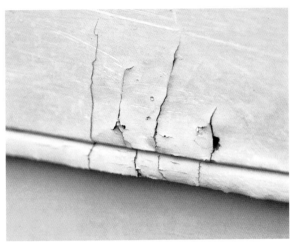

Cracked and peeling paint on hardboard composite siding is a good indication that the material underneath has started to rot.

If water gets into the end of a hardboard composite board, the entire board can swell up—sometimes to more than 50 percent of its original width.

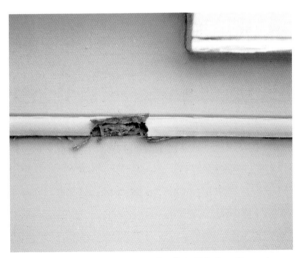

With a relatively fresh coat of paint, this hardboard composite siding board looked sound, but a firm finger push against the siding revealed that the whole bottom bead was rotted.

take an overall look at the entire wall. This makes it possible to spot general problems that you might miss close up—especially those up high. Look for edge cracks, splitting, puffed-out areas, peeling paint, large blisters, and anything that breaks the smooth, flat surface of the siding. You need to inspect all sides of the house, but pay

particular attention to the weathered side. I've seen many houses sided with hardboard composite that were fine except on this one side.

As you do your walkabout, check for the same problems that you were looking for from afar. Peeling paint and blistered areas will be obvious, but sometimes the problem will not be so immediately apparent. The wood beneath the paint can be completely rotted without any surface indication of the failure. One area that seems particularly prone to rot is the bead on the bottom edge of the board (especially the bead on the lowest course of siding). Rather than use an awl to probe for rot (you don't want to break the paint seal if the wood is sound), I recommend just pushing on the siding with your fingers. If it feels spongy, write it up.

One of the biggest problems with hardboard composite siding is that the entire board can swell up if water gets behind the paint; because the material is made of pressed composites, it absorbs water like a sponge. It's not always easy to detect the swelling on a flat board, but it can be seen when two butt ends of the siding come together. Once water enters and the swelling begins, the rot

Check for swelling and blistered areas anywhere that pipe or conduit is cut through hardboard composite siding.

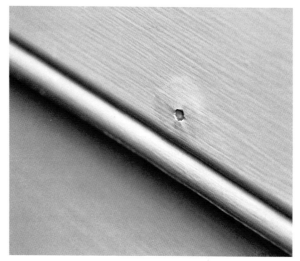

Nail holes are not immune to water penetration. The small area around the nail hole allows water to enter, causing swelling around the nail head.

Hardboard Composite Siding Checklist

- ☐ Splitting, peeling paint, large blisters
- ☐ Severe thickness swelling
- ☐ Rotted beads along bottom edge
- ☐ Missing caulk at open butt joints
- ☐ Swelling around pipes or conduit
- ☐ Dimples around nail heads

follows close behind. All butt joints are potential problem areas. Look closely where the siding butts together, where it terminates against an inside or outside corner, and especially where it butts up against a brick or block wall. These areas are main entry points for water intrusion into the siding, and all should be sealed with caulk. Log them if they aren't sealed or if the caulk is pulling apart.

Water can also get into the siding where holes have been cut for plumbing pipes or electrical conduit. If left unsealed, the cut edges of the hole absorb water and start the swelling and rotting process. You may occasionally see dimples and cracked paint around the nails that attach the siding to the house—another instance where water has penetrated the paint surface. One final area to check is anywhere something has been nailed or screwed into the siding—for example, where a handrail has been attached directly to the siding. The fasteners provide a direct water-entry path into the center of the siding.

Asbestos-cement siding

Up until the time it had to be taken off the market, asbestos cement was probably the longest-living, lowest-maintenance siding around.

It was used on houses from the 1940s through the 1970s, and the siding on some of the earliest houses still looks brand new. The problem wasn't with the performance of the material but with the health risks associated with the use of asbestos.

Asbestos is not generally considered a problem unless it is airborne. Being outside and in a solid form, asbestos-cement siding should pose no problem to the homeowner. Most experts (including the EPA) agree it should not be removed, just left alone. How do you know a house has asbestos siding? It was made in thin, wide sheets, some straight, some wavy. Most are white, but they can be painted too. Tap on the siding with the tip of a screwdriver; if the siding sounds like a pie plate, it's probably asbestos cement. For a more positive answer, call a siding specialist—preferably someone who is old enough to have installed this material.

If the house is sided with asbestos cement, make note of it on your inspection form and check for broken and missing sections (I ignore tiles with small cracks). Asbestos-cement siding is thin and very brittle, so it's not unusual to see a few broken tiles, especially at the corners. In addition, I'd mention to the homeowners that children shouldn't play immediately adjacent to the exterior walls unless it is known that the dirt is free of asbestos and it will not rub off against the children's clothes.

Fiber-cement siding

Fiber-cement siding, an offshoot of asbestos cement, is another attempt to come up with a better, long-lasting siding board. This product was developed by James Hardie Building Products, and unlike composite hardboard, synthetic stucco, and some of the other alternative siding materials, fiber cement really seems to work. Fiber-cement siding substitutes tough wood fibers for asbestos, blending them with Portland cement, ground sand, and clay. All fiber-cement siding is $5/16$ in. thick and comes primed or unfinished. Fiber-cement planks look identical to other types of manufactured siding. Available in widths of 6 in., $7\frac{1}{2}$ in., $9\frac{1}{2}$ in., and 12 in. and in standard lengths of 12 ft., this siding comes in a smooth finish, a wood-grain texture, and even a rough-sawn look. Fiber-cement panels are also available in 4-ft. widths.

Fiber cement can simulate almost any type of wood, as well as vinyl, brick, and even stucco, and you may have to take a close look at the siding to be sure it is not the real thing. To be

Asbestos-cement siding is recognizable by its thin shingles, which often have a wavy bottom edge. Check for broken edges and cracked corners.

sure, tap the siding with a screwdriver—as with asbestos cement, it sounds like a hollow plate. The siding can be installed either vertically or horizontally, and most types can be painted or stained. Fiber-cement siding has a Class 1 fire rating, which means the siding doesn't burn and produces virtually no smoke—offering increased safety and, in some areas, lower insurance rates. According to the manufacturers, it is also resistant to everything from weather to wood-boring insects and immune to ultraviolet (UV) rays.

I don't know of any significant problems with fiber cement, although given that it's a cement-based product there's the possibility that the sid-

ing may crack during installation. So, as with asbestos cement, be on the lookout for any major cracks in the material.

Vinyl siding

It's hard to beat vinyl siding for low cost and ease of installation, which is probably why it's used on more homes than any other siding on the market. Contractors like it because it requires few specialty tools. Homeowners love it because it spares them the chore of having to paint or stain the exterior of their house every few years. As a bonus, vinyl does a good job of covering rotted and insect-eaten siding. (Not that this solves the underlying

Fiber cement can emulate almost any type of siding, making it hard to tell the difference even up close. (Photos courtesy James Hardie Building Products.)

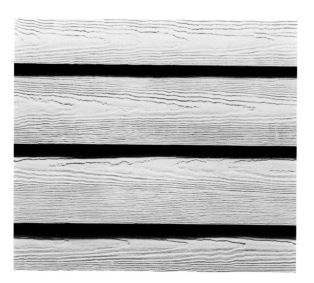

problem, but if the owner is an advocate of "out of sight, out of mind" thinking, there's nothing an inspector can do because he or she is not going to tear off the siding to check.)

As with most other types of siding, vinyl is not without its drawbacks. Most problems are the result of poor installation. Vinyl expands and contracts a significant amount due to changes in temperature; for example, a standard 12-ft. length can be a ½ in. shorter on a cold day than it is on a hot day. For this reason, vinyl is normally cut long, overlapped an inch or so, and allowed to slide. But if the installer cuts the pieces too short and they don't overlap enough, they'll pull apart and leave a gap, allowing water to get into the wall. Other times, if two sections get caught on each other as they expand, they will buckle, bow out, or break. Sometimes a section of siding just

pops away from the wall for no apparent reason. With this in mind, you need to look particularly closely at the joints between sections.

A common misconception about vinyl siding is that it is watertight. It is not. Wind can drive rain through the smallest of cracks between sections and through the inevitable gaps that will appear around windows and doors. This will be especially apparent when water gets behind the siding and then freezes. In winter, look for icicles protruding down between the siding and the wood behind.

Not all problems with vinyl are installation problems; some are inherent in the material itself. UV radiation makes vinyl brittle over time, which occasionally causes long horizontal cracks in the siding. And anything thrown against the house, such as a rock picked up by a lawn mower or an errant baseball, can punch a hole in the siding.

Vinyl siding expands and contracts a significant amount with changes in temperature. If the installer fails to overlap the siding, adjoining pieces will pull apart and allow water to get into the wall.

Check for buckled edges at the joints between sections or areas where the siding has popped away from the building.

Two other problems I see with vinyl-sided houses have to do with renovation and maintenance. On houses where the electrical system is upgraded to a higher-amperage service, the installer doesn't always put the new meter base in the same location as the old meter base. As a result, you're left with a large ugly hole in the siding—a gaping entry for rain and snow to pour in and rot the wood. The second problem occurs on the side of the house that the sun never hits—where mold, mildew, and algae can grow. Although this doesn't seem to damage the vinyl (other than causing discoloration), left unchecked mold and mildew can spread to the wood underneath and cause problems. There's really no

Vinyl Siding Checklist

- ☐ Expansion gaps between sections of siding
- ☐ Buckled, bowing, or broken sections
- ☐ Horizontal cracks in the siding
- ☐ Holes in the siding or trim
- ☐ Old meter-base holes
- ☐ Mold, mildew, and algae

When inspecting any siding, make sure you look up high on the building, not just at ground level. On this house, the wind has caught the vinyl and ripped it upward just above the lower roof. Immediately below that, the trim section has splintered and broken, probably because a ladder was leaned against the vinyl.

On houses where the electrical system has been upgraded, you'll sometimes see a hole in the siding where the old meter base was removed. Wind, rain, snow, and ice can now penetrate the siding. This house isn't without other areas of concern, including a ground wire that goes nowhere and conduit problems.

Mold growing on the side of the house that never sees the sun is a common problem on vinyl-sided houses, especially if there are bushes and trees close to the house.

Aluminum siding holds up well to the elements, as evidenced by this house, which was sided 35 years ago. Check for significant dents and any ripped sections of siding.

excuse for this other than the apathy of the homeowner—all the homeowner has to do is wash it off.

Aluminum siding

Aluminum siding isn't used much these days (vinyl siding has pretty much cornered the market), but it is still available. Most aluminum-sided houses have held up pretty well over the years: I have a neighbor whose house was sided

with aluminum 35 years old, and it still looks brand new. All it's needed during all those years has been one coat of paint.

Aluminum siding's biggest drawback is that it dents if hit by a branch, rock, or other projectile. (Although a dent is certainly preferable to the hole that you'd have gotten if the siding were vinyl.) In addition to major dents, check for any sections of the siding that have been ripped off; you're most likely to find these low to the ground. One thing to watch for as you are inspecting an aluminum-sided house is that the outside coating of the siding tends to dissolve into a fine powder that will rub off onto your clothes and hands.

Block

Block isn't normally considered a siding, but it is included here because it is an exterior wall that has to be inspected. Smooth-faced block was one of the most common building materials right after World War II. Block had a lot going for it because it went up fast; was very strong; wouldn't rot; wouldn't catch fire; lasted almost forever; and served as the footer, foundation, and siding all in one. Later, block was sometimes finished with a thin stone veneer for a more attractive exterior; today, block is available with various fancy finish faces, so the veneer is no longer installed.

A block exterior wall is just about as permanent and low maintenance as you can get. There shouldn't be much to inspect on newer block buildings; on older ones, probe the mortar joints between the blocks with an awl to check for disintegration. Also look for any broken blocks at the corners of the building and for Z-pattern cracks, which indicate that there is a footer problem. Mildew might be a problem if the house is in an area with high humidity, it doesn't get a lot of direct sunlight, or there are trees and other plantings growing close to the house.

Brick

Like block, brick is a house exterior that is durable and almost maintenance free. There are two types of brick houses: those with solid exterior brick walls and those with brick veneer. Solid-brick walls serve the same function as block walls, providing structural support and acting as the permanent finished wall. Brick veneer, a thin brick wall set to the outside of a stud wall, started replacing solid block when building codes began to require insulation in the exterior walls. One way to tell the two apart is to look immediately

A Z-crack running along the mortar joints in a block wall indicates that the footer has sunk, pulling the block apart. Make a note of it on your inspection form.

above the doors and windows. If it's brick veneer, you'll see the same pattern here as on the rest of the wall. On the other hand, solid-brick walls will typically have masonry arches or a different brick pattern above doors and windows. As you might expect, older solid-brick buildings usually take a little longer to inspect than newer brick veneers.

Inspecting brick is similar to inspecting block. Always look for Z-pattern cracks (which indicate that the footer has settled), crumbling mortar joints, and broken bricks. Although brick is a low-maintenance material, it is not ageless and will break apart over time, especially if the workmanship of the installation was faulty. Missing mortar joints should be obvious—look for dark voids where the mortar has broken loose and for conduit clamps that have pulled out of the crumbling mortar. Don't rely on your eye alone; probe with your awl to see how solid the mortar and bricks really are.

"Rotting," or disintegrating, bricks aren't always as easy to spot as missing mortar. The wall that's likely to have the most damage is the one

Block and Brick Checklist

- ☐ Missing or crumbling mortar joints
- ☐ Z-pattern or other continuous cracks
- ☐ Missing, broken, or disintegrating blocks or bricks
- ☐ Brick with missing facing
- ☐ Surface mildew

that faces into the prevailing wind. Look for brick that is losing its facing—it will be lighter in color than the surrounding brick. Sometimes the side of a house will be fine overall, but there will be missing or crumbling bricks at the corners. This normally happens when the brick is cracked and starts breaking up as a result of repeated freezing and thawing.

As you inspect the brick wall, try to see if there is a pattern to any of the cracks. Although Z-pattern cracks are usually obvious, other patterns are subtler but still possibly significant. Observe the small cracks in the mortar and brick face and then see if your eye can connect them.

Look closely and you'll see the telltale signs of a "rotting" brick wall. As seen in the close-up, the light-colored bricks are bricks that are crumbling away and have lost their face; the dark areas are where the mortar has fallen out of the joints; and the Z-pattern indicates that there's a settling problem above the lower-right window.

Small, discontinuous cracks are to be expected; but if the cracks join up, there's possibly a problem with the footer (see the photo below).

Stucco

Stucco, in use as a building material since at least Roman times, provides a durable and attractive waterproof coating; but, as with any siding, it works only if it is installed correctly. Moisture is the bane of all stuccoed houses. It gets into the exterior walls via the inevitable cracks that form on all stuccoed houses—cracks that result from improper installation, settling of the footer, shrinkage and expansion of the building frame,

The crack in this old brick wall starts at the footer and runs almost all the way up the wall. Small cracks are to be expected, but always write up any significant continuous cracks.

and seismic activity. Water also gets into the walls around doors, windows, utility access points, and anywhere the flashing has been left off or improperly installed.

There are three basic types of stucco—hard coat, synthetic, and hybrids of the two—but it's not the inspector's job to list the type of applied stucco (it's very hard to tell the difference once the stucco is applied). In the past, stucco installations had a good reputation, primarily because stucco was normally applied to a solid-masonry surface. Problems started when techniques were developed to install stucco on wood-studded walls. Today, a considerable number of hard-coat-stuccoed houses are leaking water into the stud walls, rotting out the framing members and wall joists; and an even greater number of synthetic-stuccoed houses are doing the same.

A good indication of the problems with synthetic stucco is the number of companies that have started up to sell equipment for testing for moisture intrusion that the allegedly waterproof siding invariably lets in. In industry parlance, synthetic stucco is known as EIFS (exterior insulation and finish system). EIFS is a layer of Styrofoam glued or nailed onto a wood backerboard (typically plywood or OSB), followed by a layer of Fiberglas mesh, a base coat, and a thin finish coat. There are two types of EIFS: the barrier-type and the water-managed system. Most of the problems reported with synthetic stucco are with the former type. Although the barrier system is said to be watertight, water inevitably gets in around doors and windows and other breaks in the wall. The water then gets trapped under the EIFS and cannot get back out—which is how the rot begins (the water-managed system gives any moisture that gets behind the stucco a way to get back out).

What is most confusing for the homeowner and most frustrating for the inspector is that stuccoed walls with water intrusion rarely show signs of the rot that is occurring within. An almost guaranteed leak spot is where the roof of a lower story, a garage for example, butts up against a synthetic-stucco wall. If there is no flashing

It always pays to be wary when inspecting a stuccoed house. From the outside, nothing appears to be wrong with this house, which is sided with barrier-type synthetic stucco (below); but the moisture problem was readily apparent when the interior facings were removed (right).

The intersection between a synthetic-stucco wall (visible above the rotted soffit) and a garage roof is a potential leak spot. Here, water followed the stuccoed wall down, and because there was no kick-out flashing at the bottom, the water drained straight into the soffit. (Photos this page courtesy of Stucco Pro.)

between the two, then the wall is probably rotting out from the roof/wall interface on down. Other likely leak spots are around double-hung windows and doors, with rot occurring immediately below.

Another potential problem with synthetic stucco is termite damage. If the stucco is in direct contact with or within a few inches of the ground, termites will migrate up into the water-soaked Styrofoam and into the damp sill plate and studs. Carpenter ants may also chew out large areas of the Styrofoam to nest in. Insect damage normally occurs when the wall is not finished properly and/or is less than 6 in. from the earth.

So what should the home inspector do when confronted with a house that has stucco—especially synthetic stucco? Moisture meters are available to check behind the stucco, but they are expensive and it takes a little practice and experience to use them properly. In my opinion, only certified inspection specialists should do these tests. If you are not experienced in this area, recommend that the seller or buyer call in a certified specialist for a comprehensive inspection.

Stucco Siding Checklist

- [ ] Obvious cracks in the stucco
- [ ] Stucco peeling off applied surface
- [ ] Old, caulked cracks that have reopened
- [ ] Rotted areas around doors, windows, and pipe penetrations
- [ ] Discoloration or damage due to excessive moisture in the wall
- [ ] Missing flashing
- [ ] Damage to interior wall facing

Of course, it is acceptable and prudent to observe and list the obvious, such as cracks in the stucco, areas where the stucco is peeling off the wall, caulked cracks that have reopened, missing flashing, discoloration on the wall, and any rotted wood. But under no circumstances should an uncertified inspector make a judgment about whether or not water has penetrated the wall. Some professional stucco inspectors can give the homeowner a national warranty, called Moisture Bond, against water intrusion.

Doors

As you walk around the house checking the siding, you should also make a note of the condition of the exterior doors and windows. The front door is the focal point of the house, and you should take your time inspecting it. If there are other exterior doors, check these as well. You won't normally inspect the interior doors until after you've finished outside and have begun your inside inspection.

The first thing to note is the type of front door. The three most common types are solid wood, steel with an insulated foam core (known as "steel insulated"), and fiberglass. No matter what the material, there are a few basic checks common to all. Observe the door's condition. Is it warped, split, or dog scratched? Is the glass cracked? Make

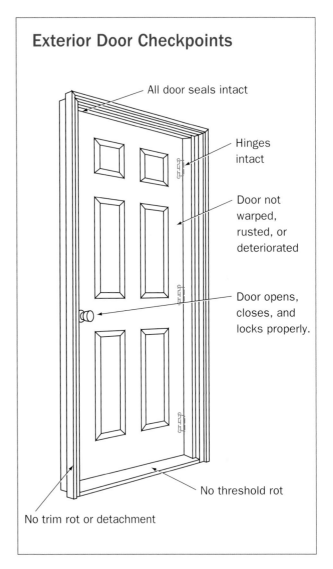

Exterior Door Checkpoints

All door seals intact

Hinges intact

Door not warped, rusted, or deteriorated

Door opens, closes, and locks properly.

No threshold rot

No trim rot or detachment

sure the door opens and closes properly and that both the handle and the locking mechanism work. Does the door shut and latch easily or do you have to push it in to make it latch? Are the hinges secured to the frame? Observe the seals with the door both opened and closed. Does part of the door seal and part not? If so, either the door is bowed or the frame was installed out of plumb.

Solid-wood doors

Solid-wood doors are an attractive choice but they tend to warp. I've seen many that warped so badly immediately after installation that, from the

Check the bottom of exterior steel-insulated doors, especially those left primed but unpainted. They sometimes rust on the bottom where salt has been thrown on the front step.

On steel-insulated doors, check the condition of the plastic trim and glass separators. Exterior doors that face the sun are particularly susceptible to broken and cracked trim.

inside of the house, you could see outside with the door shut. As with any wood building material, solid-wood doors can crack, split, delaminate, or rot. Sometimes the problem will be obvious, other times you'll have to probe more closely. Another problem with solid-wood doors is their low R-rating, which means they provide only minimal insulation against the cold (but there's no check for this, of course).

Steel-insulated doors

Steel-insulated doors with a sandwich of foam insulation were developed as a low-cost, energy-efficient alternative to solid-wood doors. Most come from the factory with a gray primer coating—and many stay that way. Unpainted, it is possible for the doors to rust, especially in coastal areas or around the bottom where salt is thrown on the front step to prevent ice buildup.

Although steel-insulated doors rarely warp, UV light can destroy the plastic trim around the door's edge and glass center. Look for broken and missing sections of trim. If that happens, the real problems can start—for example, the foam-core insulation may disintegrate and fall out of the door.

Steel-insulated doors use magnetic stripping to help seal out the cold. The problem is that many manufacturers use inferior plastic to house the magnet, and the magnet rips right out of the brittle plastic frame and stays stuck to the door. Other times you'll see strips that have been ripped out by dogs and cats trying to get back inside the house.

Look closely at the magnetic seal of a steel-insulated door. The photo above shows how a magnetic seal (the small white ridged area between the door and the door frame) is supposed to look. The photo at right shows a magnetic seal that has been ripped out of its plastic cover by a cat clawing to get into the house.

Storm doors tend to have a problem with the damper arm, which either gets bent or rips out. A telltale sign that this is a recurring problem on this entry door is the bare wood on the door frame where the damper support has been ripped out and reattached many times before.

Fiberglass doors

Fiberglass doors should go through the same basic inspection as solid-wood doors, but with a couple of additional checks for fading and fiberglass splinters. If the door is on the side of the house that has the worst weather—hot sunshine and driving rain—check the door closely. Fading will be obvious, but not the fiberglass splinters. Look for scores of tiny spears just barely sticking out from the outside door face. Don't rub your bare fingers across the face of the door to check, or you may take a few splinters home with you.

Storm doors

If there's a storm door, check it in the same way as you would any exterior door. In addition, the

Door Checklist

Exterior doors

☐ Won't open, close, or lock properly

☐ A gap between the door and the seal when the door is shut

☐ Solid wood:
    ☐ Split
    ☐ Warped

☐ Steel insulated:
    ☐ Rusting
    ☐ Broken away plastic trim
    ☐ Ripped off magnetic seal

☐ Fiberglass:
    ☐ Faded
    ☐ Splintered

Interior doors

☐ Damaged

☐ Won't close or lock properly

storm door may have a damper arm (a cylinder-like mechanism that shuts the door slowly and automatically), which has a habit of bending and ripping out of the door frame when a strong breeze catches the door's flat surface. Be sure the damper is in good condition and securely attached to the door and frame. If there's a screen door in place, make sure the screen is intact and not ripped or clawed.

Interior doors

These days, most interior doors are hollow wood, though on higher-end houses you'll still find solid wood. Whatever the material, simply check for the obvious. Are the doors intact? Do they open and close, latch and lock? Always check behind the door to see if the handle has made a hole in the wall.

Windows

Inspecting the windows of a house is a two-part process: first, a visual inspection of the condition of the windows, which is part of your exterior walkabout; and second, a manual check to make sure the windows function as designed, which is part of the interior inspection. Although you need to look at all the windows to determine their condition, you probably won't have time to open and close every window. Therefore, you need to check a representative number—maybe a window in every room, or at least one on each side of the house.

The most common problems for all windows are obvious ones: cracked, broken, or missing panes. But don't get so caught up in the glass inspection that you overlook some other important checkpoints. Be sure to check the wood around the window frame to see if it is rotting out or in need of paint. One item that's commonly missed is the sealant around the window frame. If there's visible caulking between the window frame and the siding, check to see that it has not pulled away from the siding, allowing water to get

Check the frame around the window for signs of rot. If you see a windowsill this bad, write it up.

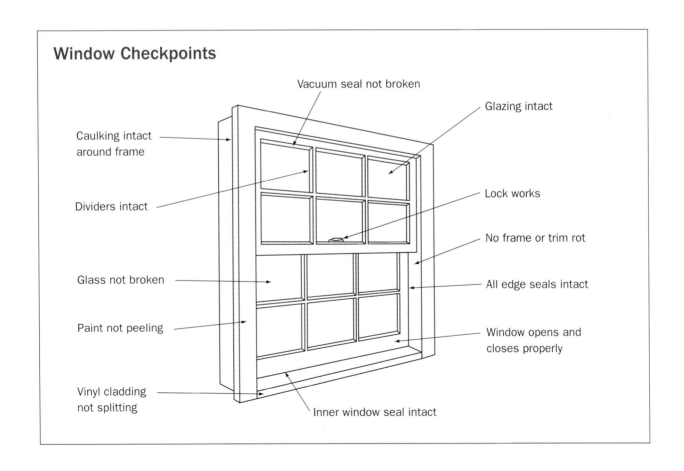

Window Checkpoints

Vacuum seal not broken

Glazing intact

Caulking intact around frame

Dividers intact

Lock works

No frame or trim rot

Glass not broken

All edge seals intact

Paint not peeling

Window opens and closes properly

Vinyl cladding not splitting

Inner window seal intact

Look closely at vinyl-clad windows, especially on the side of the house that gets the most sun. Vinyl has a significant expansion:contraction ratio, and mating pieces can pull apart at the corner of a window, allowing water to enter and destroy the wood interior.

Insulated windows are infinitely better than single-pane glass to help keep the heat in, but they can lose their insulating gas or vacuum barrier. Look for moisture between the two panes and white streaks left by evaporated water.

into the wall. On vinyl-clad windows, check for any corners where the vinyl has pulled apart.

Although windows come in an almost infinite number of designs, the most common are fixed, double hung, horizontal and vertical sliders, casement, and a category I refer to as "leave-alone." Regardless of the design, a smart prospective buyer will want to know two main things about the windows. First, are the windows insulated (also called double or triple glazed) or single pane (also called single glazed)? Second, if they are insulated, do they have low-E glass? Both are important because of energy considerations.

Insulated windows

Windows have R-ratings just like walls—the higher the number the less energy you lose through them. A typical exterior wall has an R-rating of around 15. Compare that to a single pane of glass that has an R-rating of only 0.89. The only thing a single pane of glass is good for is to stop the wind from coming through. To raise the R-rating, window designers have come up with double- and triple-pane insulated glass. It's considered insulated because there's a vacuum between each pane. In an attempt to improve on the vacuum models, some manufacturers use argon and/or krypton gas between the panes. The typical R-rating for insulated windows is between 3 and 5.

Low-E, or low-emissivity, glass has a film on its surface that allows certain wavelengths of light through and reflects others. What this means to the homeowner is that the glass blocks some of the summer heat but allows winter sunlight energy to enter and stay inside. It's not always obvious if the windows are low-E (although the owners will probably let you know because low-E windows are a good selling point).

Although insulated windows are clearly desirable, they can eventually lose their vacuum. Moisture droplets and mist between the two panes of glass are signs that the seal is broken. Also check for white stains or streaks (mineral salts) that are left over from water as it evaporates.

Window Styles

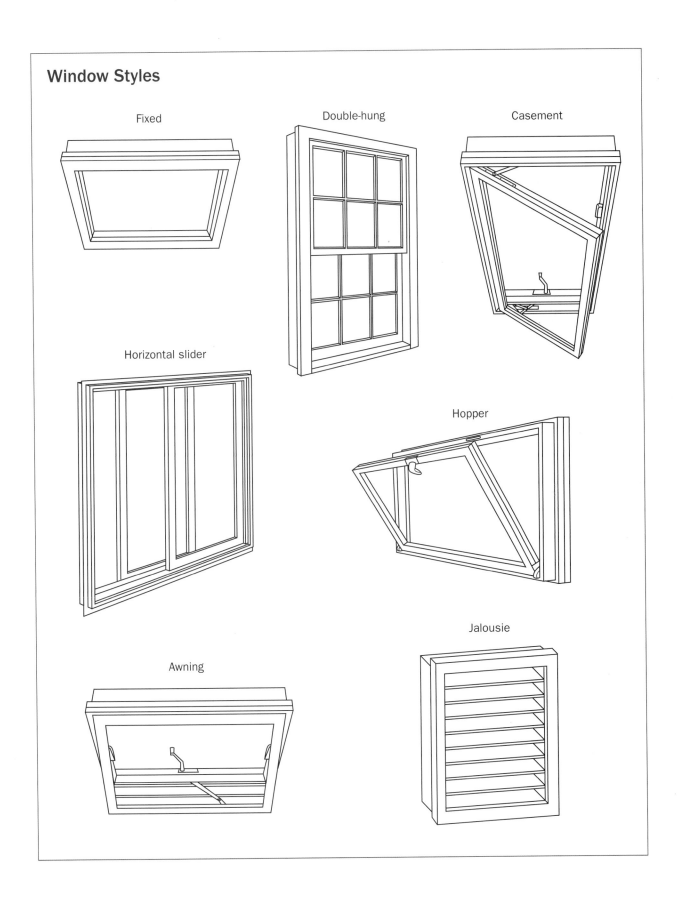

Fixed

Double-hung

Casement

Horizontal slider

Hopper

Awning

Jalousie

If you see "after-thought" flashing like this installed along the top of a window, it's a good indicator that the window leaks.

On old-style double-hung windows with a pulley, sash cord, and weight mechanism, check that the cord is present and not worn.

Fixed windows

Fixed windows are the easiest to inspect. They usually consist of a wood frame with one or two single or double panes of glass. They can be stand-alone windows or be incorporated with operable windows—such as a large fixed pane of glass between two double-hung or casement win-

dows all in the same frame. Because there's nothing to operate, simply check the glazing (if there is any) and everything that surrounds the glass. Pay particular attention to the sill, which may be water damaged as the result of condensation.

Double-hung windows

Double-hung windows, the most popular design on the market, have an upper and lower sash, or window, which slide up and down on separate tracks. Note the condition of the window and check to see if it functions. Old double-hung windows, which have a pulley, rope, and weight mechanism to aid in raising the bottom sash, are rarely in operating condition. By the time you inspect them they've probably been painted several times, which can make them very hard if not impossible to raise or lower. On older windows, also note if the ropes are still intact.

Horizontal and vertical sliders

Sliders are low-end windows that typically have aluminum frames. Unlike wood, aluminum will not rot, but it can corrode; and if enough trash gets in the tracks, the window will jam open or closed. Aluminum windows and frames sweat a lot, and as the water drains from the tracks it may rot out the adjoining wood. Be careful when checking to see if vertical sliders are operable: These windows have a habit of coming down fast and hard when you least expect it, with the risk of trapping your fingers and breaking the glass.

Casement windows

Casement windows open via a hand crank. Check to see if there's a handle on the crank, and then turn the crank to see if the window opens smoothly (make sure the latches are undone first). If the handle slips on the crankshaft, don't keep turning or you'll strip the grooves off the internal gear. If the window doesn't open as you turn the handle, gently push on the window to help break the seal. If it doesn't open with a gentle push, do not force it—just log that it won't open. On some

Window Checklist

- ☐ Broken, cracked, or missing glass
- ☐ Glazing that has broken away from the window
- ☐ Water damage at sills, rotted sills
- ☐ Wood framing in need of paint
- ☐ Caulking pulling away from the window trim
- ☐ Vinyl splitting at the corner of the vinyl-clad window
- ☐ Windows that are jammed or painted shut
- ☐ Double-hung windows with broken sash cords
- ☐ Casement windows with missing handles and ripped weather seals
- ☐ Missing, broken, or ripped storm windows and screens

On casement windows, check that the weather seal between the window and the frame is intact. This one has ripped out.

casement windows, the weather seals tend to rip out, which will be detectable by a small piece of plastic hanging out from the window.

Leave-alone windows

Awning, hopper, and jalousie windows fall in the category of leave-alone windows. All these windows have a tendency to corrode or jam in place; and even if you do get them to open, they may not be easy to close. My advice for all three is to check the condition of the glass and frame in the normal manner but otherwise leave them alone.

Storm windows and screens

Storm windows add another barrier between the inside and outside. They have the same R-rating as the single-glazed panes of glass they are installed in front of. One of the biggest problems with storm windows is heavy condensation on the inside, which means there must be a way for

Notice anything odd about these two double-hung windows? Look closely at the storm windows; the one on the left was installed upside down.

the water to leave and drain back outside. This is done via two weep holes or slots at the bottom of the storm window. If the holes get plugged, the water cannot drain, and the sill may rot. Be sure to check for this. If screens are in place instead of the lower storm windows, check for rips and tears in the screening and verify that the frame is not warped. If there are no screens, simply log it.

Chapter 4

ROOFS, GUTTERS, AND GRADING

INSPECTING THE ROOF

GUTTERING

GRADING

This inspection was one for the books. I was looking at a roof with my binoculars when I spied a small, furry head popping in and out of what appeared to be a hole. Eventually I saw his entire routine. He would climb a tree, jump to the roof, run along its peak to a hole he had gnawed through the roof at the dormer—then dive in. Apparently that was home.

The house had just gone on the market. I was there doing an inspection, and the owner was standing next to me. He had a reputation for being a little eccentric, and I was seeing the roots of it firsthand. "You have a squirrel in your attic," I told him.

"I know," he replied.

"But he's chewed a hole in your roof."

"I know," he repeated. "He's been quite a nuisance. I've tried everything to get rid of him."

"Do you really want your home to be inspected when it has a hole in the roof? I think that will lower the amount of money anyone is going to offer."

The guy thought about it for a moment. "How about coming back in the morning?" he suggested. "I'll have him gone by then. I guarantee it."

The next day I saw that the hole was patched and the squirrel was nowhere in sight. Later, while inspecting the attic, I noticed that there were six holes in the roof, which were letting in little light beams. They looked like lasers criss-

crossing in the dark, dusty attic air. After the inspection, I asked the owner how he'd rid himself of the squirrel. He smiled a broad smile and said he shot at it with a .22 bolt-action rifle—he didn't kill it, but he scared it away. "It took only three shots," the man bragged.

I informed him that there were now six holes in his tin roof just about the size of a .22 bullet. He thought about it for a moment. "Can you come back again tomorrow?" he asked. To this day that tin roof has six holes in it patched with six globs of silicone. The scary part wasn't that he shot his roof full of holes trying to get rid of the squirrel—the scary part was that he was a professor at the local university.

Inspecting the Roof

Not all roof problems will be as evident as the .22-scarred, squirrel-infested roof that I came across, but it's important to do a thorough check of the roof, because this is one of the main potential water-infiltration points into the house.

All roof inspections are done in two parts: the walk-about inspection and the attic inspection. The latter won't be done until you move onto the interior inspection—after all, you don't want to be constantly walking in and out of the house— but I've included it here so that all roof-related information will be in the same chapter.

The walk-about inspection

The walk-about inspection is the same no matter what type of material is used on the roof (asphalt shingles, cedar shingles, tile, slate, and so on). Walk around the house with binoculars and inspect the roof for any obvious problems, such as a hole in the roof or missing shingles or tiles, and for specific problems that apply to the type of roof material.

One of the first things you'll notice on a roof inspection is the peak, or ridge, of the roof. The ridge should be straight, not bent down like a swayback horse; problems here are likely caused by a cracked or rotted ridge beam. Also be on the

As you do your walkabout of the exterior, check the ridge of the roof. It should be straight, not swayback like this roof.

Wavy roofs typically occur where the underlying roof sheathing is too thin, rotting out, or delaminating.

How to Inspect the Roof

A roof inspection requires a close look at the roofing material to verify its condition. No matter what the material, it will take a beating from exposure to sun, wind, rain, and snow. But for insurance reasons, you're probably not allowed to get onto the roof—many roofs are dangerous to walk on because of their pitch or type of covering. There's also the risk of caving in the guttering or the edges of tiles or shingles with the ladder.

A good alternative is to use a pair of binoculars to inspect the roof, flashing, and chimney. If necessary, I climb an 8-ft. stepladder so I can get a better look at the roof with my binoculars. But be careful when you're setting up a stepladder in the yard because it can easily tip over if the ground is uneven. If you insist on using an extension ladder to get a closer look at the roof, and your insurance company is okay with that, you have to figure a way to lean a ladder onto the building without crushing the guttering. I use a special bracket that I built onto my ladder that goes over the guttering and leans on the roof itself. Stabilizer bars are also available for this purpose.

lookout for wavy roofs. Low bidders sometimes install thin sheathing on the roof, and the result can be a series of gentle undulations over the surface. A long time ago, $^3/_4$-in. plywood was the standard roof-sheathing material. When that got to be too expensive, $^1/_2$ in. became the norm. Now even $^3/_8$-in. plywood is used as sheathing. I've seen entire subdivisions with this wavy roof problem.

Wavy roofs can also be caused by delamination of the roof sheathing or excessive moisture rotting out the sheathing. On older houses, wavy roofs can result when new asphalt shingles are placed over old shingles and the roof can't support the weight. As an inspector, it isn't important to know what's causing the problem, just to note that it exists. I list roofs with a rippled surface as slightly, moderately, or very wavy.

As you do your walk-about inspection, don't get so caught up in inspecting the surface of the roof, that you forget to look at the guttering (see p. 93) and the soffit, fascia, and rake boards. Many soffits are installed with thin untreated wood, and they start rotting and pulling away from the building almost immediately. The problem is likely to be exacerbated if a drip cap wasn't installed (see the drawing at right). In squirrel country, it's not unusual for a squirrel to chew its way into the soffit to make a nest or to store some food.

Anything that protrudes through the roof is a potential leak source. Using your binoculars, look around attic vents, plumbing vents, gas vents, and chimneys that go through the roof for missing, raised, or ripped flashing. Make note of any skylights in the roof (these are notorious leakers), and check for signs of water infiltration below

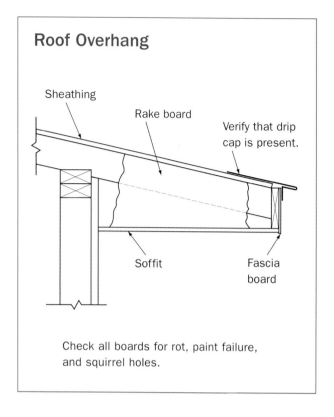

Roof Overhang

Sheathing

Rake board

Verify that drip cap is present.

Soffit

Fascia board

Check all boards for rot, paint failure, and squirrel holes.

Squirrels one, humans zero. Although squirrels don't keep score in the games they play with humans, they normally win. This one decided to make himself right at home in the soffit.

Flashing Checkpoints

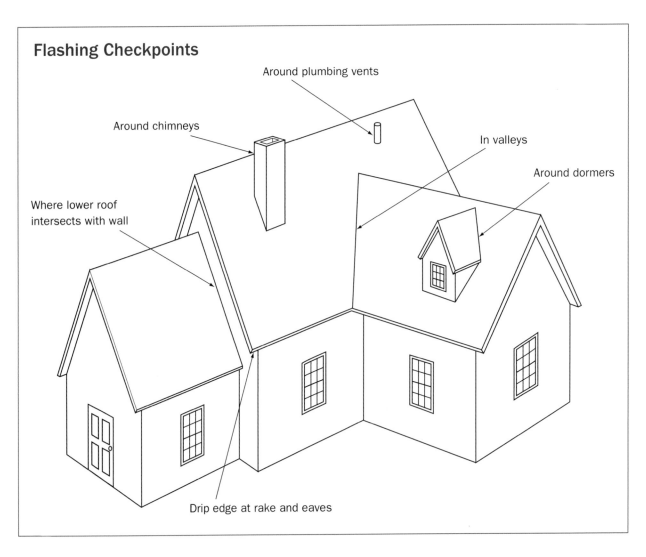

Around plumbing vents

Around chimneys

In valleys

Around dormers

Where lower roof
intersects with wall

Drip edge at rake and eaves

Make a note of any sky-
lights as you do the exterior walkabout and be
sure to check for leaks
under the skylight when
you inspect the interior.
Look for water tracks
along the skylight frame
inside the house and
water stains on the floor.
Be careful not to confuse
a leak with condensation.

Chimney Flashing

One of the main causes of leaking roofs is failure of the flashing around a chimney. Chimney flashing fails for two basic reasons: It is either punctured or torn, typically as a result of old age and corrosion, or the two-part overlapping flashing system, which consists of the step flashing beneath the shingles and counterflashing embedded in the chimney brick, has come loose or been damaged by wind and ice.

Other than spotting obvious problems, such as flashing flapping in the breeze, it's difficult to detect flashing failure from ground level, so it's important to do a thorough check from the inside when you do the attic inspection. Stone chimneys are notoriously difficult to flash because of the irregular shape of the stones; check these carefully. If the chimney is on the down slope of the roof, there should be a cricket, or saddle, whose purpose is to prevent water from pooling on the back side of the chimney. If there is no cricket, look closely for signs of leaking on the upper side of the chimney when you do the attic check.

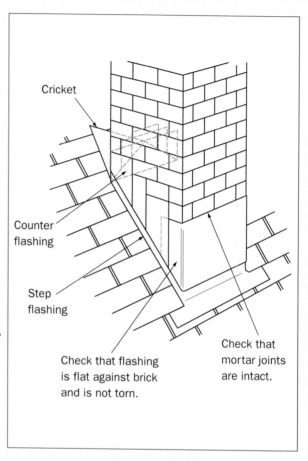

Cricket

Counter flashing

Step flashing

Check that flashing is flat against brick and is not torn.

Check that mortar joints are intact.

and around the skylight when you do your interior inspection.

Flashing is always a potential problem with roofs. Some places you can see it (as around a chimney), others you can't (as in a "woven" roof valley), so you can't always tell if it's there. (The drawing on the facing page shows the main roof-flashing checkpoints.) All you can do is try to verify that flashing is present where you think it should be, such as the drip edge around the edges of the roof sheathing. If it is there, look closely to see if it is in good condition.

Sometimes two roofs intersect, typically where an addition has been added. It's not always easy

General Roof Checklist

- ☐ Obvious holes in the roof
- ☐ Missing, broken, or torn shingles or tiles
- ☐ Sagging ridge
- ☐ Wavy roof surface
- ☐ Missing, raised, or ripped flashing
- ☐ Rotted or damaged soffit, rake, or fascia boards
- ☐ Damaged or inadequate guttering and downspouts

The intersection between two roofs is always a potential leak spot. On this house, the sheathing of the new addition was placed right on top of the shingles of the old building, with silicone caulk placed along the sheathing edge. Over time, the caulk will probably drop away, allowing water to saturate the sheathing and eventually rot it.

to see if there's a problem from the outside, but make note of the intersection on your exterior inspection and be sure to check immediately under this seam (inside the attic) to verify that there's been no leakage where the two roofs come together.

Asphalt shingles

Asphalt shingles are the workhorse of the roofing industry. In most areas of the country, the majority of houses you'll inspect will have asphalt shingles—also known as composition roofing or laminated shingles. One great advantage of

shingle roofs is that they can be reapplied over existing composition shingles (up to three layers in most states) without the need to strip off all previous layers. This brings the inspector to one important inspection—some roofs cannot take the weight of three layers of shingles and the roof will be sagging. It will be up to the inspector to catch this problem.

Asphalt shingles are categorized as either organic or fiberglass based; both are composed of a mat with weather-resistant granules. Early organic shingles were made by saturating rag felts with asphalt. Some time in the 1940s, the felt-mat base content was changed to incorporate cellulose, such as recycled paper and wood fibers. More recently, many manufacturers began producing shingles using a fiberglass mat to replace the felt. Fiberglass-based asphalt shingles are manufactured with a mat composed entirely of glass fibers of varying lengths and orientations. This fiberglass base is then surfaced with a specially formulated asphalt coating, followed by weather-resistant mineral granules.

Old age can get to any type of shingle. Over time, organic asphalt shingles disintegrate, cup, curl, buckle, crack, and break apart—after all, they are just ground-up paper. However, many die a premature death. Heat buildup from a poorly ventilated attic can shorten their life significantly. Most of us have seen evidence of this—shingles that look like puffed-up marshmallows or rough bark on a tree. Asphalt shingles tend to disintegrate more quickly in hot climates than in cold climates; similarly the side of the roof with the greatest sun exposure is likely to fail first.

Watch out for small raised areas called pop-ups. Nails pulling out of the roof and metal fasteners that used to hold the roofers' walkway bend the shingles up like small pup tents. Leaks immediately follow, and wind caught under the edge will rip and tear the shingle.

Specific things to watch for with organic-based asphalt shingles are rotting, blistering, and curling. Rotting is caused by absorption of moisture by the cellulose mat at the core of the shingle.

Left: If an old asphalt shingle roof looks this bad, write it up. The shingles need to be replaced. Below: A close-up look at the shingles reveals that the sand coating is completely gone in some areas and the shingles are rounded off and disintegrating.

Typically, an early sign of rot is rounding of the shingle edges, especially between the tabs. Blistering is caused by moisture soaking into the upper layer of the shingle and is visible as bubbled-up areas on the shingles, some of which may have broken open. Curling can occur if there is insufficient back coating on the shingles and can be part of the general aging process due to shrinkage caused by UV light. If you see rotting, blistering, or curling shingles, the roof is probably already leaking or will be leaking soon, so always write it up on your inspection form. Also make note of any areas on the roof that have been patched.

Loss of granules from the surface is another problem with asphalt shingles, but it's not something you have to write up unless the problem is significant. Granule loss doesn't affect the service life of the shingles unless the asphalt or fiberglass mat is exposed. One area to look for significant loss of granules is where an upper roof drains down to a lower roof (without a gutter).

Missing shingles caused by improper fastening and/or exposure to high wind will be obvious as you inspect the roof, but also make a note of any shingles that have their tabs waving loose—these are likely to blow off in the near future. The newer fiberglass shingles seem particularly prone

If the shingles are failing on a roof, there's a good chance that the flashing will have problems too. Here, a nail through the flashing under the window has worked itself back out of the roof deck and the flashing is pulling away from the roof.

to "fly-away" problems, in part because they are lightweight and do not adhere to each other as well as organic-based shingles. You're looking not only for missing shingles but also for shingles that have torn either vertically or, more commonly, horizontally along the exposure line. The cause of the tear is much debated—manufacturers blame the people who install the shingles, in-

Some fiberglass shingles are so thin that they tear right off the roof in high winds. The lower half of the shingle rips loose right at the interface with the one above it.

Fly-Away Shingles

Using an air nailer saves a tremendous amount of time when installing roof shingles, but it can cause problems down the road if used incorrectly. If the air pressure is adjusted too high, the nailer will shoot the staples in so the nail head goes through the shingle. If the roof seems to have an abnormal number of shingles breaking loose, that could be what the problem is. Many homeowners are now requesting hand nailing for the shingles. But the same logic applies for hand nailing; if not done properly, you can still have problems with fly-away shingles.

This house is not very old, but one section of the roof is constantly in shade, encouraging the growth of algae over the surface.

stallers blame the manufacturers; the bottom line is if you see torn or missing shingles, write it up.

One final problem to check for is algae, a green growth over the surface of the roof (and the siding). It normally occurs on the side of the roof that gets little sun or on any side where large trees grow close to the building. If not removed, the algae will eventually rot out the shingles.

Wood shingles and shakes

Wood shingles (which are machine sawn) and wood shakes (hand hewn and rougher looking) are made from cedar, redwood, southern pine, and other woods. Shingles and shakes are undeniably beautiful; but, as with almost any roofing or siding material, they are not without

problems and controversy. High-quality shakes can come with a 30-year plus treatment warranty, but lower-grade shakes are nowhere near as long lasting. You'll find these curling and splitting not too long after they are installed. Some people believe that the newer cedar shingles are short lived compared to the older products.

When inspecting a roof with wood shingles or shakes, look closely for rotted, cracked, and broken shingles. Just because they are cracked doesn't necessarily mean there is a leak (you won't know until you get into the attic), but make note if there are any areas of excessive cracked shingles. The risk of fire is another concern with wood roofs, so ask the owner if the shingles have been treated for fire. A unique problem that has just surfaced with cedar shakes is thay they can "dissolve" under the right conditions. One incident in Virginia has traced the problem allegedly to using a catalytic converter with a wood-burning stove. You will note the shingles tapering and getting thinner and large holes forming in the wood. One final point on shingles and shakes: I strongly recommend that you never walk on wood roofs—they can be very slippery.

Standing seam

Standing-seam roofs were very popular at the beginning of the 20th century, and they are slowly making a comeback. I put a standing-seam roof on my own house many years ago, and the roof still looks brand new. Standing seam comes in many metals: copper, terne, tin, and stainless steel. Don't confuse standing seam with aluminum sheets, which you may occasionally find in some parts of the country. The latter will normally have Vs bent into them for support and come in short sections, which are held down by rubber-gasketed nails placed through the V into the wood underneath.

Standing-seam roofing comes in 20-in. and 24-in. rolls, 50 ft. long, which are cut to length to fit the roof. One side gets bent up 1¼ in. and the other, 1½ in.; this is called a pan. Once on the roof, the short bend of one pan is placed adjacent to the long bend of the next pan. Using a hand anvil and wooden mallet, the ¼ in. extra is bent over to connect one pan to the other. Then the seam is bent over again for a double-bend joint. The advantage of a standing-seam roof is that no nails penetrate the roofing material, so there are

If the standing-seam roof looks as bad as this one, list it as an area of concern. Although this tin roof is not leaking, it needs to be cleaned and repainted.

This standing-seam roof was built back when roofing was an art form. It has a couple of small spots that need to be taken care of—note the rust streaks on the right-hand side of the roof—but otherwise the roof is in good condition.

The aluminum of this attic vent is reacting with the tin of the roof, causing the latter to corrode.

fewer potential leak spots. Small strips of metal are folded into the seam and nailed underneath.

Where I live, standing seam is called 100-year roofing because it lasts such a long time (I don't know of any warranty that comes with this type of roofing). What the inspector is looking for is excessive rust or corrosion, denoted by dark-colored splotches or rust-colored stripes. A standing-seam roof doesn't have to be painted, so don't write it up if it is not. Standing-seam roofs sometimes have a problem with aluminum flashing, which can corrode the roof. To check for this, look immediately below the flashing for rust stains that are bleeding down the roof.

Slate

Slate is one of the oldest roofing materials around: as of 1915, more than 85 percent of all mined slate was used for roofing and chimneys. Although slate roofs are not as common as shingle roofs today, you'll no doubt find a few to inspect in your area. Slate is a hard, dense rock that splits into thin slabs. Its biggest benefit is its durability—as long as the quality of the slate is good, it's not going to wear out. In addition, it is completely waterproof and fire resistant.

But—and there always seems to be a *but* with roofing or siding—a slate roof is not maintenance-free. Slate can split in half, and its corners crack off fairly easily. Sometimes a poor-quality slate,

called ribbon slate, is used as a roof covering. The ribbons within the individual shingles are softer than the standard roof slate and will cause the shingles to crack along the ribbon after a few years. As well as looking for cracked or broken off tiles, also look for any areas that have been patched with asphalt cement. This material has a tendency to dry and crack and requires periodic reapplication.

Tile roofing

Tile stands with slate as one of the oldest roofing materials in existence. Modern tile is either fired clay, concrete, or fiber cement. It is molded or extruded and then hardened into a brittle, inert material for use as a roof tile. Clay or terra-cotta tile is the standard glazed flowerpot-type material—commonly seen as the half-barrel tile on Spanish-style homes. Concrete tiles and fiber-cement tiles are those that attempt to simulate other roofing material—such as slate. When inspecting any type of tile roofing look for tiles that have cracked, split, or broken free. Concrete tile has a tendency to fade over time, but this has no harmful effect on the material's performance so just ignore it.

There's nothing much to inspect on a tile roof, save for any tiles that have cracked or broken free. Don't worry about small chips on the edges of the tile.

Inspecting the attic

A roof inspection isn't complete without a check of the attic. Once inside, you'll be able to check on all those potential leak spots that you noted during your exterior walkabout and on the general condition of the sheathing and rafters. There are also a couple of additional checks that have nothing to do with the roof itself, such as the presence of insulation and the condition of any maintainable equipment that is located in the attic.

Into the Attic

Access to an attic might be via a regular stairway, a pull-down ladder, or a tiny scuttle hole in the closet, so in some houses the first challenge for an inspector may be simply getting into the attic. If access is via a scuttle hole, set your ladder (I like to use a fold-up ladder for this purpose) below the hole and gently push up and shift the panel to one side. You never know what's going to be above the panel—maybe cellulose or some other loose insulation—so proceed with caution as you move the panel; it's also a good idea to wear some protective glasses at this time.

Once the access panel is removed, shine your flashlight around (assuming there's no fixed lighting in the attic) to make sure there are no boxes or wires to trip over. I typically work with two diving lights in the attic—one I set down to provide general illumination and another I carry around to light up specific checkpoints. Some inspectors, myself included, bring in plywood panels to stand on to avoid putting a foot through the ceiling. Also check overhead for nails coming through the sheathing directly above the entry hole. If the thought of standing up and running your head into a nail makes you squeamish, you might think about wearing a hardhat for this part of the inspection.

The first thing to check is the underside of the roof deck (the sheathing) and the rafters. Look for any obvious cracks in the supporting structure and for any signs of insect damage, rot, or water penetration. Also check for any sagging areas. Sagging rafters indicate that the rafters were probably undersize when the roof was built or the roof is just too heavy. Sagging between rafters usually means that there's a problem with the sheathing: It could be too thin, delaminating, or the third or fourth layer of asphalt shingles applied to the roof was just too much added load. The sheathing could be rotted or cracked as well. Don't be afraid to probe for rot with your trusty awl.

Look for any stains on the underside of the roof and for any black spots or fungus. In cold climates, water penetration may be visible as icicles in winter. Pay particular attention around all the roof penetrations, such as plumbing vents and chimneys, to see if there are any water tracks running down. Trying to find the source of a leak in an attic can take some detective work, but good places to look are where you noted flashing points and patches when you did your exterior inspection of the roof. If the source of the leak isn't immediately obvious, don't spend a lot of time searching for it—simply write it up that there are signs of past or present leakage.

Often what appears to be a leak is in fact condensation, which is a sign of inadequate ventilation. Proper attic ventilation reduces heat gain in summer and helps prevent condensation in winter. Normally, it's best to evenly distribute half the vent area near the peak and the other half near the bottom at the soffit. This creates a convective airflow from bottom to top. Ventilation will typically be in the gable ends of the building; extra venting is done through the roof with turbine vents and the like. Different parts of the country will use different types, so you'll need to know which type is common in your area. As well as checking that the ventilation is adequate, also make sure that the vents are screened to keep out squirrels, bats, and other small animals.

Another thing to check while you're in the attic is the insulation. Each area of the country has a specific amount of insulation that is supposed to be in the attic, so make note if it is adequate. If there are recessed can lights in the ceiling below the attic, check whether there is any insulation around them. If there is, you need to verify the type of light by going back downstairs and looking into the light itself: IC fixtures may be completely covered with insulation; on non-IC (or T) fixtures, the insulation must be kept at least 3 in. from the housing. Also be on the lookout for bare electrical splices. Be very careful about moving the wiring around any lights whose outlet boxes extend up above the ceiling—you may create a loose connection.

You'll also need to check any equipment that is in the attic (in which case, write it up if there's no switched light here). Some people like to put the heat pump in the attic, which, in my opinion, is a bad idea because sooner or later a heat pump will leak. If a heat pump leaks in the basement, the water will go into a drain or be noticed quickly. If it leaks in the attic, you'll probably lose the ceiling. One final attic check is the bathroom fan vent. One contractor I know has a habit of installing bathroom fans without venting them to the outside: He leaves out the ductwork and buries the fan housing under several layers of insulation in the attic (see p. 221).

Guttering

I tend to think of guttering as a necessary evil. Standard, low-cost guttering isn't particularly attractive, and it leaks, fills up with leaves and other debris, and has a short life span. Drive down almost any road and you'll likely see it falling off someone's house. Part of the problem is design; the other part is the installers not following the manufacturer's installation instructions.

Allegedly, the purpose of guttering is to collect rainwater (not leaves and pine needles) off a roof and send it away from the house. In the north, this definition applies only until the onset of the first heavy snow. Then the ice and snow slide down the roof and, more times than not, literally tear the guttering right off the house. There's also the problem of what happens to the water the

Attic Checklist

- [ ] Rotting, splitting roof sheathing and/or rafters
- [ ] Sagging roof
- [ ] Signs of water penetration
- [ ] Excessive condensation
- [ ] Inadequate insulation
- [ ] Insulation around non-IC can lights
- [ ] Bare electrical splices
- [ ] Maintainable equipment without operable light
- [ ] Bathroom vent terminating in attic

gutter collects. At worst, the water runoff doesn't flow away from the house but into the basement via wall seepage or down through the window wells (see chapter 7). In the winter, the gutter runoff can form an ice rink around doors, walkways, and patios—and sometimes put a pool of water so deep around the garage door that it freezes closed. And repairs don't get made, until—you guessed it—the home gets put up for sale and the home inspector pays a visit.

Checking the downspouts

The first checkpoint for guttering is the downspouts. The downspout sections must be solidly connected to each other and to the building to hold the heavy weight of the water running through them. Sometimes the problems will be obvious, such as when neither end is connected or is simply destroyed. The water flow at the bottom should be diverted away from the building, not just allowed to saturate the area around the building. At best, the water should enter some type of pipe (black corrugated pipe is most commonly used) and be taken away from the

Guttering Checkpoints

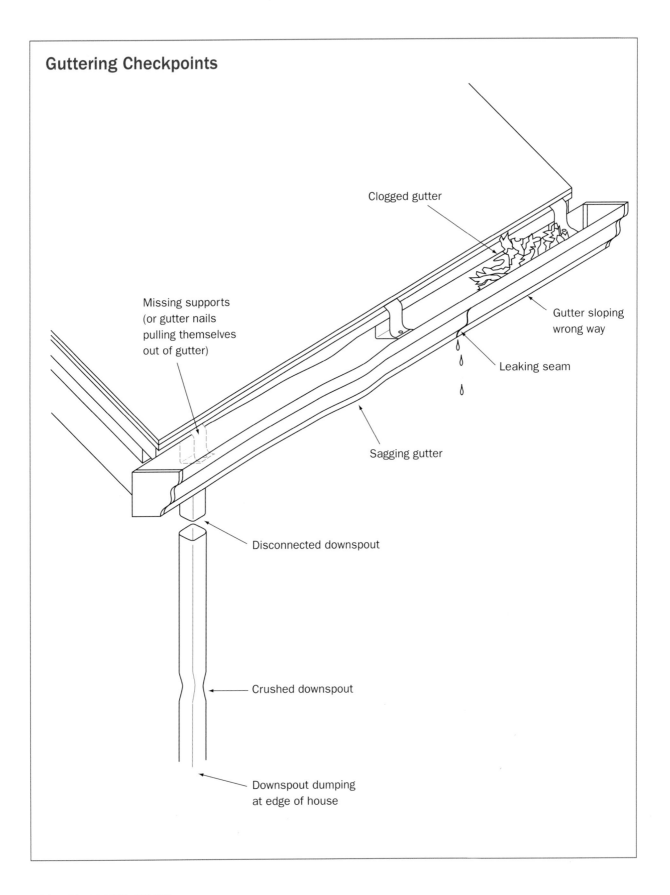

Clogged gutter

Gutter sloping wrong way

Missing supports (or gutter nails pulling themselves out of gutter)

Leaking seam

Sagging gutter

Disconnected downspout

Crushed downspout

Downspout dumping at edge of house

Check the downspout at the top, bottom, and all connections to make sure it is secure. This downspout is in good shape, but there is nothing tying it to the post.

Always check where the downspout connects to the gutter. The problem here is obvious—a tree limb crashed into the gutter during an ice storm.

Don't assume that the bottom end of the downspout is connected—this one came loose and was never repaired. Just imagine the ice that forms on this deck in the winter.

house. At least, there should be a short rain diverter to send the water away from the house. Make sure the pipe that takes the gutter water away is not clogged—if it is, it's useless.

Some areas have codes that dictate how far the water must be diverted away from the house (3 ft. to 5 ft. is typical); it's up to the inspector to know if his or her area has such codes. A loophole in the code is the uphill side—diverting water 3 ft. to 5 ft. uphill from the house just brings it right back, so note any such instances on your form. Here you need to follow the intent—not the letter—of the code. Codes are not an excuse to do something wrong.

Checking the gutters

The most common type of guttering installed today is K style. It's normally 5 in. wide (but

sometimes 6 in.), and thousands of miles of this paper-thin, seamless guttering are installed by contractors every year using a special machine that forms the guttering at the home site. K-style is also available for do-it-yourselfers in 10-ft. and 20-ft. preformed sections (in plastic as well as

K-style guttering comes in plastic as well as aluminum for do-it-youselfers. This one appears to be holding up well.

Be on the lookout for gutter spikes that have worked themselves out of the fascia board behind the gutter.

aluminum). The seamless is preferable to the seamed guttering, and the inspector should indicate on the form which type is installed on the house.

Walk under the guttering to observe any seams that appear to be broken. Seams leak under the best of conditions, and the thin metal sometimes

cannot hold all the water without bending in the center and having it spill out (in areas with heavy snowfall, the whole gutter may be bent down). The best time to check guttering, of course, is during a rainstorm. Alternatively, you can also direct a stream of water from a hose to the roof to check the guttering—but that takes a lot of time and is normally left up to the new homeowner.

A lot of guttering isn't installed properly. To state the obvious, the gutter should run downhill to the downspout (a standard downward pitch is $1/16$ in. per foot). But that doesn't always happen. Some people install the guttering level for aesthetic reasons, and I've seen countless gutters where the low end is the wrong end and the gutter is filled with standing water. Another common installation problem is putting too much roof runoff on the gutter. A rule of thumb in some areas is that you need a downspout for every 30 ft. of gutter. But the amount of square footage on the roof also counts. I have two downspouts for my roof that has 50 ft. of guttering. During a hard rain the guttering cannot always take the runoff from the roof and will overflow in the middle.

One of the biggest problems with guttering is the attachments to the house. There are several

Gutters that are integral with the soffit are prone to rot; not all problems will be as obvious as this one.

ways to attach guttering to the house, but spikes seem to be the most common (at least with K-style gutters). However, spikes have a habit of working themselves out and allowing the gutter to fall or sag. Be on the lookout for spikes that extend out beyond the gutter edge. If the gutter is attached to the building with support straps, check for loose straps.

Another type of gutter you might come across is the half-round gutter (which drains water better than a flat design). Half-round gutters come in a variety of materials, so be sure to list what is on the house—for example, copper, galvanized, or plastic. Copper is installed on a lot of high-end houses because it is both beautiful and durable (but very expensive). However, nothing is perfect, and copper can stain anything it drips or drains on a greenish blue. This can make a beautiful siding job look spotty. Galvanized half-round guttering will rust as its zinc coating deteriorates. Plastic half-round guttering is installed by home-owners and do-it-yourselfers, which means you have potential leak spots at the abundant seams and the entire assembly may fail if it wasn't installed properly.

If you see weeds growing in the gutter, there's no need to bring out the ladder—it's safe to assume that the gutter is clogged.

Older houses may have wood guttering built into the edge of the roof itself. This type of gutter is easily spotted because the downspouts come right out of the soffit. Having the guttering integral with the roof is an aesthetically pleasing option, but this kind of guttering is very prone to rot (unless it is made of redwood or lined with copper or lead). Always be particularly vigilant with any house that has built-in guttering.

One final problem with gutters, regardless of type, is that they get clogged with debris. In most cases, you'll need a ladder to verify that the gutter is clogged (but, as stated previously, your insurance agency may not allow you to use a ladder). However, if you see weeds and even small trees growing in the gutter, it's safe to assume it is clogged.

Gutter Checklist

- [ ] Downspouts breaking apart and falling off building
- [ ] Broken seams in gutter
- [ ] Guttering sloped in wrong direction
- [ ] Sagging gutter
- [ ] Gutter strapping or spikes coming loose
- [ ] Rotted wooden gutter
- [ ] Weeds growing in gutter

Grading

Grading, elevation, and site orientation are among the most important considerations when it comes to picking a house's location, yet these factors are often ignored. Houses get built in some of the most illogical locations. I've seen them built on flood plains, in the middle of a significant acreage runoff, and so close to the trees that the sun never hits the house and mold grows all over it.

As you approach the building site, observe the grading around the house. If the house is in a low-lying area, make a note of it and check for any flooding that may have occurred around the building; telltale signs include bent grass, mud around tree trunks, debris caught in tree limbs, and excessive erosion. Grading is not just a problem in rural areas. Architects and grading experts are famous for putting at least one house in a subdivision in such a location that runoff from the entire neighborhood flows across the property. I know, I used to own one.

If the house is at the bottom of a hill or a significant slope, you should investigate how the water gets around the building. It's common to bury a drain along the footer to send the water

This house has a unique grading problem. The surrounding land sends all its water runoff directly to the building, and when it rains three large rivers flow into the crawl space and half basement. After giving up on sump pumps to get rid of the water, the owners dug a ditch and ran a large pipe from the half basement all the way to the roadside.

around the house to the low end and then over the hill. Immediately above the drain and against the back wall, some contractors put 1 ft. or 2 ft. of gravel. At my house (which I built into the side of a mountain), I took the gravel all the way up the wall to the surface—logic being, any water flowing down the mountain and against the wall would immediately filter down through the gravel and into the drain. If the water can't pool, it can't leak into the house. If the water pools at all, I write it up. In the worst-case scenario, if the water flows into the basement or under the house, the inspector needs to note if it is doing any damage.

Another typical grading problem occurs when a driveway is added immediately above the house. Before the driveway went in, there may not have been a grading problem. But once the driveway is added, the water drains down to the house, where it either hits the building and goes down and saturates the basement walls or is trapped and pools in front of the house. Look for water from the guttering flowing onto the pavement and the runoff flowing into an open seam between the driveway and the house. In cold areas of the country, this water will freeze and cause a large horizontal crack along the basement wall.

Having the water flow under the house is just as bad as having the water leak into the basement. A woman I know has water that flows from two fields directly under her old house. The house used to be steady. Now, however, when she walks across the floor, the house shakes; the piers (piles of rock) that support the house are being undermined and are no longer stable. For more information on grading, see "Types of Garages" beginning on p. 114.

Water from this downspout flows into a crack between the driveway and the basement wall, causing water problems below.

Chapter 5

FOUNDATIONS, STRUCTURAL SUPPORTS, AND DECKS

THE FOUNDATION

DECKS

A foundation can be loosely defined as whatever the house box sits on to support the weight of the structure. The foundation or supporting structure can be anything from solid block or concrete to posts and columns, wrought iron, or rock taken from the property. It has been said that as long as the foundation is in good shape, almost anything in the house can be fixed. That may be an exaggeration, but it does stress the importance of making sure the foundation is sound.

Vertical columns that support overhangs from porches to living areas can be considered to be the foundation of the overhead structure, and I normally inspect these at the same time as the rest of the foundation. I also inspect any wrought-iron railings around the front steps or porch, as well as the deck (if the house has one).

The Foundation

The bottom line in foundation inspections is that prospective buyers want to be assured that the house will not fall down once they move in. And I've inspected more than a few houses that looked as though they could. I recall one inspection

The brick foundation of this house is tilting forward. In an attempt to prevent its collapse, the owner drove metal pipes into the ground next to the foundation and patched up the Z-crack at the corner. In the close-up photo you can see that the house has separated from the foundation so much that someone has been able to run an extension cord between the two.

where the top of the brick foundation wall had tilted so far out that it looked as though the entire front of the house would come crashing down at any moment. In a futile attempt to stop the inevitable, the seller had driven a couple of 1-in. metal pipes into the ground in front of the foundation (see the photos above).

To keep a foundation from tipping over or to keep posts from sinking into the ground like spears, a footer is required. This is a flat base at least twice the width of the foundation that is normally installed deep in the ground below the frost line. If the foundation is continuous, the footer must be continuous too. The footer has to be wider than the foundation above it so it can spread the building's weight out onto the supporting earth below. In the old days, large buried rocks served as footers; today we use concrete pads. Because you cannot see into the earth to verify that the footer is both deep enough and wide enough, the only way to check for possible footer problems is to observe what is happening to the foundation.

Solid foundations

A solid foundation forms a continuous skirt around the building that supports the structure above it. There are many types of solid foundations, but you'll be checking for the same things regardless of type: namely, cracks or breaks in the foundation, bowing or tilting, and signs of disintegration. There's a good deal of overlap between inspecting a foundation and a basement wall, and the main causes of failure are the same for both. These include poor construction, frost-

Foundation problems aren't always evident until you go into the basement. This block foundation wall is caving in from the constant pressure of the earth pushing against it. You can see moisture coming through the lower blocks.

Over time, the constant pressure of earth against a block foundation can cause the wall to bow in and the mortar joint to fail.

related damage, settling or shifting of the ground under the footer, and a high water table or water infiltration caused by improper grading and guttering.

As you do your exterior inspection, make note of any conditions that may allow water to accumulate around the foundation, such as improper grading, missing or damaged gutters, cracked driveways and walkways, and so on. Then when you go into the basement, you can verify whether these problems are causing problems inside. Also note any significant cracks in the foundation and check to see if these cracks run all the way through the wall when you're inside. (For more on basements, see chapter 7.)

A solid, continuous foundation that extends from the footer to the framing can be of almost any material: rock, block, poured concrete, brick, or wood. Many old country houses sit on a continuous footer of rock taken from the planting fields. The rock itself lasts forever, but the mortar used to seal the openings between the rocks disintegrates over time. Use an awl to check for disintegration, and look for any long gaps between the rock and the foundation beams it is supposed to be supporting.

Block foundations are rarely problematic unless the footer is inadequate. If the footer moves or sinks, a typical structural defect is a Z-pattern crack through the block or the mortar joints. Ignore minor "old-age" cracks, but be on the lookout for long vertical or horizontal breaks that form a continuous pattern. As with other solid foundations, the constant pressure of the earth against a block foundation, along with excess water, can cause the foundation to bow in and the mortar joints to fail.

Brick foundations are subject to the same problems as block, but an additional check is for disintegration of the brick itself. New brick should be sound, but watch for old brick foundations or new foundations built with recycled brick, which usually isn't as hard as new brick. Use an awl to probe for signs of disintegration in the brick and the mortar. Be sure to check the foundation on all

Foundation Checklist

- ☐ Bowed or leaning foundations
- ☐ Excessive water around perimeter of foundation
- ☐ Gaps and major cracks in the foundation
- ☐ Crumbling or missing mortar joints
- ☐ Disintegrating brick
- ☐ Peeling stucco

If part of a footer settles and part does not, a stairstep Z-crack will work its way down the foundation wall. Write it up.

sides of the house; as with siding, the foundation may be sound on all sides except one—the side that gets the heavy weathering.

Many solid foundations have a surface covering such as stucco. In cold climates, repeated freezing and thawing can peel off this covering (which is good, in a way, because now you can get a good look at the real foundation). Whenever I inspect a foundation that has a stucco covering I always make a note to check in the basement to see if there are problems on the inside of the foundation wall. Many times, the stucco is applied over the exterior of the foundation to conceal cracks and other defects.

Piers and columns

Not all houses are supported by a solid, continuous foundation. Many are held up by a system of piers or columns placed strategically around and within the house perimeter. These individual structural supports may be of rock, brick, block, concrete, wood, or steel. Rock piers are the oldest of these, and they should be in just as good a condition as they were the day they were installed. Most of these foundations were not constructed with mortar, so there was nothing to disintegrate. For those that have it, probe into the mortar to verify that it isn't crumbling or breaking apart. One common

Settlement or shifting of the ground under the footing is one of the major causes of foundation failure. This crawl-space foundation, which used to be continuous, is breaking apart (as is the sidewalk next to it).

When stucco is applied directly to the foundation without wire, scratch coat, or brown coat, it doesn't stay on long in areas that undergo extremes of climate. Peeling stucco shouldn't have any structural effect on the building, although it may be concealing problems in the foundation itself.

Rock piers are the tradi-
tional standby for foundation support in old hous-
es. Be on the lookout for
shims that have fallen out
from the top of the pier,
allowing the floor beams
to sag or break. This wood
shim is still in position.

Brick support columns are prone to disintegrate—
especially if the builder used old brick to begin with.

problem with rock support structures is that a
wooden shim may have been wedged in at the
top of the pier between the last rock and the
horizontal support beam. This wedge may have
slid out and the pier is no longer supporting the
house. Therefore, when inspecting rock piers
always shine your light to the very top to verify
that something is making contact with the
building.

Piers made of brick are fairly common on old
houses, and sometimes the bricks are disintegrating. Old bricks were often made locally, and
they are not always up to today's standards. In
some cases, the bricks used in the piers were
recycled from other buildings, and these are
particularly prone to decay. Most of the time the
disintegration will be obvious; if in doubt, probe
the bricks or mortar with an awl.

Whenever wood comes in contact with concrete or dirt, it is a simple matter of time until it
rots. Treated foundation posts last longer than
untreated posts, but all will eventually succumb.
Below ground, wooden posts will probably stay
intact for quite a few years, but at the earth's
surface they will rot and fall apart. We have
finally learned our lesson and now break post
contact with the earth or concrete by placing the
column on a small raised, platform. But not all
localities require this platform, and in many
places you'll still find the posts sitting right on
the moist concrete or, worse still, on the dirt.

Check for obvious problems in the posts such
as rot, cracks, or excessive mildew; and use your
awl to verify that the wood is sound. Be especially
wary of hard-to-see posts within brushy areas that
rarely see sunlight, posts that are in areas that
flood (look for mud rings around the post), or

Pier and Column Checklist

- [ ] Rock or brick piers that have begun to disintegrate
- [ ] Wood columns that are rotted at ground level
- [ ] Concrete piers that have major cracks

posts sitting on concrete pads that are level with the ground. These will rot quickly.

On the coast, on steep hillsides, and in areas where houses are built over loose soil, you'll often see giant pole and circular concrete piers holding up the buildings. Disintegration of the wood columns will be obvious (make sure you check a few inches below ground level for rot), but problems with the concrete piers will be harder to detect. Check for a shear crack that goes all the way around or through the pier. If the concrete has broken or cracked all the way through, the only thing that is keeping it from shearing in two is the rebar within.

Low foundations

All houses have some kind of foundation, but on some buildings the foundation is so low to the ground that the floor joists are literally sitting in the dirt. In some parts of the country in the early 20th century, it was common to build the floor right into the ground. As illogical as this seems to us today, it was considered a viable option back then when wood was denser and less prone to rot. (Pine, considered a soft wood today, was so dense that it was difficult to drive a nail into.) The wood would rot, but not in the homeowner's lifetime. Unfortunately, it is rotting in ours, and the inspector needs to take a close look when the floor is at or close to ground level.

As you do your walk-around inspection of the exterior, observe how high the foundation is above ground level. If it is level with or below the ground, there's a good chance that the floor joists

Top: Whether treated or untreated, a wooden support post that's in contact with concrete (or the ground) will eventually rot. The inspector should probe into the post to see how far along the rot has progressed. Bottom: This post has been extended off the concrete by a raised platform—it shouldn't rot.

Porch Columns

Wooden columns and posts that support porch roofs are prone to rot, especially around the base where water runs off the roof and splashes back against the supports. Sometimes you'll see simple 4x4 posts holding up a structure, other times you'll see giant vertical columns reminiscent of old plantation homes of the South. Simple or grand, all columns will rot if they are in contact with the ground or concrete.

For a physical check of the support columns, you'll need an awl to probe the wood to see if it is solid or spongy. Check first at the base (where it rots the easiest) and then overhead to make sure the column is securely attached to the building. I usually give the column a gentle push to verify that it is tight to the building, but go easy here—you don't want the porch roof to come crashing down if there's a problem.

Some porch columns are a combination of brick and wood. The problem with these is that the two materials react differently to settling or shifting of the house structure. The upper wooden part can move and bend slightly if the footer or house shifts; but the rectangular brick section is "set in concrete" so to speak, and it cannot move. Instead, it starts to break up and come apart with the stress.

Plantation-style porch columns are particularly prone to rot where the base is in contact with concrete.

More common than giant columns, this simple home-made post is being eaten away by rot, mold, and mildew.

For a combination brick-and-wood column, it's always a race to see which is going to come apart first: the wood column or the brick base. This race was won by the brick.

You'll see this quite often in rural areas: a low foundation over a crawl space too small for a person to get through. This means that the floor joists are either in the dirt or an inch or two above it.

The upper end of this house has the full width of the floor joists in the dirt. The bottom skirtboard has fallen away, exposing rotted wood behind, which extends through the bottom plate and into the studs.

If you see a newly installed and freshly painted skirtboard, be aware that it might be hiding some major problems.

and other support beams are sitting in the dirt and rotting. Make a note of it and, when you go inside, look for major dips in the floor, indicating that the beams may be rotting and are no longer able to support the weight of the floor. If the foundation is a crawl space, note if there are any vents. If there are no vents, the joists are probably rotting. Although this is normally a problem only in older houses, I've also seen new homes with

large crawl spaces rotting out for lack of venting. (For more on crawl-space inspections, see chapter 7.)

On the outside, look for rotting skirtboards at ground level, which likely indicate that there's a problem with the support beams behind. I'm also suspicious if I'm inspecting a house on which the skirtboard has recently been replaced. More often

Wrought-Iron Supports and Railings

Wrought iron is used as a support structure on some houses and more commonly as a hand railing around front steps and other parts of the building. The major problem with wrought iron is that it will eventually rust. One of the worst spots for rusting is where the iron is in contact with a porous concrete floor, as, for example, on the front steps of a house. Also check for rust through at the weld joints between railings.

Although major rust through will be obvious, it's important to check more than just the metal of the railing. You also need to look at the screws and/or bolts that hold the brackets to the walls, ceiling, and floor. If these rust through—and sometimes they are the first things to go—the railing is an accident waiting to happen.

Pay particular attention to stair and balcony railings, which people are likely to lean on. Look closely at the attachment brackets. Put your weight against them to verify that they are securely attached to the building and floor. Also be on the lookout for temporary fixes to rusted railings. I've seen hand railings attached to wrought-iron posts with everything from belts to metal ties. None of these will hold for long. Observe and report.

Wrought-iron stair railings have short life spans in cold climates, where salt, thrown down on the steps to melt the ice, also eats through the metal.

Wrought iron used as a support structure or railing is both decorative and functional, but it has one drawback—it rusts. Carefully check where the wrought iron attaches to the building and to the floor.

The screws used to attach this railing to the house have rusted through, causing the railing to the right of the door to come loose—a dangerous situation.

than not, the owner will repair obvious problems in an attempt to sell the house, while ignoring the major structural problems that the new boards conceal—such as rotting sills and floor joists.

Decks

Building a deck is one of the most popular projects undertaken by do-it-yourselfers; but unfortunately, not all decks are constructed soundly. Although many are built to high standards, I've seen more than a few that are constructed contrary to both code and common sense. Typical problems fall into three main categories: the support posts and attachments, the railing, and the decking boards. In addition, you need to watch out for decks that are built in unsafe or illogical locations: I've inspected decks that were built just a couple of feet below the utility service drop and several that had the decking boards butting directly against the utility meter. And if a deck is installed immediately over an air-conditioning/heat pump unit, there will need to be 5 ft. minimum between the grill and the decking.

Support posts and attachments

The deck inspection should begin at the support posts. Treated wood posts and masonry posts are the most common. Verify that wood posts are in

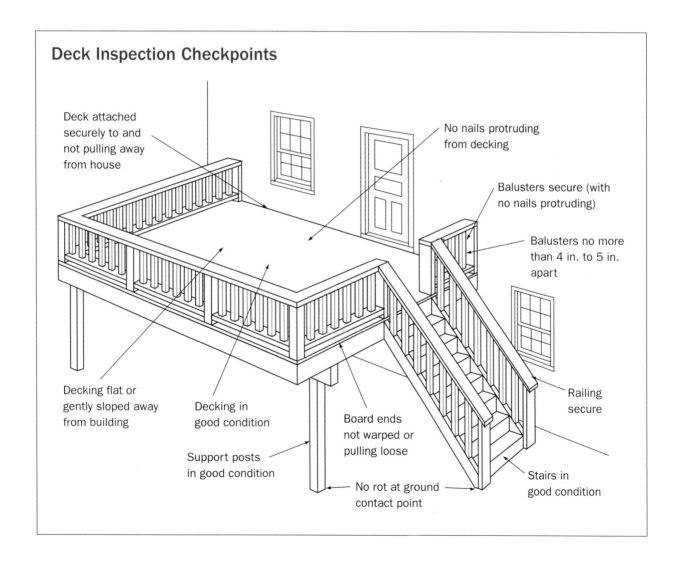

Deck Inspection Checkpoints

Deck attached securely to and not pulling away from house

No nails protruding from decking

Balusters secure (with no nails protruding)

Balusters no more than 4 in. to 5 in. apart

Decking flat or gently sloped away from building

Decking in good condition

Board ends not warped or pulling loose

Railing secure

Support posts in good condition

No rot at ground contact point

Stairs in good condition

The support structure and decking boards of this deck are in good condition, but the deck has been secured to the house with nails, which do not provide as strong an attachment as lag bolts. The entire weight of the deck and people on it are supported solely by the shear strength of just a few nails, which have a habit of working themselves back out.

These two threaded bolt ends are protruding from the deck support just a few feet off the ground on the yard side of the house (instead of toward the house). Be sure not to let something this dangerous get by you.

good condition without warp or major fracture and that they are securely attached to the structure, preferably with bolts. Masonry posts need to be checked for broken block or brick and deteriorating mortar joints. Don't overlook the obvious, such as one or more missing support posts; believe me, if it can be built wrong, you'll see it.

The support posts need a footer or concrete pad underneath to prevent them (and the deck) from sinking into the ground. You won't always be able to see the pad because it may be underground, but a clue that there's a problem is if the deck slopes noticeably toward the house (the support posts closest to the door usually take the most downward pressure). You can also use a long awl to check for the presence of an underground pad or footer. It's normal to build a slight slope into the surface of the deck so that rain and snow will drain away from the house. But be aware of severe slopes, especially at the corners, where a support post may be sinking or the dirt under the post may be eroding.

Codes normally require decks to be either independent of the main building or securely bolted to the structure. If the deck is attached to the structure, it should be with threaded bolts or lag bolts, not nails. Although local codes may not require a bolted deck-to-house attachment, I always write it up as an area of concern if the deck support structure is simply nailed to the house. Problems associated with nailed attachments include shear weight limitations, the risk of the deck pulling away from the building, and nails working themselves loose over time. When bolts are used on the deck support structure, they should be installed with the threads toward the inside of the deck. If the threaded ends protrude from the supports, there's the danger that someone will catch his or her clothing or legs on them.

Railings

Most codes require that decks higher than 3 ft. off the ground have a railing around them to keep people on the deck from falling off. Just as important is the spacing between the vertical supports (or balusters) on the railing. If the balusters are too far apart, children might fall through or get their heads stuck. Most codes require the balusters to be placed no farther apart than 4 in. The same requirements apply to the stair railings leading to the deck.

Also check that railings are sound (not rotting) and are securely attached to the deck, stairs, and

Check to make sure that the gap between balusters complies to the local code (typically the gap should be no greater than 4 in. to 5 in.). If in doubt, measure, don't guess.

Decks such as these are a death trap for small children and the elderly. All decks over 36 in. high need railings and balusters to keep people from falling off.

This 2x4, the main support for the stair railing, was poorly installed and the railing wobbles when any one leans against it.

house. Make sure that the railing doesn't wobble back and forth and that there are no exposed nails.

Decking

On the earliest decks, decking boards were typically made from trees cut right on the property. Although some of the boards, like hard oak and

Mold and algae can make a deck as slick as ice as well as shorten the life of the deck.

locust, last a long time, eventually weather and insects take their toll. Newer decks are made of treated wood or a composite material, which is supposed to be a step in the right direction, although I've seen treated decks last less than a decade. Regardless of the material used, first check that the decking boards are sound and not rotted or broken (don't forget to check the treads on the stairs leading to the deck as well). Pay particular attention to boards that are under trees or in continual shade from the house. Such shady locations are a haven for the growth of algae, which the not only shortens the life of the deck but also poses a safety risk because it makes the deck slippery.

Safety also comes into consideration when decks, especially wrap-around decks, are installed below steep roofs in cold climates. Nobody thinks about this until the first heavy snow fall. The snow accumulates on the roof and then slides down onto the deck, with the risk of seriously injuring anyone caught in the avalanche.

Most deck surfaces, even pressure-treated decks, need some type of treatment to prevent water from penetrating the grain. Decks of treated wood

This deck looks sound enough, but there's a hidden design problem here. The deck extends beyond the roofline, so any snow that accumulates on the steep roof will eventually slide down and bury anything (or anyone) that happens to be on the deck. An additional problem is the rain runoff from the roof, which will speed the deterioration of the deck.

Check for warp at the ends of decking boards. If they are not securely fastened, the ends have a tendency to buckle.

Deck Checklist

- Deck built immediately below electrical wires or over an air-conditioning/heat pump unit
- Warped or fractured wood support posts
- Deteriorated masonry posts
- Missing support posts
- Support posts that are sinking into the ground
- Deck securely attached to house or independently supported
- Bolts mounted head out and thread end in
- Railings and steps installed, if required, and secure and sound
- Maximum gap between balusters not exceeded (typically 4 in. to 5 in.)
- Decking in good condition and securely attached

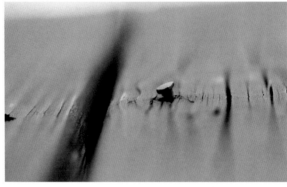

Look for deck nails that have worked their way back out of the decking as a result of extreme fluctuations in temperature.

that have been ignored and left to absorb whatever the weather throws at them will turn gray and have their grain pulling out of the wood; nontreated boards may be dark and look permanently wet in shady areas. Pay particular attention to the ends of the boards, which are prone to severe warping.

Decking boards can be fastened down in a number of different ways, but the best way is to use stainless-steel screws attached from the top or bottom. I learned this the hard way on my own deck: I used coated spiral decking nails, and they are coming right back out of the decking boards. The temperature extremes in the mountains of Virginia where I live force the nails out of the wood. When it is very cold outside, I can hear the nails popping up from the surface—it sounds like a rifle going off. The nail heads are raised only about $1/4$ in. from the surface of the deck, but it's high enough to trip someone or to snag a bare foot.

Chapter 6

GARAGES, DRIVEWAYS, AND WALKWAYS

TYPES OF GARAGES

INSPECTING THE EXTERIOR

DRIVEWAYS AND WALKWAYS

The garage, driveway, and any walkways are typically the last things I inspect on the exterior before I move inside the house. Garages have come a long way since the carriage houses of yesteryear, and it's important not to treat the inspection lightly. In more and more homes, at least some part of the garage is given over to living, working, or playing; and many garages are fully equipped with electrical and plumbing facilities. This means that there's sometimes as much to inspect in a garage as there is in a small house. The importance of making a thorough inspection is compounded by the fact that many house fires start in the garage, so if the two are attached, it's important to verify that the garage-to-house interface is fireproof (see "Garages and Fire Safety" on p. 115).

Types of Garages

The first thing you'll need to indicate on your inspection form is the type of garage. There are typically three categories: detached, attached, and detached with breezeway. These can be further broken down into those with and without living quarters.

Garages and Fire Safety

With gas fumes, oil spills, half-empty paint cans, paint thinner, and air that doesn't move, fire is a potential hazard in all garages. It's important that any fire that breaks out in a garage doesn't spread to any living space above or to the attached house. To contain the fire within the garage, surfaces between the garage and living spaces must be fireproof. The definition of fireproof is normally given as being able to hold back a fire for a certain period of time.

When inspecting garages, you need to be familiar with the terms *fire wall* and *fire door*. A fire wall is a wall made of nonflammable material used between the garage and any living area. A fire wall can be solid, such as a brick or block wall, or it can be a stud wall covered with a nonflammable material such as $\frac{1}{2}$-in. or $\frac{5}{8}$-in. drywall (facing the garage area).

A fire door is a fire-resistant interior door at least $1\frac{3}{8}$ in. thick (some rated for fire, some not) between the garage and living area. Local codes vary on what constitutes a fire door, but typically metal clad (without windows) doors, solid-wood doors, and doors covered with some type of metal (sheet metal, tin, etc.) on the garage side are acceptable. Not all areas require fire doors between the garage and house, so you need to be familiar with your local code.

Although it's usually easy to see if a fire door is present, it can be trickier to recognize a fire wall. If the wall is covered with drywall, you need to verify that the thickness of the drywall meets your local jurisdiction's requirements. To check the thickness, remove a receptacle cover on the fire wall and observe the cut edge of the drywall. Brick and block fire walls will usually be obvious, unless they are integrated within the wall. In this case, you'll have to check in the attic to see the masonry wall, which is required to extend all the way to the roof.

Detached garages

The old-style, single-story detached garage is normally a small building used only as a garage and storage building. The structure may or may not have electricity. This type of garage is usually the easiest to inspect because it's separate from the house and, therefore, doesn't require a fire wall. If it has electricity, it's likely to be minimal. Most detached garages don't have any plumbing—at least in cold climates.

A two-story detached garage will quite often have its upstairs area turned into living quarters or a studio/workspace, which means that the building will take a significant amount of time to inspect—after all, you're essentially inspecting another residence. This type of garage has to have

A single-story detached garage is quick to inspect. It typically has minimal or no electricity and no fire wall requirements. In this example, the driveway slopes away from the building, as it should; but note that the rear of the garage is built into the hill, which might indicate that there are water infiltration problems.

Detached garages sometimes have living quarters above the garage space. In this case, the building requires a fire wall between the garage and the living quarters. The driveway slopes down and away from the entrance to the garage, so water infiltration should not be a problem here.

A garage that's built as part of the house—either at the side or underneath as here—is the most common garage design. The overhead garage fire wall must be present and intact (with no openings created for plumbing repairs).

Attached garages

The most common design is a garage that's built into the house. By sharing a common wall, considerable material and expense can be saved. If the garage you're inspecting is attached to the house, a fire wall is required between the two. The fire wall must extend from the floor all the way through the attic to the ceiling (the idea being to slow or stop a garage fire from spreading to the house).

As well as checking for the presence of a fire wall, you must also verify that there are no openings in the wall through which fire could spread from the garage to the house. Cutting a hole for a light switch or receptacle outlet on the garage side is acceptable because the outlet box that goes in the hole has a two-hour fire rating, which means that it's supposed to hold the fire back for two hours. But if there's an electrical box on the other side of the wall facing the living area, you may have a problem. Most jurisdictions do not allow two boxes in the same stud wall cavity because if fire does get into the wall (as it could if it went around the box), it has a way out into the adjoining room via the other outlet. So if the house you're inspecting has switches or receptacles back to back in the common wall

some type of fire wall on the ceiling (typically ½-in. or ⅝-in. drywall) and a fire-resistant door, if there is access to the upstairs from the garage. A detached garage with living quarters will normally have full 100- or 200-amp service either feeding off the main house or a service separate to itself.

This detached garage is connected to the house via a breezeway with an attic. With this design, you must verify that there's a fire wall between the garage and the breezeway attic and that it extends all the way to the roof.

Garage Type Checklist

Detached

☐ No living quarters above

☐ Living quarters above:
   ☐ Fire wall present on garage ceiling
   ☐ Fire-resistant door present (if required)

Attached

☐ No living quarters above

☐ Living quarters above:
   ☐ Fire wall present on garage ceiling and common house wall
   ☐ Fire-resistant door present (if required)

Detached with breezeway

☐ Fire wall isolating breezeway attic from garage

between the garage and the living area, make a note of it on the report.

A similar problem may occur if a hole was cut in the fire wall to allow access to water and drain lines (to repair a leak, for example). As with the wall that surrounds it, this access door or panel must be fireproof (drywall is fine, plywood is not). One other thing to check for is the presence of an overhead access panel, if there is a hatch in the garage ceiling/upstairs living area floor; if the panel isn't in place, fire could spread to an upstairs living area very quickly. Panels, whether in the wall or ceiling, should be attached securely and not just hang down by a single screw. Verify that the panel is screwed or nailed directly to the drywall ceiling, not held up by wood trim like a picture frame. If the wood frame is the only thing that holds the drywall panel against the ceiling or wall, the panel will fall as soon as the wood frame burns through.

Detached garages with breezeway

A third garage design is a detached garage connected to the main house via a roof with a storage attic continuous from the garage to the house. In this situation, there has to be a fire wall between the garage and the storage area over the breezeway. Otherwise, if the garage catches fire it can travel through the breezeway attic and into the main house in seconds.

Inspecting the Exterior

Thus far, we have focused our attention on checking for the presence or absence of fire walls and fire doors, but there's a lot more to inspect on a

This driveway slopes down toward the garage. A small concrete apron in front of the door prevents runoff from entering through the door, but the water is damaging the building as it flows off to the right side.

garage than that. Whether the garage is attached or detached, the exterior will need to go through the same inspection procedure as the house: siding, roof, guttering, foundation, and so on. It's important not to overlook the grading: I've seen more than a few garage floors that double as seasonal wading pools or skating rinks as a result of poor grading and drainage. Once you've done your walkabout and checked the outside, you can start on the inside.

Grading and guttering

Just because the building you're inspecting is a garage, don't think you can get by with only a cursory check of the grading and guttering. Having the water drain away from the garage is just as important as having the water drain away from the house. If the grading (or even the apron under the door) is sloped the wrong way, water can flood into the garage like a raging river.

Ideally, all surrounding land should slope away from the building, but this isn't always possible. Many garages (and houses, too) are built adjacent to a road or highway that's uphill from the building. As an inspector, it's important to recognize this design hazard and verify that it is not causing any problems.

There are two basic ways the landscaping problem can be solved. First, a dip can be carved into the driveway and landscape immediately in front of the garage on the uphill side. The problem with this method is erosion—especially with new construction, because the grass and shrubbery haven't had time to put down deep root systems. The inspector must verify that the water is running away from the building—not along it, where it can cause damage to the building, and not pooling in a lake between the garage and the highway. This pooling can cause an ice buildup on the driveway or walkway in cold climates. Also check to make sure the guttering is not draining onto the driveway, which can cause a massive ice lake.

The second way to keep drainage water away from the building is to install a buried drain system in front of the garage door. This type of system will have a grill over a rectangular box, the top of which is flush with ground level and, ideally, slightly lower than the apron. The water flows down the hill toward the garage but flows into the grill and drain box instead of into the garage. A large-diameter drainpipe is connected to the box to take the collected water downhill and away from the house.

A homemade version of the grated drain box uses a large-diameter drainpipe buried a few inches underground in a dip just in front of the garage. The pipe has a number of holes (or slits) drilled (cut) in the top to accept the water flowing

Watch Where the Water Goes

The owner of this house installed a grated drain box in front of the attached garage to carry away water that flows down the driveway. The drain flows into a corrugated line and around the house corner.

Unfortunately, the drain line got crushed and filled with earth, and the water overflowed the drain box. The water then ran along the interface between the asphalt driveway and the brick wall of the house and then disappeared under the sidewalk—almost as if the contractor designed it that way.

Once the water got under the sidewalk, it ran down the basement wall, seeping into it and ruining the wooden walls in the basement.

down to the garage; a layer of gravel is spread over the top. As the incoming rainwater pools in the dip, the water flows down through the gravel and into the pipe, and from there the water is taken away. Both the grated drain box and homemade version work fine in principle, but if either one fills with debris or the drain end is clogged, the system is useless. On a garage attached to the house, the water will end up flowing along the basement wall and some of it will eventually find its way into the basement.

And then, of course, the inspector may find that the homeowner has simply chosen to ignore the problem of drainage water flooding into or against the garage. On the outside, look for evidence of water damage around the base of the building (such as rotting siding, crumbling stucco, or muddy water stains around the building). On

This homemade version of a grated drain box has slits cut into the top of a pipe to drain the water out of the driveway before it flows into the garage. Unfortunately, the drainpipe is prone to break and cave in from the weight of the cars running over it.

Garage Grading and Guttering Checklist

- ☐ Grading slopes away from garage
- ☐ Grading directs water against garage
  - ☐ Dip in front of garage on uphill side
  - ☐ Drain box installed in front of garage
- ☐ Drain box functioning, not clogged
- ☐ Apron slopes away from garage door
- ☐ Guttering intact and diverting water from the garage

the inside, look for mud on the floor, signs of water damage, and rotting sills.

Another potential drainage problem is where the garage door meets the floor. From the contact point of the door seal to the floor, the garage floor outside the building (known as the "apron") must slope down; otherwise the rainwater that hits the door and flows down to the floor by gravity will flow backward under the door seal and into the garage.

If the garage has guttering, verify that the gutters and downspouts are intact and sending water away from the building. To cut costs, many detached garages have no gutters. If there are no gutters, verify that the massive amount of water runoff from the roof is not adversely affecting the building and that splashback from the ground is not deteriorating the siding.

The garage roof

The garage roof should be inspected in just the same way as the main roof, checking for obvious holes in the roof, missing or ripped shingles, sagging ridge lines, and so forth (see chapter 4). Human nature being what it is, you're more likely to find problems with detached garages without living spaces—homeowners tend to delay fixing a leaking roof over an unused garage, whereas they'd make the repair if someone were living or working under that roof.

One additional thing to watch for on garage roofs is the use of sheet metal as a roofing material (you'll find this on many old garages and even on a few new ones). Sheet-metal roofs come in various designs, but most are attached the same way: nails with rubber grommets under their heads (standing seam is the exception). The problem with this system of attachment is that in areas with extreme temperature variations, the nails can work themselves out of the wood. When this happens, the metal starts to rattle in the wind and the nail holes enlarge. Eventually, the seal is broken and water seeps into the building.

To check for this possible problem, look for nail heads that are raised up off the metal roofing—you will see a gap, sometimes $1/4$ in. or more, between the rubber seal on the nail and the metal roofing itself. Never walk on metal roofing that uses any type of rubber-grommeted nail. The metal can deflect down, breaking or ripping the grommet-to-metal seal and causing a leak.

If the garage is an add-on, there's sometimes a problem getting the new roof to integrate with the old building. A problem may occur where the new garage roof joins the main roof at the same level; look for possible leaks under the joint when you go inside the attic. Many times the garage is a single-story structure butted against the wall of an existing two-story structure. Be sure to check for leaks at the seam where the garage attaches to the house; if you can see the flashing, check that it's in good condition.

Structural stability

It goes without saying that the garage should be structurally sound. Attached garages will have at least one side attached to the main house structure, so they should be solid. Detached garages, on the other hand, are freestanding and, as discussed for roofs, are more likely to have problems.

A few summers ago, a homeowner asked me to come over and look at his newly built detached garage, which had just passed inspection. He wasn't happy with the work, but he wanted a second opinion before complaining to the contractor and building inspector. The homeowner took me out to the garage and slammed the side entrance door. The slamming door was his official test; and after I saw what happened, it became my first test on all detached structures from then on. The walls shook, the metal roof vibrated, and the steel garage doors looked as though they were about to fly loose from the building. The support structure was, to say the least, not only inadequate but almost nonexistent—with supports that were too small, too shallow, and spaced too far apart. I suggest that this test also be your test. If after slamming the door, you find that your eyes go wide and you feel the need to grab the structure to steady it, make a bold note on the inspection form: "Something is wrong here."

In addition to the slamming-door test, a few others are recommended. Check the supporting beams and walls of the garage—they should be solid with minimum signs of deterioration. These walls are occasionally hit by something more than just inclement weather: Look for snapped or cracked beams and studs, bowed-out walls, and so

A garage roof should go through the same inspection as a house roof. This garage roof has such a low slope that the pine needles lie decaying on the roof year-round. The resulting acidity destroys the shingles.

Garage Roof Checklist

- [ ] Obvious holes in the roof
- [ ] Missing, broken, or torn shingles/tiles
- [ ] Sagging ridge
- [ ] Wavy roof surface
- [ ] Missing, raised, or ripped flashing
- [ ] Rotted or damaged soffit, rake, and fascia boards
- [ ] Damaged or inadequate guttering and downspouts
- [ ] Nails working loose on sheet-metal roof
- [ ] Joint between garage roof and house roof or wall unsound

on, where someone has driven a car into the back wall of the garage.

If the wood framing of the garage is sitting on a concrete slab, check the interface between them. Any time wood is in contact with porous concrete, the wood should be treated or it will start to deteriorate. Look for rotting wood members, as well as signs of insect damage; the wood/slab contact area is moist and insects will thrive there. If stairs, inside or out, lead to an upstairs living area, they should be inspected in the same way as stairs inside the house (see chapter 7). Check for the distance between balusters, the height of the tread rise, and the presence of a hand rail and make sure that the stair structure is sound.

The garage floor

The garage floor check is a quick-and-easy one—simply observe any major cracks. All small cracks, known as hairline cracks, should be ignored. If the concrete is starting to disintegrate in large patches, write it up. There may be a floor drain in the garage to drain away melted snow and water. Floor drains have a habit of not working after a period of time and will need to be checked with water from a hose. If a sump pump is installed in the garage floor, it must go through the same checks as does a sump pump installed in a basement (see chapter 7). Obviously, if a sump pump is installed, it's because there's a problem with water in the garage, so try to find out what it is. Check for mud on the floor, a good indicator that the floor is being flooded.

Garage doors

The garage door is one of the more important checks of the garage inspection. You'll need to note the type and condition of the door, as well as how (and if) it opens and closes. With automatic safety features, today's garage doors have a lot more to check than the manual swing-up doors of the past, so be sure to allocate enough time for a thorough inspection.

The first thing to note on your inspection form is the number of doors and whether they are single or double. This information tells the buyer how many cars the garage will hold and how much storage space is available. Next write down what the door is made of. Most of the earliest garage doors were made of wood, which were high maintenance, requiring constant repainting and repair. Today's doors may be wood, metal,

Garage Structural and Floor Checklist

- [ ] Cracked or disintegrating foundation
- [ ] Cracked, broken, or rotting support beams
- [ ] Bowed-out walls
- [ ] Untreated wood in contact with slab floor
- [ ] Insect damage at wood/concrete interface
- [ ] Major cracks in floor
- [ ] Disintegration of concrete floor
- [ ] Sump pump, if present, is working

vinyl clad, composite, fiberglass, or metal-clad insulated.

On wood doors, look for the obvious, such as peeling paint and rotting boards; on metal doors, check for rust. If the door is a composite material, check to see if the composite is delaminating. Pay close attention to old fiberglass doors. Even when new, these doors were very thin and fragile. After many years in the sun, they can get brittle and then crack and break. Note if the fiberglass strands have started to peel off the door (but don't run your finger along its surface or you run the risk of getting fiberglass splinters).

Beyond the surface problems, also look for obvious signs of damage on garage doors, such as dents, cracks, and broken glass. I also note whether the glass is single pane or insulated and whether the door is insulated. Be sure to check the garage door seal; the door should seal well enough that you can't see under the door once it is closed.

The next step is to determine whether the door is operable—does it open and close smoothly? There are basically three ways for a garage door to open. The oldest doors have hinges and open like two giant doors—a holdover from the horse-and-buggy days. Others have overhead rollers and slide sideways; this type of door is seen in many barns. With both these older styles, it's almost

Garage doors come in a wide variety of styles and sizes. A single door is on the right—a double on the left. There are many things to inspect on modern automatic doors, so be sure to allocate enough time for a good inspection. (Photo courtesy Raynor Garage Doors.)

This garage door is literally falling apart, needs paint, and won't open. It also happens to be at the bottom of a driveway, with water flowing up against it. If the door won't open, there isn't a whole lot to check; just make note of what you see on your inspection form.

impossible to keep the cold air out of the garage—so don't expect to see any plumbing in these buildings in cold climates. An additional problem with sliding doors is the rollers in the overhead rail; they bind if any type of debris is caught in the track. Slide these doors back and forth a couple of times to see if they move easily.

The third style is a door that lifts up as one complete unit (either manually or automatically). Newer doors will be sectional, with each section or module making a small angle as it rolls up. Many of these are finger pinchers, so watch out as you close the door. Some of the newest designs have a protective cover where the sections meet, which is a safety device and a good selling feature. On manual doors that use springs to overcome the weight of the door, the door can come down fast and heavy if the springs are incorrectly adjusted, so be wary when you close the door and write it up if there's a problem. Operate the door several times to be sure all the hinges are working, all the sections fold and unfold properly, and the door isn't about to fall apart. Watch the wheels slide up and down in their track, and make sure the chain or screw isn't binding on anything.

Old-fashioned sliding doors can be difficult to open if debris gets caught in the track. When sliding the door open, grab high and push hard.

Modern garage doors have a photoelectric-eye sensing system to detect any object in the door's path. A light beam traverses the doorway and is sensed by the photoelectric eye. If the light beam is interrupted, the door should not operate. (Photo courtesy Raynor Garage Doors.)

Garage Door Checklist

- ☐ Number of doors
  - ☐ Single
  - ☐ Double
- ☐ Door material
  - ☐ Wood
  - ☐ Metal
  - ☐ Vinyl clad
  - ☐ Composite
  - ☐ Fiberglass
  - ☐ Metal-clad insulated
- ☐ Door in good condition
- ☐ Seals intact and functional
- ☐ Door opens and closes without binding
  - ☐ Automatic
  - ☐ Manual
- ☐ Safety features functional

When all garage doors were manual, testing whether a door was operable was easy—all you had to do was manually open and close the door. With today's automatic or motorized doors, there's more to check, including safety features that prevent the door from closing if there's something—or somebody—in its path. For example, automatic door openers that were installed after 1982 have a reversing mechanism that makes the door go back up if something is under it as it closes. Openers installed after 1992 are required to have a back-up system—normally a light beam sensor or a sensor built into the door seal. Nothing is as simple as it used to be.

As an inspector, you must verify that all this automatic equipment works. If the door has a light beam sensor, the light beam will be just above the garage floor where the door comes to rest. It is composed of a transmitter and receiver (automatic eye). To test this system, place a cardboard box in the light path and then press the close button. The door should not work. Take the box away and try it again; this time it should work. As the door is coming down, put the box back in the light beam and the door should reverse itself. With older models that don't have a light-beam mechanism, put a cardboard box beneath the door as it closes; it should reverse before the box is crushed. If it doesn't, write it up—it could also crush a child.

Automatic doors will have a pull-down rope that bypasses the automatic feature and allows you to open and close the door manually. This allows use of the door if there is a loss of electricity. Be sure to verify that this manual bypass works. And don't forget the obvious—the bulb in the automatic opener itself. I normally write up a missing bulb, because the bulb socket becomes hot when the door opens. Then there is the superobvious: For example, if the installer has cut through any beams or joists to allow the opener to work. If it appears that the cut is so dramatic that the structural integrity of the beam has been

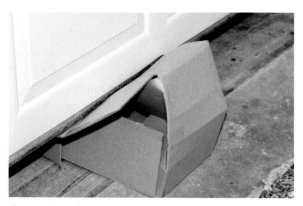

If an automatic garage door has a light beam sensor, the door should not close if a box is placed in the path of the light beam. On this door, the safety feature has failed.

On older automatic doors without the light beam sensor, the door will attempt to close. But once contact is made, the door should reverse itself before the box is crushed.

Carbon Monoxide Problems

Carbon monoxide, sometimes known by its chemical formula CO, is a colorless, odorless gas emitted as a by-product by open-flame appliances. If inhaled in sufficient concentration, it can be fatal. Symptoms of overexposure include headache, dizziness, weakness, nausea, vomiting, and sleepiness.

Unlike smoke detectors, carbon monoxide detectors are not yet required in most areas, but it's a good idea to recommend them to a client who's getting ready to buy a home you inspect. CO detectors are inexpensive, easy to install, and require very little maintenance. Some detectors feature a digital display that indicates the readout of CO levels from 0 to 999 parts per million. A loud horn sounds a warning when excessive quantities of the deadly gas are detected.

Potential sources of CO in a home include automobiles running in a garage, poorly vented or clogged fireplaces and chimneys, gas water heaters, gas furnaces, portable kerosene space heaters, and cracked or broken furnace heat exchangers. A common source of CO is incomplete combustion within a gas water heater. Installed in garages and other small airtight spaces, gas heaters can produce CO when the garage door is completely down and the heater combustion runs out of sufficient oxygen. How fast the oxygen is depleted depends on how big the garage is, how airtight it is, and how big the burners are. A small airtight garage can use up the available oxygen within 24 hours. In addition, rust can fall from the flue pipe onto the burner causing incomplete combustion. When this happens, the flame sound will change and noxious fumes will start to permeate the building.

Any open-flame device in a garage has another problem the owner will have to deal with—the danger of igniting flammable gas, such as gasoline vapor. This is why gas water heaters are required to be at least 18 in. off the floor (depending on local codes). For some illogical reason, a gas dryer does not have the same requirement in many areas. Pay particular attention to the flue of a gas dryer (or a water heater or woodstove) in a garage and have it pass the same inspection as you would in a house.

Fluorescent lights don't work well in an unheated garage in cold climates. A close look at the ballast reveals why: The ballast has a minimum starting temperature of 50°F.

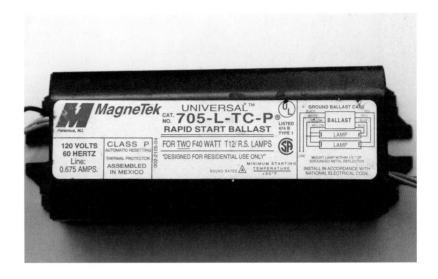

compromised, it should be checked by a qualified structural inspector.

Electrical inspection

Garages are not required to have electricity; but if they do, the inspector needs to verify that they are wired safely. Just because you're inspecting a garage, doesn't mean you should use a lower standard to evaluate the electrical system than you would in the main house.

In my experience, the most significant electrical problem in the garage is using fluorescent lighting. Standard ballasts are not designed for cold-weather climates, and the lights will not come on consistently at temperatures below 50°F. Cold-weather ballasts are available, but they are expensive and may have to be special ordered. Add corrosion, damp air, and condensation forming inside and outside the light, and it's a wonder they work at all. If the weather is cold and the lights are blinking, make note of it on your report form. The best lights for a cold-weather garage are simple incandescent lights.

The next most common problem in a garage is incomplete work. Homeowners have a habit of leaving wiring projects in the garage unfinished. Check for open splices and missing splice covers; also inspect the incandescent lighting and

Check for incomplete electrical work in the garage, such as open-faced splice boxes without cover plates.

switching. The electrical cable should be attached to the framing, not just hang loose.

It's quite common to have the wire protected by thin-wall conduit as it enters the switches and receptacles. If this is the case, the inspector should verify that the conduit and metal boxes the switches and receptacles are in are grounded. As it enters the box, the ground wire must connect onto the metal box via a screw—preferably a green grounding screw that is installed just for that purpose. The conduit connected to the box is then grounded as well. You're not allowed to run the ground wire to the receptacle and then have the receptacle ground the box and conduit. However, it can be the other way around. You are allowed to ground the metal box with the incoming ground wire and then have the receptacle get its ground from the metal box. To do this, some receptacles have special metal tabs on the long receptacle attachment screw so that when the receptacle is tightened up against the box a secure ground is obtained.

If the garage has electricity, there should be at least one receptacle outlet. Even though it isn't required for older houses, suggest that any receptacle in the garage be ground-fault protected. Newer garages will have ground-fault circuit interrupter (GFCI) protection for all their general-purpose receptacles. You'll need to use a GFCI tester to verify that the protection mechanism is still working—GFCI receptacles seem to have a short life span in cold, moist environments. An easy way to verify which receptacles are protected by a GFCI breaker is to trigger the breaker via the push-in button on the checker and then see which receptacles don't work.

You also need to verify proper polarity, which means that the black and white wires are connected to the proper terminals on the receptacle. Check all standard receptacle outlets and GFCIs with the plug-in checker to verify that they have been wired properly. Sometimes it pays to have two different brands of plug-in checkers to check

Garage Electrical Checklist

- [ ] Lights working
- [ ] No open splices, missing splice covers
- [ ] Conduit grounded
- [ ] Receptacles grounded and wired correctly
- [ ] Receptacles ground-fault protected
- [ ] Subpanel has neutrals and grounds separate

one against the other in case something doesn't look right, such as a dim light or a flashing light.

Even though you may be inspecting a newer building that is required to have GFCI protection, all receptacles are not required to be protected. If a table saw, freezer, or similar item is plugged into a common duplex receptacle (and is accessible for use), it probably is not on a GFCI. This is common because dedicated outlets are not required to have ground-fault protection. The receptacle will have to be changed to a single receptacle if it is to remain non-ground-fault protected. Or if it was allowed, the installer might have broken off the internal tabs of the receptacle to kill the unused receptacle half and make it unusable. Therefore, don't write up that the duplex receptacle needs to be replaced by a single until you verify that both parts of the entire receptacle are hot. If this is the case and the receptacle half is dead, the installer is following the intent of the code (safety) but not quite the letter.

An attached garage will probably have a circuit or two tapped into the main service panel that is in the house. A detached garage will likely have its own panel that feeds off the main panel. If the number of circuits used in the garage exceeds six, the garage is required to have its own panel. This panel, separate and fed from the main panel, is considered a subpanel. What this means to the inspector is that you must verify that the subpanel is wired like a subpanel; that is, it must have a four-wire feed—hot, hot, neutral, and ground. You will probably often find that a garage doesn't have the four-wire feed, so write it up. The neutral must not be connected into the grounding circuit. In addition, verify where the neutral bus is and check that it is on plastic standoffs. The ground wires cannot connect into this bus, nor can the panel-frame connection; it is for neutrals only. The panel will have to go through the same checks as a main panel—checking for overfused wires, and so on. (For more on the service inspection, see chapter 2.)

If there are heavy-duty machines in the garage (such as table saws, bandsaws, and compressors), they need to be grounded. If the garage is old and has not been rewired, all these machines are probably using a cheater plug to operate. Write it up—there is no grandfather clause. The building needs to be rewired. (The exception would be if the cable was BX with a steel sheath around the wires being used as ground.) However, if the machines are leaving with the seller and the buyer is not going to be using grounded tools and appliances in the garage, there is nothing to worry about.

As in any other part of the house, you cannot glue PVC (this type of PVC is gray) to the black ABS pipe. However, for some unknown reason, many people think they can get by with it in the garage.

Plumbing problems to watch out for in a garage, or in any other part of the house, include use of PVC as a potable hot- or cold-water pipe. PVC is not approved for water distribution.

This installer not only glued PVC pipe to ABS pipe, which is against code, and used the wrong type of elbow (too short a sweep) but also forgot to glue the elbow onto the vertical pipe. Every time the toilet above is flushed a small amount of water leaks out and drains down the pipe, leaving a white calcium deposit.

Plumbing

Any plumbing in the garage should be taken through the same inspections as the plumbing in the rest of the house (see chapters 7 and 9). However, if the garage is in a cold climate, you might well ask yourself what keeps the plumbing from freezing in the winter; write it up if the answer is not satisfactory. If the heat has to be kept on in the garage all winter to keep the pipes from freezing, the new owner will want to know. Some garages have a heat source to keep the plumbing from freezing, and this needs to be listed.

Plumbing in the garage is very common in warm climates, and as in the basement, most of it is exposed for easy inspection. For some reason, many do-it-yourselfers think that because the drain lines are in the garage, they don't have to follow the same rules as those in the house. The inspector should be prepared for anything.

The most common garage plumbing problem is not technically in the garage—it's in the living space immediately above the garage. If the builder puts a bath and utility room above an unheated garage in a cold climate, the plumbing's not likely to make it through a hard freeze. Almost as illogical an installation is when an outside water line drops down from the second floor to feed an outside faucet that's in the mini-wall between garage doors. The water line is inside an outside wall with freezing temperatures on both sides of the wall. It is only a matter of time before the line will freeze and break.

Another possible problem to be on the lookout for in the garage is a damaged vertical drain

The homeowner took this pipe with him as he tried to leave the garage in a hurry. A pipe that has snapped off at floor level is obvious, but also be on the lookout for cracked pipes and for inadequate repairs (with glue, duct tape, and so on).

line—you see them all the time running from ceiling to floor. These sometimes get hit when someone drives a car into the garage (or more likely when they back out). The pipe may snap at the concrete floor (and thus cannot be ignored), but other times the damage is less obvious. Check for cracks in the line and the smell of sewer gas. Look especially closely at the point where the line goes into the floor. It is here that the line will most likely crack, because it cannot flex at the point at which it goes into the concrete.

Garage Plumbing Checklist

- [ ] Water lines located (or insulated) so they will not freeze if garage is unheated
- [ ] Water lines not leaking
- [ ] Drain lines not cracked, broken, or leaking

Driveways and Walkways

Over the years, I've observed that some buyers are very picky about driveways and walkways, whereas others hardly seem to care about their condition. Nevertheless, the type and condition of the driveway and walkway are things you should make note of. Typical materials are dirt, gravel, asphalt, concrete, patterned concrete, and pavers such as cobblestone, brick, and concrete.

Driveways

Dirt and gravel are common in the country, where driveways tend to be longer. Asphalt is less expensive than concrete but softens and gouges easily in high temperatures. It's also subject to

Long country driveways tend to be gravel and dirt; this one is in good condition. Potholes are unavoidable; the author doesn't make note of them until they are deep enough to blow a tire or to be called a sinkhole.

degradation from gas and oil spills. Its black color absorbs heat, which makes it more popular in cold climates to melt snow and ice. Asphalt also seems to be the favorite of disreputable contractors who want to create a "throw and go" driveway that's lucky to last a year of two because they didn't compact the subsoil. These driveways break apart in many irregular sections, looking like a schoolbook example of plate tectonics movement.

A slab driveway costs about twice as much as an asphalt one. Properly detailed, concrete is extremely durable. A subcategory for higher-end homes is the exposed-aggregate driveway. This type has pebblestone in the top layer of concrete, which gives good traction.

Water destroys driveways. If the land around the driveway doesn't shed water, the driveway will start to break up, especially in cold climates. If the driveway is surrounded by saturated soil, freezing temperatures will cause frost heave and make the driveway buckle. Long driveways going downhill are especially vulnerable to erosion, because of the amount and velocity of water that races downhill alongside and over the driveway. This is why you may see what look like speed bumps built into long, downhill gravel and dirt roads. These cutouts channel the water off the driveway before it picks up enough mass and velocity to erode and destroy it.

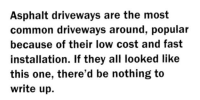

Asphalt driveways are the most common driveways around, popular because of their low cost and fast installation. If they all looked like this one, there'd be nothing to write up.

The inspector should note any major cracks and degradation of the driveway surface. Small cracks are inevitable and should be ignored. Major potholes and any shifted sections large enough to trip over should be noted. Any driveway adjacent to the building that has a basement should be suspect. As the car packs down the soil it pushes in on the basement wall. If there is an abundance of water due to poor drainage and guttering, the problem is aggravated even more. It's quite common to find that the guttering is draining at the same spot, pouring into a crack between the driveway and the basement wall, and then leaking into the basement.

Driveways of flagstone or brick have a tendency to be wavy if the subsurface was not prepared properly. This driveway has been in several years and is still flat. If any bricks or stones are cracked or disintegrating, write it up.

Walkways and sidewalks

I think of a walkway or sidewalk as a miniature driveway and inspect it in the same way. Small cracks I ignore, but if I can stick my finger in the crack or if a sidewalk section has shifted up enough that I can trip over it, I write it up. As with everything else around the house under inspection, pay particular attention to how the grading and guttering affect the walkway. One of the most significant design errors in houses is having rainwater or snowmelt flow over or settle on the sidewalk. In the winter, the sidewalk becomes a very dangerous place to walk.

Ignore hairline cracks on concrete driveways, but write up anything that's big enough to trip over.

Driveway and Walkway Checklist

- ☐ Major cracks and deterioration of surface
- ☐ Major potholes
- ☐ Low areas that saturate and hold water
- ☐ Raised sections

Be on the lookout for low-lying muddy areas on walkways where water pools when it rains. This walkway is breaking up because water has saturated the area under the walk and is heaving the rock and concrete up at different rates.

BASEMENTS AND CRAWL SPACES

I always tell people never to go into a flooded basement. The worst basement I ever inspected was also the most dangerous. As I entered, I could see the water on the floor, visible as dark stains against the light gray concrete. But wet basements are nothing new where I work, so I went against my own advice and walked in. The leak appeared to be coming from the opposite side of the basement, so I casually walked over, splashing water all the way, curious to see what the problem was.

What I couldn't see was that a botched splice on a water line upstairs behind the refrigerator was sending a torrent of water down the wall into the basement. The water was pouring into the top of the main service panel and out the bottom. The service panel lid had been removed, and I could see green algae growing on the neutral bus. I turned and walked out as fast as I could, fully expecting to feel the familiar tingle of electricity coursing through my body at any moment. I had the meter pulled before I went back into the basement again and resolved that in future I would listen to my own advice about staying out of flooded basements.

You have to be just as careful in crawl spaces. A few things I've encountered over the years include giant aggressive spiders, skunks, cats, and dogs as well as broken glass, overhead nails, and bare wires. If there's a water heater in the crawl space,

Always be careful when entering a crawl space: You never know what you're going to find lurking in the dark.

expect to find a snake or two in or around it. And I suppose in Florida and Louisiana, you might even find an alligator or two lurking in the shadows.

Types of Basements

There's probably more to inspect in the basement than there is in any other part of the house. Checking for water damage, cracked concrete walls, and the condition of joists, gas lines, water lines, drain lines, and appliances (see chapter 8) is all part of a basement inspection. It's important to allow enough time for this inspection, because whatever affects the basement also affects the rest of the house.

When inspecting the basement, the first thing to note is whether it is finished, unfinished, or a combination of the two. A finished basement is one that it is livable, with finished walls and ceiling as opposed to bare studs and concrete. Unfinished basements have bare exterior walls—the concrete block or pour will be visible. Any inside walls will be stud walls, and all utilities will be visible. Overhead you'll see the floor/ceiling joists, plumbing, wiring, and ductwork.

Many basements, however, are a combination of the two. The owner never got around to finishing the project, so you'll see some things

The advantage of inspecting an unfinished basement is that all the utilities are visible, making it easy to spot problem areas. Here, white plumbing pipe is connected to black pipe, which is not allowed because the two materials have different expansion and contraction ratios.

finished and others unfinished. If walls are up but the floor is still a bare slab, the basement is typically considered unfinished—at least it is as far as the electrical inspection is concerned, because you'll still be standing on bare concrete. (The one exception would be a concrete floor that has been finished with an epoxy coating.) And that means that all receptacles (except dedicated

Inspection Checkpoints for Basement Water Damage

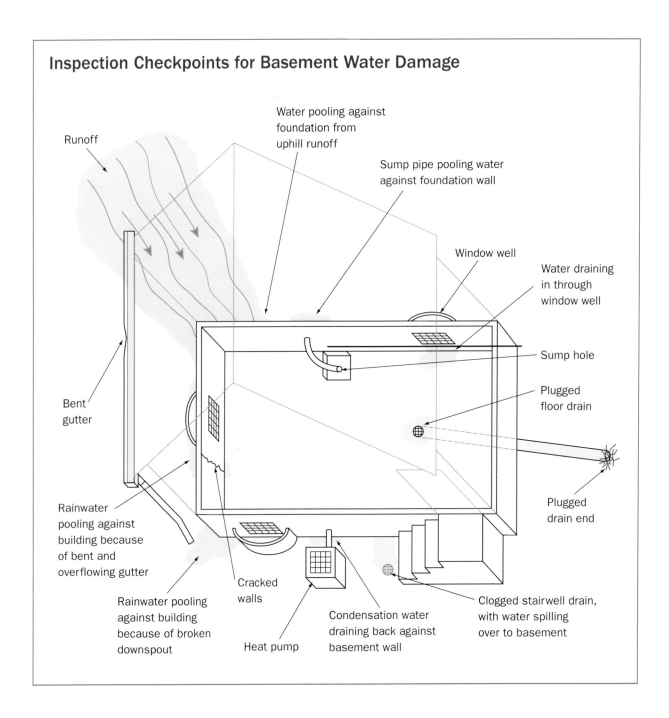

Runoff

Water pooling against foundation from uphill runoff

Sump pipe pooling water against foundation wall

Window well

Water draining in through window well

Sump hole

Plugged floor drain

Bent gutter

Plugged drain end

Rainwater pooling against building because of bent and overflowing gutter

Rainwater pooling against building because of broken downspout

Cracked walls

Heat pump

Condensation water draining back against basement wall

Clogged stairwell drain, with water spilling over to basement

and inaccessible) should be ground-fault protected.

It's important for the inspector to pay particular attention to the quality of work in basements that are only partially finished. Normally you ignore the quality, reporting only the facts, but you can do so only to a certain point. Many homeowners like to tackle basement remodels themselves, whether they're qualified to do the work or not. Look for receptacle boxes extending too far out of the wall or set too far in, drywall seams that aren't taped, walls that are bowed, paneling that's starting to pop off its nails, and other telltale signs of an unprofessional job.

Basement Water Damage

Because all basements, whether finished, unfinished, or a combination of the two, are below grade, the most significant problem is water damage. As you walk in, look for obvious signs of flooding, such as muddy walls and wet floors. Most flooding is the result of improper grading and the building's faulty guttering. However, in the country it's also not uncommon for there to be springs and wells in the basement. If the basement is flooded, don't go in: It's too dangerous to be walking in water that could be electrified at any moment. Many times the floor will be dry when you inspect the basement, but there will be signs of flooding such as mud rings on the wall and around the appliances. I've seen mud rings halfway up water heaters.

Inspecting the basement walls

Researchers at the University of Minnesota Underground Space Center have shown that over a period of four months 30 gal. to 50 gal. of water will seep through the porous walls and floor of a typical basement built in well-drained soil whether the foundation is block or poured. Therefore, the amount of moisture coming through the walls and floor owing to poor drainage and less well drained soil would have to be significantly more.

The most common type of moisture damage in basements is the result of intermittent flooding or, at a slower pace, water seepage through small cracks in the porous foundation walls. Most of these problems can be corrected by diverting the sources of water away from the house. But sometimes the moisture problem comes from an appliance within the house: the dryer vent. Many houses have the dryer venting directly into the basement or attic—I've even seen them vented

Rust and flaking paint on the bottom of this water heater indicate that the basement has a moisture problem (and possibly a flooding problem).

Symptoms of a Humidity-Sick Home

Summer
- [ ] Dampness, even during dry weather
- [ ] Musty odor in basement
- [ ] Mold and mildew buildup
- [ ] Possibly allergic discomfort, especially for infants and children
- [ ] House doesn't cool down during the evening or on cooler days

Winter
- [ ] Fogged-up, sweaty, icy windows
- [ ] Water on windowsills
- [ ] House slow to heat up

Year-Round
- [ ] Headaches, nausea for occupants of house
- [ ] Water seepage on floor
- [ ] Damp, musty basement
- [ ] Visible mildew or fungus
- [ ] Peeling paint
- [ ] Warped paneling or wood
- [ ] Loose floor tiles
- [ ] Rust at furnace and water heater base
- [ ] White powder (efflorescence) on walls and furniture

As water seeps through the basement wall it evaporates and leaves behind a white mineral residue known as efflorescence. If you see white powder on the walls of the basement you are inspecting, it's a sure sign there's a moisture problem.

grow. Many molds reproduce by releasing spores into the air, which then settle on organic matter and clothes, are taken into the lungs, and grow into new mold clusters. Such airborne mold spores are far more numerous than pollen grains and when inhaled can produce allergic reactions and sickness. Mold and mildew can irritate the eyes, nose, and throat; produce nausea and headaches; and cause allergy-related diseases, digestive disorders, influenza, and other infectious diseases.

Finished basement walls present a special problem in that leakage may be occurring that you cannot see. Be on the lookout for water damage that might be originating behind the finished walls. Most often this will be visible as dark stains on the drywall or rotted paneling. Pay particular attention to stains at the bottom edge of the wall and trim because this is where the water will settle and destroy the finished wall. Look for wood that's starting to crumble, mold growing on the finished walls, and mildew stains. Make note of how the basement feels: Does it feel damp and cold from excessive moisture? Is there a dehumidifier, and if so, is it working?

As you inspect the basement, you may also need to check outside to locate potential sources of water damage. Pay particular attention to the following: exterior stair wells and window wells, walls adjacent to gutter downspouts or faulty guttering, and cracks in the walls (either in the basement walls themselves or at the interface between the wall and the floor).

Exterior stair wells and window wells
Basement stair wells can collect hundreds of gallons of water when it rains. There should be a drain at the bottom landing to take all this water away; if it is plugged up, all the rain water will spill over into the basement. Sometimes debris is covering the drain grill, other times the far end of the drain is plugged with weeds and roots. Mud rings around the well walls are one indicator that the drain is plugged, but the best test is to run a hose into the drain and see if it backs up.

between the ceiling joists. The dryer must vent outside—there are no exceptions (see chapter 8).

A good indicator of excessive moisture in a basement is a white powder residue, known as efflorescence, on the walls. The residue is the leftover salts or minerals after the water has seeped into the building and evaporated. Look for efflorescence along the basement walls—in particular at the corners—and on plastic or leather furniture.

It's imperative that you make note of mold and mildew on the inspection report. Molds are living organisms that need moisture and nutrients to

Exterior stair wells can trap water at the bottom and flood the basement. If there is a drain, verify that it works.

Window wells can sometimes be more trouble than they are worth. In this basement, they are channeling rainwater directly into the basement every time it rains.

At times, window wells are nothing more than water collectors for the basement. Look for brownish red water tracks under the windows. And if it's raining, of course, watch for the incoming water.

Walls adjacent to gutters People have a habit of not repairing damaged downspouts and letting the water collect along the foundation, not realizing that the basement walls are porous and the water seeps in. Another problem is that, even if the downspouts are sound, the water is not diverted far enough away from the house. (Improper lawn drainage can also force water from the surrounding area against the basement walls.) If the basement walls are finished, look for discoloration on the finished wall surface and

perhaps a bit of rot at the bottom. If the walls are unfinished, look for mold and mildew and perhaps water on the floor every time it rains.

Most guttering is so flimsy that if the downspout ends plug up, the gutter can't take all the weight of the water. It bends and overflows at its center. Other times the run is too long and again, it can't take the weight of the water coming off the roof. This presents the same problem as broken downspouts—the water saturates the ground along the basement walls and leaks into the basement.

Wall cracks Cracks in the walls of a basement can be caused by a number of different factors, but the result is always the same: a point of entry

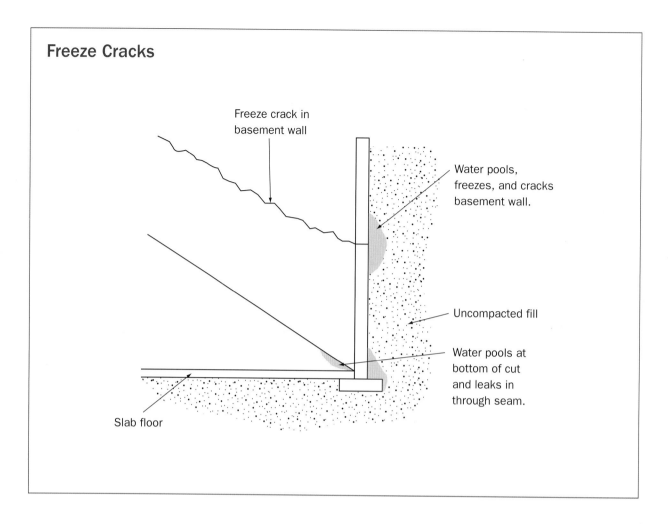

Freeze Cracks

Freeze crack in basement wall

Water pools, freezes, and cracks basement wall.

Uncompacted fill

Water pools at bottom of cut and leaks in through seam.

Slab floor

for water into the basement. Freeze cracks show up as long horizontal cracks along the exterior walls caused by pooling of water in uncompacted or saturated fill. The water freezes, expands, and cracks the wall. Adhesion adds to the problem: Earth sticks to the wall and lifts as the fill freezes.

Over time, due to weak concrete or too much exterior pressure, the basement wall can no longer take the weight bearing against it and it will crack and start to bow in—or just snap along a horizontal section. Within the bow there'll be both major and minor cracks in the concrete. Through these large and small cracks come anything from minor seepage to a river of water. Look for patches over cracks that are disintegrating or doing nothing but slowing down the incoming water. Eventually, the crack will widen and cause a complete sheer of the wall. The only way to

stop such water is to eliminate the source, which is on the other side of the wall, by diverting the water away from the wall.

A common area of seepage is where the outside wall comes into contact with the floor itself. Water flows down the outside walls and pools at the bottom of the wall. Eventually, this pool seeps through the porous concrete and onto the basement floor.

Unvented basement shower In some older homes, it's common to have an open basement shower. It's just as common not to vent it. A downstairs shower will put a lot of moisture into the air that can do a lot of damage. If the shower is functional, it needs to be vented (or there needs to be a working dehumidifier to remove all the airborne moisture).

Sump Pumps

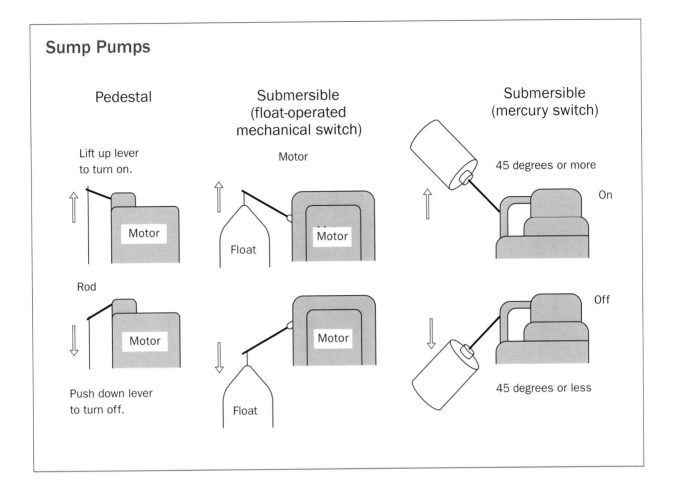

Pedestal

Lift up lever to turn on.

Motor

Rod

Motor

Push down lever to turn off.

Submersible (float-operated mechanical switch)

Motor

Motor

Float

Float

Submersible (mercury switch)

45 degrees or more

On

Off

45 degrees or less

Inspecting the basement floor

If the floor is a bare slab, observe and report any major cracks, whether they are leaking or not. Ignore minor hairline cracks—all slabs will have these. If there has been any major flooding from overhead pipe breaks, it will normally appear on the floor as a circular stain on the slab. Small overhead drips from the plumbing will appear as reddish iron stains or greenish blue stains.

Floors in finished basements are typically indoor/outdoor carpet, standard cloth carpet, or linoleum. Of the three, only cloth carpet will stain from a leak. As you make your inspection along the exterior walls, check for stains or pooling water where the carpet meets the concrete exterior wall. Linoleum that was installed in squares may be starting to pull loose. If water has saturated the carpet pad, the carpet will "squish" when walked on.

Sump pumps If there's a sump pump in the basement, it's a good indication that the basement floods or has water seepage problems—otherwise there's no reason for the pump to be there. As part of your basement inspection, you must test the pump to see if it works. The old-fashioned type of pump looks like a pedestal. It has the pump end down in the sump hole and the motor on a rod several feet above. As water enters the sump hole it lifts the float, which in turn pushes up a rod that engages the motor switch. To test the pump manually, you simply pull up the float rod.

The submersible sump pump won't be so obvious—you won't be able to see it, because the entire assembly is in the sump hole. There are several types of submersible sump pumps. One of the most common has a mercury float switch on a short cable that's attached to the pump. As

Testing a Sump Pump

Use a garden hose to check that basement floor drains are working.

1. Does the pump turn on automatically as the water raises the float?
2. When the pump turns on, does it give a high-pitched squeal? (This indicates that the bearings are bad.)
3. Does it just hum and not pump? (This indicates a jammed impeller.)
4. Once the pump is on, does the water leave the sump hole? (If not, the pump slots may be clogged with debris.)
5. Once the water starts leaving the sump hole is there water dripping or spraying out from the fittings (indicating a leak)?
6. Where does the water go? (It cannot go into the sewer or adjacent to a basement wall.)

water enters the hole, the float switch rises. Because it is attached to the pump, the float must invert, and as it does, the switch closes and the pump turns on. To engage this switch manually, you have to reach down to the pump and raise the mercury float so that it points up. A second common type of submersible pump has a white plastic torpedo float that's attached to a mechanical switch—it raises and lowers to push a switch up and down. If either type of submersible sump pump doesn't turn on, write it up.

All sump pumps have a large-diameter pipe that leaves the pump and exits out a side wall to discharge the sump water. If the water is pumped to the outside of the building only to have it drain along the basement wall and come back in, it isn't doing a lot of good. I've seen this happen more times than I can remember. In addition, most codes prohibit the discharge of sump pumps into the sewer system. This overloads the system with water.

There are a number of things to check on a sump pump. The best way to test the pump is to run a hose into the sump hole, turn on the hose, then watch and listen. If you don't have access to

water for the test, use a manual test (described previously) to verify that the pump will turn on. It won't hurt the pump to have it run for a second without water. Make a note that it turned on but that there was no water available for a complete test. One other type of sump pump, the diaphragm pump, will be hard to test. This pump has no rod to lift, but instead uses water pressure that goes into a port on the pump itself to turn the pump on. The hard part is getting the water pressure. Use a hose and raise the water level only to where the drain pours into the sump hole. Stop there—any more water will backflow into the drain pipe and flood the area it is intending to drain. If it hasn't turned on by then, observe and report.

Basement floor drains Basement floor drains are always a problem. Most simply don't work. The only way you can tell for sure is to run a hose to them, but you'll have to stay by the hose in case the water backs up. Many times, the blockage is at the drain exit, and it takes a few minutes for the water to reach it and then start backing up. Never go away and leave the hose running—you run the risk of flooding the basement. If possible, ask the owner about the drains before you test them with a hose, because it is possible to put water in one drain and have it come out another. (Write it up that the owner indicated that the drains worked/did not work.)

In some areas, basement drains are allowed to flow into the sewer system; in other areas, they are not. There's no way for the inspector to know where the drains go for sure; therefore, it's a good idea to ask the owner if the drains flow into the sewer or just over the hill. For drains that flow into the sewer, there'll be a problem of trap evaporation, which results in sewer gas coming into the house. (Mineral oil poured on top of the water seal helps eliminate the problem.) Others are kept primed (full of water) from the discharge from an appliance.

If there's a heat pump in the basement you're inspecting, be sure to trace the condensation drain that comes out of the pump. Heat pump installers run these lines almost anywhere from underneath the slab to outside along the basement wall where it can flow back down the wall and leak into the basement. Both are wrong and should be written up. The condensation drain should go into a drain trap via an air gap or be drained away from the building. (For more on heat pump condensate lines, see "Cross-Connections" on p. 248.)

Basement Wall and Floor Checklist

- [ ] Type of basement:
  - [ ] Unfinished
  - [ ] Finished
  - [ ] Partly finished
- [ ] Signs of moisture damage
- [ ] Cracks in the wall
- [ ] Cracks in the floor
- [ ] Sump pump functional (if present)
- [ ] Floor drains functional

Basement Lighting

If there are inside stairs leading to the basement, these stairs should have three-way switched lighting at top and bottom. If you have to cross the stairs in the dark to get to the switch, make note of it, because this is a safety hazard. Once you enter the basement, there should be some type of switch or light to illuminate the surrounding area. If the basement is considered unfinished, the light can be anything from a pull-chain to switched lighting. If there is no lighting at all, make note of it—especially if there is maintainable equipment in the room. If the basement is considered finished, it should have switched lighting at each point of entrance and/or exit. All open light fixtures, such as the keyless type that contain power when switched, need to have a bulb so no one can stick his or her finger into a hot socket.

As in garages, fluorescent fixtures in basements have a habit of not working particularly well. The moist and sometimes wet environment is not well suited for fluorescents, especially the common four-footers, whose small terminal pins corrode easily. Make a note if the lights take an unusually long time to warm up and turn on or if they don't do anything except flash on and off as they attempt to start.

Basement Structural Inspection

The advantage of inspecting an unfinished basement is that you can see the overhead joists. Look for any obvious dips; upstairs the finished walls may be cracking if the floor is sagging. Numerous screw posts in the basement indicate that such a problem has been noted and corrected.

Ceiling joists in basements are typically in much better condition than joists in crawl spaces (see p. 152), because they are not exposed to the elements. One thing to watch for, however, is

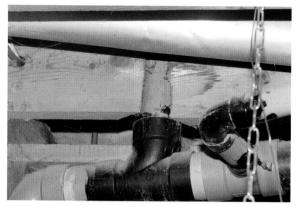

The person who installed this toilet cut the entire floor joist in half rather than moving the toilet a few inches off to the side. This was a major error.

Cutting a small notch in a joist to make room for a plumbing connection is acceptable.

This stringer, resting on the basement floor, is suffering from major rot as a result of gutter water entering the basement via the block walls.

Basement Stairs Checklist

☐ Is there a handrail?

☐ Is the handrail secure to the wall and in good condition?

☐ Are there balusters on the steps?

☐ Is the gap between the vertical balusters 5 in. or less?

☐ Are the steps secure top and bottom and not pulling away from their support?

☐ If the basement is a living area, do the steps leading down to it have a kickplate installed on the step risers (to prevent a small child from crawling between the steps and falling behind the stairs)?

where a utility installer has cut through a joist in an overzealous installation. As a rule, going horizontally (never vertically) through the center of a joist is acceptable, and taking a little off the underside edge is also okay. Cutting a third or more off the edge is not.

In worst-case conditions, it's possible that overhead joists could be damaged by either wet or dry rot. Walk under the joists observing any damage. Also check for insect damage—visible as numerous small holes in the joists or as powder on the floor underneath the joists (see "Insect Damage" on pp. 58–59). If you cannot see the overhead joists, or any other structural component, because something is blocking the view, make sure to note it on the inspection form.

Pay particular attention to the stairs leading from the basement to the first floor. These stairs are often overlooked, because they are not in a highly visible part of the house. Basement stairs should be in sound condition, with no signs of rot or other structural defects. Be sure to check the stair stringer (the board the steps are nailed to) where it touches the concrete floor to be sure it is not rotting out. Other than rot and cracks, the most common problem with basement stairs is the hand rail and balusters. In many houses, they are simply missing or installed in a haphazard manner. Also pay particular attention to the last step. If it is shorter than the rest, it could be a trip hazard. The most important checkpoints are listed in "Basement Stairs Checklist."

Basement Electrical Inspection

If the basement is finished, its electrical system should be inspected in the same way as in any other room in the house. In an unfinished basement, you have the advantage of being able to see how a considerable amount of the wiring is run. Look for ripped and damaged wire, bare wire, and open splices and covers that are not on the splice boxes. In many basements, you'll find wires just trailing off to nowhere, their ends hanging down from the joists; write it up. Be sure to note any broken receptacles or switches and any missing cover plates.

No two basements are quite the same, and each one you inspect will present a whole new set of items to check. Pay special attention to old, unfinished basements—they've had a lot more time

to collect items that are unique and beyond code. Many features may at one time have performed a purpose, but perhaps now they are doing more harm than good.

Knob-and-tube wiring is still being used in many old houses, and you may come across these old wires run through and along the basement joists. There is nothing wrong with this kind of wiring, and it shouldn't be condemned just because it is old. Knob-and-tube wiring consists of two insulated wires run independently a few inches apart. One wire is a hot conductor and the other a neutral return—two wires with no ground.

Many years ago, this ancient battery used to power the doorbell to the house. No one took the time to remove it, and the chemical fumes have reacted to the copper pipe where the low-voltage wire is lying on it. It's only a matter of time before a pinhole forms in the pipe and the basement floods.

It's not uncommon to find wires that go nowhere in the basement. Be sure to note them on your report form.

Old knob-and-tube wiring has two separate conductors—one for the neutral and one for the hot conductor. As long as its insulation is intact the wiring is still usable, albeit without a ground.

Messy but not dangerous. All these little wires are low voltage and commonly left open. The high-voltage cable feeding the transformer is inside the metal splice box.

As long as the insulation is intact, I don't recommend that it be replaced, unless the new owner wants to modernize or have grounds on all the outlets. I make the buyer aware that it is old wiring and still usable—but with no ground.

Grounding in unfinished basements is of primary importance because you are always standing on a moist wet floor. Just because the house has old ungrounded wiring is no excuse—even with knob-and-tube or the old two-conductor duplex cables. Grounds can be added without having to replace all the wire.

You'll probably come across a lot of low-voltage wiring in the basement, used, for example, for doorbells and thermostats. The low voltage comes from the secondary winding of a small transformer—it is wired with 120 volts on its primary winding, which sends 20 to 30 volts to its secondary. These sometimes look very messy, with small secondary wires going every which way and not even in a splice box; but as long as the wires to the primary are not accessible, I don't write it up. It may look messy, but the low voltage is not considered an electrocution hazard.

New houses will have ground-fault circuit interrupters (GFCIs) in the unfinished basement. Suggest GFCIs for older houses as well. GFCIs do not need a ground to work, so they can be in-

stalled and function just as well in older homes as in the new. Check these receptacles with a GFCI plug-in tester. GFCIs compare incoming to outgoing current and "kick" if there is even a small difference. The tester creates the difference when you push the little button.

Be sure to check all three-prong receptacles for proper grounding using the standard plug-in tester. If a three-prong receptacle is installed, it must be grounded, unless the receptacle feeds off the load side of a GFCI receptacle (ungrounded GFCIs are allowed). But even here, the ungrounded receptacle must be labeled "no ground." Many homeowners and do-it-yourselfers install a three-prong receptacle on old two-wire ungrounded cable just to be able to plug appliances in—this is not allowed unless, as previously stated, it is fed by a GFCI.

Basement Plumbing Inspection

Water lines and drain lines are visible in an unfinished basement, so you'll be able to see what has happened to the plumbing since it was installed. Slow leaks will appear as stains on the pipe and on the floor below. Look for leaks at all male and female adapters. One of the most common pressure-line leak locations is immediately above the water heater.

Water lines

Before you get picky on the water-line plumbing, it's important to know what's approved for your area. Approved pipe differs from locale to locale. Copper is approved everywhere. Chlorinated polyvinyl chloride (CPVC) is approved in most states but not all. Polybutylene (PB) is banned throughout the United States, and the homeowner may be required to replace it before the house is sold. Rural houses that have had every do-it-yourselfer within a country mile work on the plumbing will probably have a little of everything—and many of the joints will be leaking. One pipe that is not approved for inside plumbing is black rolled plastic, or polyethylene. And it's something I see all the time; it's the pipe that holds together with stainless-steel clamps. Polyethylene (PE) pipe can come into the house to the water pressure tank or main turn-off valve, but it must stop there.

Copper pipe There's no such thing as a perfect water line—they all give trouble over time. For example, copper water lines can spring pinholes. Sometimes the water leak will be a small spray off to the side—other times it will just flow down the pipe and drip off. Soft copper that comes in rolls tends to change its diameter when it freezes. As the water turns to ice, it expands the pipe slightly, pushing the sides out. Once thawed, no copper fitting will go over the pipe. Another annoyance of using copper is that it can dissolve from the inside out if the water is slightly acid. This shows up as the greenish blue stains that you see on tubs and sinks.

Plastic pipe CPVC, also called plastic pipe, is pale colored. The white plastic pipe is polyvinyl chloride (PVC), which is not normally used for water lines throughout the house but is commonly used to bring water into the house from the well or city water main. The problem with all plastic pipes is that they crack easily—especially

Check for leaks at male and female adapters. This leak must have been dripping for a long time for such a buildup of mineral deposits to occur.

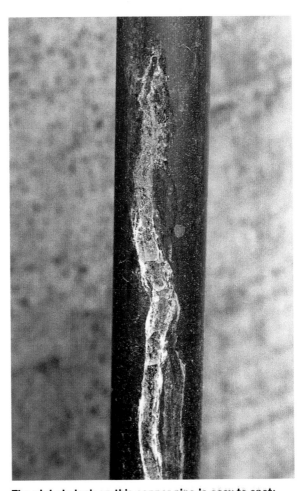

The pinhole leak on this copper pipe is easy to spot: the small dot with greenish blue deposits trailing down the pipe. The pinhole was caused by acid water eating away at the inside of the pipe.

Be especially wary when inspecting plastic pipe. CPVC gets damaged easily—this pipe got hit, and the male adapter pulled out on one side.

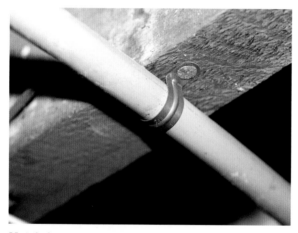

Metal clamps are not approved for PB pipe, because the sharp edges can cut into the flexible pipe as it expands, creating a leak.

Finished Basement Ceilings

A finished basement has one inspection advantage over an unfinished one—overhead leaks are easy to detect. Whether the ceiling is drywall or a drop ceiling, an overhead plumbing leak is easily spotted by the brownish red stains. Be careful removing any overhead tile. If they've been damaged by water, they'll easily crumble, break, and fall in your face. Note any missing or broken tiles. Be careful working around fluorescent lights in drop ceilings: They are supposed to be individually supported with wires going up to the joists, but some owners just lay the lights on the drop ceiling grid and they'll easily fall if you take down the ceiling tiles.

when cold. And the older the plastic gets, the more brittle it gets. By far the worst problem with plastics is that they cannot take a significant freeze while pressurized with water. The water expands as it turns to ice and the plastic pipe splits in long sections.

As with all types of pipe, be sure to check the male and female fittings for leaks. CPVC and PVC are especially prone to leaks at the fittings, because they are very easy to cross thread. Furthermore, the plastic is subject to damage when it's hit or bumped into.

For a long time, some CPVC manufacturers didn't make female fittings, which was a good thing. If you screw a metal pipe into a female plastic fitting, it tends to crack. But plastic female fittings have been on the market for quite some time now so be on the lookout for problems. What you will see is a slow drip coming from a hairline crack that may be too small to be visible. Water tracking is a telltale leak sign. Look for the red rust stains where the water has been slowly following the pipe till it drips off to the floor. If the floor is concrete, you might see water or a water stain there as well.

PB is a flexible gray pipe that has had problems with its fittings. It is now banned in new construction. Make note if the PB pipe is leaking at the ring joints and if it was installed properly. It is not supposed to be glued or tightened down with hose clamps. The crimped rings should be smooth to the touch—not bent with sharp edges. PB valves have a habit of leaking where the top and base screw together. Another installation problem I've encountered with PB pipes is the support clamps—you are not allowed to use metal clamps

Cheap valves are a source of leaks. Some leak through the handles, others at the pipe interface points. This valve was made so cheaply it split right across its body.

Always be on the lookout for patched pipe and fittings. Before this valve was removed, it leaked around its sides, and the owner tried to patch it with a piece of rubber and a clamp.

to hold up the soft, flexible PB because it cuts into the pipe.

Galvanized pipe and fittings The worst problem with galvanized pipe is that it can rust on the inside of the pipe where you cannot see it. As the rust builds up, it can totally cut off the water flow. You'll note this as reduced water pressure throughout the house. On the outside it will rust through at the threaded joints where the zinc coating has been cut away for the threads. The rust particles have a habit of breaking off on the inside pipe wall and then flowing through the pipe before getting stuck in toilet refill valves and washer screens. At its worst, I've seen rust collect and totally block off the shutoff valves under the sinks.

The quality of plumbing fittings leaves a lot to be desired these days. One manufacturer came out with a set of brass ball valves that had shoulders so thin that they either would split when you screwed in a galvanized pipe nipple or, if you were lucky enough to get the valves installed without them breaking, would split on their sides. I've had the same problem with galvanized 90s. Be on the alert for patches on pipes and fittings of all kinds. This is where the pipe or fitting has sprung a leak, and rather than replace it the owner has put something around it in an attempt to stop the leak.

In older houses, it's not uncommon to see a basement sink drain into a floor drain. This type of hookup is acceptable in most locales. The trap shown here, however, is useless.

In unfinished basements and crawl spaces, look up. That's the only way to verify that there is no leak around the toilet flange. The fitting shown here is okay; if there were a leak here, the wood would be stained a darker color or rotted away.

Basement faucets If there are any faucets in the basement, such as in a laundry tub, check them as well. Turn the faucets on and off to observe the water flow. Feel how the handle moves—does it turn smoothly or grind metal to metal? Then observe the spout after you shut it off. Did it stop all the water or keep on dripping? Did any water come from around the handle? Check the drain and water lines under the sink for any leakage or old water tracks.

Drain lines

Drain lines are not without their fair share of problems. To begin your inspection, walk under the drain lines and look for anything obvious—white pipe glued into black, fittings that are cracked, pipe stuck into joints without the proper fitting, and so on. Look for anything odd or out of place: large-diameter pipes that feed into small ones, pipe runs that make no sense, Ts and Ys that are installed backward in the sewer line, and so on.

To check for leaks in the drain lines, turn on the upstairs water and then look for obvious leaks at the joints. I once saw an entire drain system that was fitted together and never glued; it leaked every time water flowed down the lines. The basement floor was dirt, so the owner never bothered to change it; he was hoping the new owners

How *not* to support a drain line. Top left: Using one drain line to support another works only until someone bumps against the support. Top right: This electric cable is not just running under the pipe, it is supporting it. Left: The long span draining from the kitchen sink has started bowing in the center; food debris will settle there and eventually clog the pipe.

would fix the problem—assuming they ever noticed it.

Be sure to look up at the toilet floor flange and all the shower and tub traps—these are the likely leak spots. If the toilet seal is leaking, the wood around the flange area will be wet to the touch; once dry, the wood will be stained and possibly crumbling away. Look for water stains on the floor, water tracks on the pipe, and any pipes that appear to be wet. Leaking traps will have droplets of water falling from their lowest point—you may have to run water in the tub/shower to find a current leak.

Sometimes tub/shower leaks are the result of the enclosure flexing when someone steps into it. If the enclosure wasn't securely supported on the bottom, the unit may flex as much as ¼ in. This

eventually creates a leak at the drain fitting or trap.

Note how the drain line is supported. Is it held up securely by metal strapping or by something that looks as though it could fall at any moment? I once saw a brand-new house lose its entire sewer line system because the supports were too far apart and not strong enough (the piping system wasn't glued together very well, either). The sewer line system had passed inspection, and the owner had already moved in when the pipes fell. Look for long sections of unsupported pipe and pipe supported by things it should not be held up by (pantyhose, string, and so on). Also look for pipe that has sagged in the middle between supports and pipe that is running uphill.

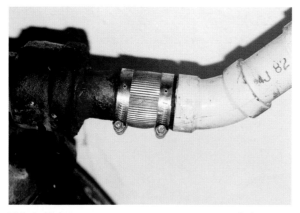

This is the proper way to connect two types of pipes together—any type of banded or flexible coupling is acceptable. However, be sure to check for leaks.

Although large-diameter pipe is generally preferable to small diameter, it shouldn't drain into a smaller-diameter pipe. Here, a 4-in. pipe drains down to a 4-in. coupling that connects to a toilet flange that connects to a 3-in. T. Technically, the T is also in violation—you are not allowed to put a T on its back facing up.

Basement Bath or Shower

All homes have a problem with moisture in the bathroom; but when you put a bath in the basement, the problems are magnified. If this room has a shower, it should also have a vent to take the water vapor outside; but, in my experience, vents are rarely installed.

Most codes state that if the bath has an openable window, a vent is not required. This is illogical, because no one is going to open a window when they're showering in the middle of winter. The result is that paint and wallpaper peel and mold and mildew thrive if the moisture is not removed. Therefore, if there's a bathroom in the basement, perform the same checks you would for any bath (see chapter 10), but pay particular attention to venting, mold, and moisture problems.

Check for leaks where one type of pipe connects to another. You must use some type of banded or flexible coupling because you are not allowed to glue different types of pipes together (although you can screw them together). Look closely where steel drain lines connect to cast iron—the steel has a tendency to rust through at this point. Also keep a lookout for the cleanouts, which need to be accessible.

You can make note of drain pipe and trap diameters, but it's not something you need to write up unless you know for certain that your area requires a particular diameter. Although it's true that 1¼-in. pipe and traps will block up faster than 1½ in., you're not there to calculate the dfus (drainage fixture units that the drain line pipes are designed with).

The water main

The main water entrance into the house needs to be looked at closely. Most areas require some type

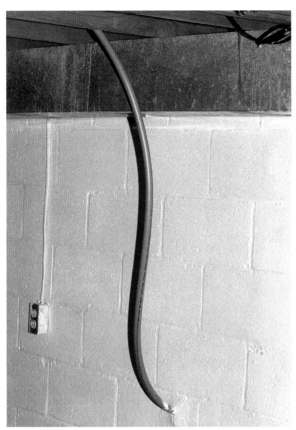

There are four things wrong with this main water entrance into a city house: (1) This type of PB pipe is not listed for outside burial, (2) you are not supposed to use concrete around the entrance pipe, (3) there is no main shutoff valve, and (4) there is no antibackflow device.

Radon

Radon is a radioactive gas that comes from the natural decay of uranium that is found in nearly all soils. It typically moves up as a gas through the ground to the air above and drifts into the house via cracks in the floor and walls, around drain and water lines, and through holes drilled for house wiring.

The amount of radon gas in the air is measured in picocuries per liter of air (pCi/L). The average indoor radon level is estimated to be about 1.3 pCi/L; about 0.4 pCi/L of radon is normally found in the outside air. The U.S. Environmental Protection Agency (EPA) has set a level of 4 pCi/L as a reference—anything higher generally indicates that action should be taken to reduce the radon level. Each state, however, has set its own reference level. Southern states, such as Texas and Florida, typically have low rates, whereas many northern states that border Canada have high rates.

Because the radon problem is not universal across the United States, some areas of jurisdiction require radon gas testing, but others do not. Contact your state radon or health department for general information about radon in your area. If your area is known for high radon, then you should suggest the test if it is not already required.

Although radon is an invisible gas, testing for it is easy. The disadvantages are that you have to buy a kit, you must conduct the test over a period of time (typically two to four days), and you will have to return to the house to pick up the kit. So you might take these factors into consideration before you suggest a radon test, and you may have to charge extra for the test to cover all your costs.

There are many kinds of low-cost, do-it-yourself radon test kits available. Make sure you buy a test kit that either has passed EPA's testing program or is state certified.

of check valve or antibackflow device. The purpose of such a device is to keep one house from contaminating an entire city block of water lines (see "Cross-Connections" on p. 248).

Also at the main water entrance, you need a shutoff valve—every house is required to have one. If the house you're inspecting has one, I'd advise you not to test it. The valve might be a gate valve—a type of valve that has a habit of breaking at the threaded connection to the internal gate. When this happens, the valve will be stuck in a permanent off or on position. If the house doesn't have a shutoff valve, write it up.

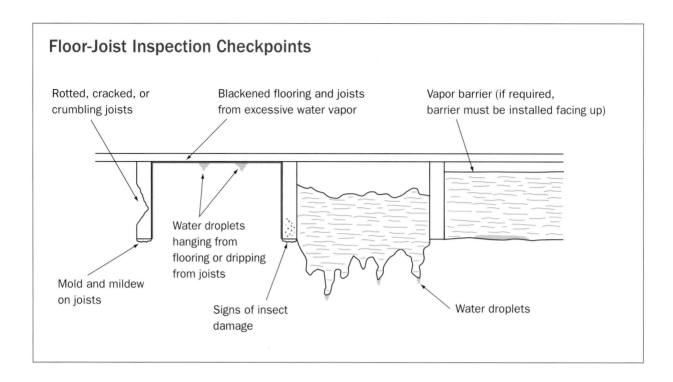

Floor-Joist Inspection Checkpoints

Rotted, cracked, or crumbling joists

Blackened flooring and joists from excessive water vapor

Vapor barrier (if required, barrier must be installed facing up)

Water droplets hanging from flooring or dripping from joists

Mold and mildew on joists

Signs of insect damage

Water droplets

Excessive water vapor in a crawl space causes the growth of mold and mildew on exposed floor joists. Anything this bad deserves some serious probing.

Crawl Spaces

Almost everything that applies to a basement inspection also applies to a crawl space. The most significant difference is that a crawl space needs some type of ventilation. If the exterior foundation is solid, this is normally done via adjustable louvers spaced every few feet in the

wall. Crawl space head room varies from almost nothing up to full basement height. It may not be safe to enter a low basement (some inspection organizations have a 3-ft. height restrictions, below which you shouldn't go into a crawl space). If the crawl space is low or there is no access to it, simply make note of it along with the fact that nothing could be inspected. If you do go in, it's a good idea to wear coveralls and to carry a powerful flashlight so you can see as much as practical in the crawl space.

Many newer houses will have a plastic tarp on the ground (typically 6-mil plastic) to help minimize the transfer of moisture to the wood and insulation above. (I always recommend putting down a plastic tarp for older houses that don't have one.) In houses without a tarp, high moisture has been known to bring down all the insulation in a crawl space. If the insulation has deteriorated to the point that it looks as though there are thousands of stalactites hanging from it, that's what the problem is. Observe which way the insulation vapor barrier has been installed—it should always be closest to the warm side of the house—which in a crawl space (or basement)

The pipe in this crawl space has one support for its entire length; it should have one support a minimum of every 4 ft. This pipe hasn't sagged yet because the house is new and the slope is high, preventing the hot water that runs through the pipe from settling and making it soft.

Crawl Space Checklist

- [ ] Adequate ventilation
- [ ] Plastic vapor barrier over ground
- [ ] Insulation present and in good condition
- [ ] Insulation vapor barrier installed correctly
- [ ] No rotted, cracked, or broken joists
- [ ] Water lines and drain lines installed correctly
- [ ] No leaks in water or drain lines

means facing up. It's common to have it reversed (stapled to the bottom of the joists); this is incorrect and should be written up. A few times I've been able to push up on the vapor barrier and hear a river of water sloshing between the joists.

Although not all inspectors are going to pull down the insulation and measure its thickness, you do need to log whether it is present and in what condition it is in. It's not uncommon to see sections of insulation pulled down and lying on the ground as a result of past plumbing repairs. Large areas of missing insulation may be an indication of major plumbing repairs, such as of burst pipes due to freezing. This should also tell you that the plumbing is susceptible to freezing.

At the same time you look at the insulation, check the joists for severe sag, rot, and insect damage. Although rot is usually more of a problem in houses with shallow crawl spaces where the joists are close to the ground, homes with deep crawl spaces are not exempt from rot. I've seen many new homes with large crawl spaces rotting out for lack of venting and excessive moisture. On one 2-year-old house I inspected, the entire crawl space was dripping with condensed water. The problem was that the house had been designed and built with only one large vent on one side of the crawl space; as a result, there was no air circulation—just stagnant moist air.

While in the crawl space, also check the water lines and drain lines. Look for water dripping from any of the water lines, but don't confuse a leak with condensation. (Both will appear as drips, but the condensation drip will slow down and disappear as the water in the pipe warms to air temperature.) Small spray leaks, such as from a pinhole in a copper pipe, can sometimes be heard as well as seen. Drain lines need to follow the same rules as if they were in the house: All lines should be intact; sloped downhill; and securely supported every few feet, with no sag between supports and without different types of plastic—specifically PVC and acrylonitrile butadiene styrene (ABS)—glued together. Sometimes it is a good idea to have someone flush the toilet to observe the drain line for leaks.

Chapter 8

UTILITY ROOM APPLIANCES

WATER HEATERS

DRYERS

CLOTHES WASHERS

WATER CONDITIONERS

The utility room typically houses the water heater, washer, and dryer. Not all homes have a dedicated utility room, of course; and these appliances can be located in the basement or on any other floor of the house. In warm climates, they might even be in the garage or on the porch. If the appliances are in the basement, the first thing to check for is visible water or moisture damage. This will normally be evident as rusting out of the bottom of the appliances. Rust can be caused by intermittent flooding or just by excessive moisture. For future reference, you might recommend to the homeowner that it's always better to install any appliance off the basement floor by setting it on concrete blocks, brick, or treated wood.

Water Heaters

The first thing to bear in mind when inspecting a water heater is size. A typical family of four needs a 50-gal., 4,500-watt heater to provide enough hot water. The gas equivalent is 40-gal., 32,000 BTU. Therefore, if the house you're inspecting has a smaller-than-standard heater, such as a 30-gal. or 40-gal. model, you might mention that it may not be satisfactory to meet a family's hot water needs.

The standard inspection

Whether the water heater is gas or electric, there are a number of standard checkpoints that are the same for both types. First I'll first discuss the

Check for leaks where the water pipe screws into the water heater. This heater is almost completely rusted out around the connection because of a long-existing leak.

standard inspection and then go on to look at the checkpoints specific to gas and to electric water heaters.

Water line connection The first thing to check for is leaks at or around the water heater—in particular, at the pipe connection into the heater itself. The water heater and the pipes around it are subject to drastic temperature changes as the water heats and cools, making the pipe connection at the top of the heater more prone to leaks than other areas. Some installers, however, make the problem even worse by screwing plastic male fittings into the female threads of the heater. Most codes prohibit this. As the heater expands during its heating cycle, a leak inevitably forms at the male/female junction.

Water temperature It's important to check the water temperature because of the risk of scalding, which is why most manufacturers of water heaters have lowered the preset water temperature from 150°F to 120°F. Rather than take the access cover off the heater to check the thermostat setting, simply put a thermometer that can measure in the range of 100°F to 200°F under the faucet closest to the water heater to check the temperature. If it exceeds 120°F, there's the possibility of scalding, so write it up. Also make a note if the water doesn't warm up at all.

Use a large-dial water temperature probe to check the hot water temperature at the faucet closest to the water heater. If the reading exceeds 120°F, it is an area of concern.

Water Temperature

Temperature	Time in contact before scald burn	Setting on water heater
150°F	1 second	High
140°F	5 seconds	High
130°F	30 seconds	Medium
120°F	5 minutes	Low

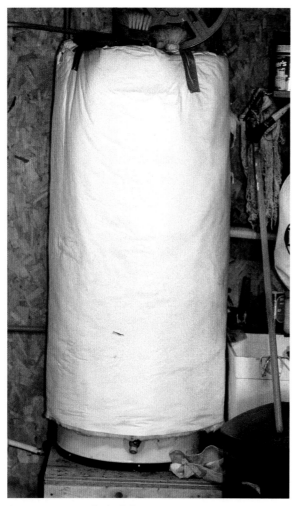

Contrary to popular opinion, you are not supposed to place an insulation jacket around a water heater; by covering up the warnings and access panels, you violate the manufacturer's warranty.

Every water heater should have a T&P valve and a discharge pipe extending down to a few inches off the floor.

One area of particular controversy is the water heater insulation jacket. Some codes require a jacket, but manufacturers will void the warranty if one is installed, because it covers the scalding warnings, instructions, and element openings. Most water heater installation manuals prohibit their use, and all codes insist that you follow the manufacturer's installation instructions first. So what should you do if the water heater you're inspecting has an insulation jacket? To be on the safe side, always write it up as an area of concern.

Temperature and pressure relief valve Every water heater is required to have a temperature and pressure (T&P) relief valve; as an inspector, you must verify not only that the T&P valve is there but also that it is installed properly. The T&P valve is the last line of defense against a catastrophic water heater failure—namely, an explosion.

Two other protective devices have to fail before the T&P valve kicks in. The first is the thermostat, which controls how long the element receives power. If the thermostat fails to turn off and power stays applied to the element, naturally the water will overheat. If this happens, the overload, which is the device with the red button attached to the top of the upper thermostat, will sense the high-temperature water and open both circuits (both 240-volt legs) applying power to the heating element. When this happens, the red button will pop out about ¼ in. If this device fails as well, the water continues to overheat until it reaches a preset temperature or pressure. At that time the, T&P valve will release the hot, pressurized water to the atmosphere to keep the tank from exploding. The valve does not release the water all at once in an explosion but as a steady drip or sputter.

If the water heater has a T&P valve installed in its body, everything should be okay if the other protective devices fail—but very old water heaters did not have a place built in the tank for the valve. In the old days, plumbers installed them separately in the water lines themselves—on the cold water side as well as on the hot. Though it may seem illogical to have the valve on the cold water line, these old valves sensed water pressure only, not water temperature. Because the pressure is the same on both hot and cold sides, it didn't make any difference which line the valve went on. If I come across a pressure valve on the water line, I still write it up as an area of concern because the valve is so old that it probably doesn't work anymore.

One of the more obvious water heater checks is to verify that the T&P valve is not dripping (assuming that the valve or pipe end attached to the valve is visible). A slow drip can indicate a bad valve. Other times, the problem can be a malfunctioning thermostat or one that is adjusted too high. Be aware, however, that on old water heaters the T&P valve can kick off without the thermostat's malfunctioning. I've seen this happen a number of times. On one inspection I did years ago the T&P valve was dripping because the dryer vented into the basement. The heater was coated with condensation, which cooled the metal tank and gave a false temperature to the thermostat. (If the surface of the tank is cool, the

On very old heaters, the pressure valve may be installed on the cold water pipe, as shown here. Suggest that a new T&P valve be installed on the hot water side—or that the owners replace the water heater.

thermostat won't turn off when it's supposed to, thereby overheating the water.)

On another inspection, the thermostat was pulled slightly away from the metal tank so there was an air gap between the two—the sensor couldn't sense the temperature if it couldn't touch the tank. Several other water heaters I've inspected were so old that a heavy buildup of rust and debris on the inside of the tank made it take too long for the sensor to receive the heat and remove the power. By the time that happened, the T&P valve had started dripping.

The T&P valve can even kick off because of problems outside the house. In Riner, Virginia, a new city water tank was installed at the top of a large hill. Once the tank was put on line, the T&P valve on the water heater in each residence on the road immediately below the tank started dripping. The dripping occurred only when the water heater would cycle on. During the off cycle, there wasn't enough pressure to open the valve. The problem was solved by installing a pressure-reducer valve on each house to lower the excessive water pressure that the new tank produced. Most codes state that if the incoming water pressure exceeds 75 lb. to 80 lb. per square inch (psi), a pressure-reducer valve is required; but in the case cited, the pressure before the new city water tank was installed did not exceed that amount, and the town put the new tank on line without warning the residents.

If the T&P valve does ever kick off, you don't want it to drip or spray scalding water all over the tank or in anyone's face. Therefore the valve needs to have a pipe extending from the T&P female threads down to a few inches above the floor. This pipe must not be reduced in size from the female thread size in the valve, which is normally ¾ in. Almost any pipe will do—even plastic CPVC—but the pipe cannot be threaded on its bottom end.

So what happens if the T&P valve malfunctions along with everything else in the water heater and the element never stops heating? If the hot and cold water pipes connected to the tank are made of a plastic derivative, they normally melt and you have a flood on your hands. If the pipe is copper, the solder can melt. I had one valve malfunction that sent the pipe skyward for over 40 ft. (it was on a test demand-type heater I made outside). The big problem comes when the house pipe is galvanized—that's when the tank explodes. Any pressurized tank is a potential bomb, and a water heater is no different. In another example, the tank exploded, destroyed the house, went through the ceiling and roof, then traveled over 100 ft. and landed in a neighbor's yard. The bottom line is to make sure a T&P valve is installed—either in the tank or in the hot water line immediately after the tank—and to visually check that it works.

A question that often comes up is whether you should raise the little arm on the T&P valve to release some hot water to check the valve. The answer is no, because you run the risk of having the valve drip continually or jam completely open after the test. Sometimes the problem is that the valve is broken, other times rust and debris gets caught in the valve mechanism; either way, you'll have a mess on your hands.

Pan The pan is exactly what it sounds like—something the water heater sits in to catch the water if the heater leaks. It's a good idea to have one installed if the heater is located in or above an area where the floor or ceiling can be damaged. Some areas require a water heater pan as code; others do not. If there isn't a pan in place, I always mention it to the homeowner and explain what would happened if the heater did leak.

I once responded to a customer complaint that he had a water-line leak upstairs in the house he had just bought; the water pooled over the living room ceiling until it caved in, ruining everything in the living room. The water line was repaired and the drywall ceiling replaced. The very next week there was another leak and the homeowner lost everything again. This time it was not a water-line leak but a water heater that was on the second floor. The leak followed the newly repaired pipe down to the living room ceiling. Needless to say the owner wasn't happy. If there had been a pan under the heater and it in turn fed to a drain, this second round of damage wouldn't have occurred.

Grounding jumper All water heaters with metal pipes need to have a heavy-wire bonding jumper from the cold water line to the hot water line immediately above the heater. The jumper is normally placed immediately above the heater. Very few inspectors I've talked to write this up,

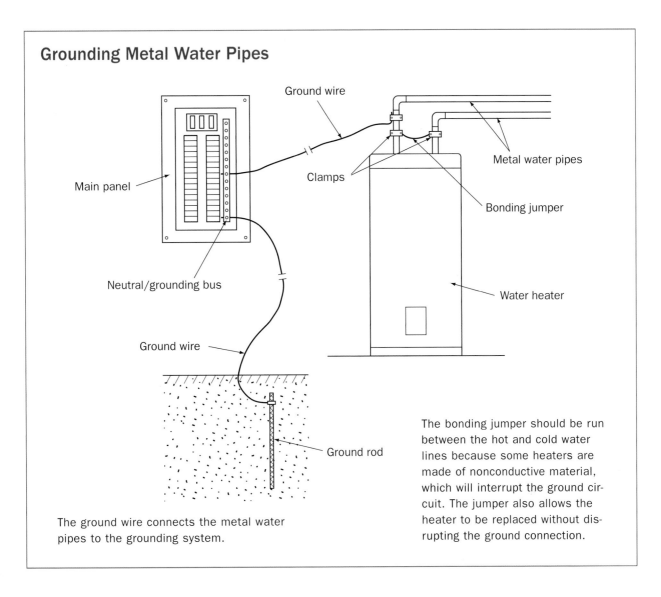

Grounding Metal Water Pipes

Ground wire

Main panel

Clamps

Metal water pipes

Bonding jumper

Neutral/grounding bus

Water heater

Ground wire

Ground rod

The ground wire connects the metal water pipes to the grounding system.

The bonding jumper should be run between the hot and cold water lines because some heaters are made of nonconductive material, which will interrupt the ground circuit. The jumper also allows the heater to be replaced without disrupting the ground connection.

but they should. The purpose of the jumper is to continue the ground connection from the hot water pipe to the cold water pipe, or vice versa. All voltage then gets bled to ground by another heavy-duty ground wire that connects one of the metal pipes into the house grounding system (see "Grounding Metal Water Pipes"). If there is no jumper, the assumption is that the metal of the water heater is making the connection between the two. For two reasons, this sometimes doesn't happen. First, all water heaters are not metal and, therefore, cannot make the required connection from one pipe to the other. Second, you would

lose the ground the minute you cut the lines to replace the heater. If there is no jumper, the danger is that excessive voltage buildup on one pipe could jump to the person installing the heater.

Gas water heaters

Gas water heaters require a few more checks than their electric counterparts. The first thing to check is that there are no flammable materials stored around the gas heater—especially in front of the access plate at the bottom of the heater. Also check that the access plate is in place. I've seen

Flammable materials should never be stored around the front of a gas water heater because they present a fire hazard.

The access plate is missing on this heater. Without it, flames can jump up the side of the heater.

Water Heater Checklist

☐ Adequate capacity?

☐ No leaks at water line connections

☐ Water temperature no higher than 120°F

☐ Insulation jacket

☐ T&P valve correctly installed, not dripping

☐ Water heater in pan

☐ Grounding jumper from cold water line to hot water line

Gas heater

☐ No flammables stored nearby

☐ No gas leaks

☐ Flue pipe tight and in good condition

☐ Draft hood installed

☐ Approved piping

☐ Valve and dirt leg installed

Electric heater

☐ Heater grounded

☐ Wired with 10-gauge wire (4,500–watt heater)

flames pour out of an open access hole and leap several feet up a heater. If any flammables are around when this happens, a fire will start. Flammable materials aren't just cardboard boxes and paint cans: Also check that there is no lint accumulation around the heater that might be coming from a nearby dryer vent.

Checking for leaks Leaks around gas fittings are fairly common. There are a couple of ways to check for leaks. A low-cost method is to apply a soap/water mixture to the fittings; if there's a leak, you'll see bubbles. This method can get a little messy. A more professional method is to use a "sniffer" (see the photo on p. 182). This hand-held device has a wand that is held close to the fitting. If gas is detected, the sniffer will sound an alarm (normally a beeping noise). Never check for gas leaks using any type of flame.

Checking for leaks not only requires you to sniff but also to listen. If the flame sounds intermittent—if it makes a noise and then burns quietly and then makes a noise again—there's something wrong. Write it up. It either isn't getting enough combustion air (called secondary air) or there is rust debris all over the burner plate. When this happens, a variety of toxic gasses are emitted; some of these you can smell, others

Gas Water Heater Inspection Checkpoints

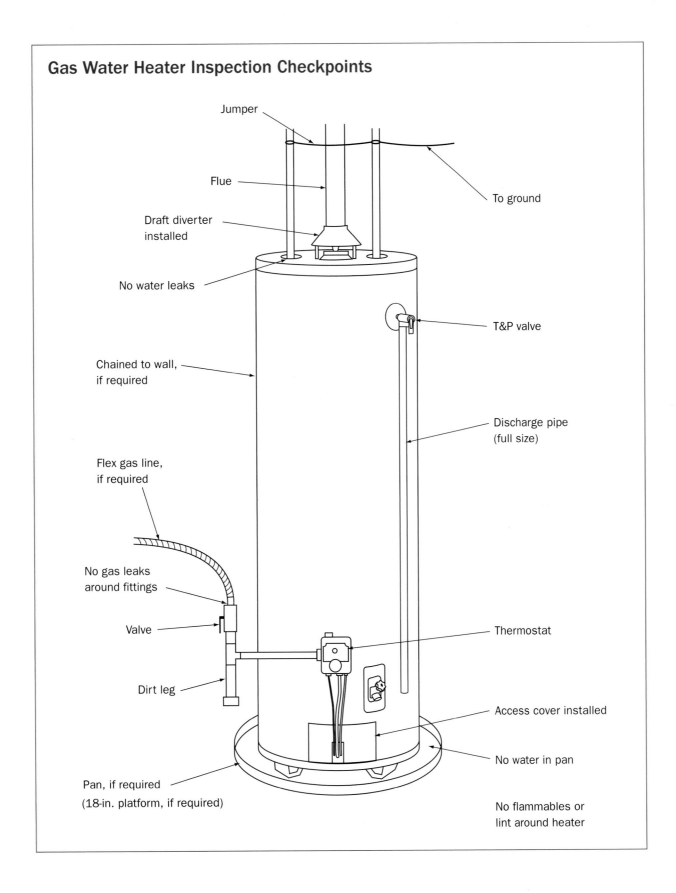

Jumper

Flue

Draft diverter installed

No water leaks

Chained to wall, if required

Flex gas line, if required

No gas leaks around fittings

Valve

Dirt leg

Pan, if required
(18-in. platform, if required)

To ground

T&P valve

Discharge pipe (full size)

Thermostat

Access cover installed

No water in pan

No flammables or lint around heater

Top: Single-wall pipe, the most common flue pipe, should be kept at least 6 in. away from flammable material. Bottom: Double-wall pipe is required if you cannot maintain a 6-in. clearance from flammables.

burn your eyes, and some you have no idea about until it's too late (see "Carbon Monoxide Problems" on p. 125).

Secondary air is the air that the heater burns along with the gas. If not enough air is available, incomplete combustion that produce massive amounts of noxious and poisonous gases will be the result. This is not a problem if the heater is located in a large open area or one that's well ventilated, but it is dangerous if the water heater is located in a small room. Some owners get around this by installing louvered doors as op-

posed to solid doors; others cut holes in the door. If the latter is done, there need to be two holes—one at the top of the door and one on the bottom—roughly 1 ft. square, depending on the BTU of the heater. The exact hole size is listed in the heater instructions.

Checking the flue The flue pipe at the top of the water heater should be inspected carefully. The sections of pipe should be tight and not falling apart. If single-wall flue pipe is used, it needs to be kept at least 6 in. away from flammable materials (drywall is not considered flammable; studs and joists are). Double-wall pipe should be used if the 6-in. clearance cannot be maintained, but it should not be installed any closer than 1 in. to flammables. Class B venting (double-wall flue pipe) has a metal outer shell, an air space, and a second metal inner shell. A significant advantage of using double-wall pipe is that it doesn't sweat like single wall. Single-wall pipe sweats on the inside and the acid condensate runs down into the heater and rusts everything out.

The flue pipe should not connect directly to the heater but should attach via a draft hood (also known as a draft diverter) to allow air to enter the flue and travel up along with the gasses vented from the heater. In general, the flue pipe should slope uphill until it exits the building; the actual angle is not important, but the pipe cannot go up and then back down. Once it exits the building, the pipe should have a cap on the outside to keep out the rain.

Gas piping Many types of pipes can be used for gas: flexible copper, galvanized pipe, black iron pipe, corrugated stainless, and even approved plastics. Flexible copper pipe is used for gas, because it installs quickly and easily. Some people still think that copper cannot be used for natural or propane gas, and I've even seen this stated in other books on home inspection. But this is plain wrong: I've used copper pipe for gas all my working life, Canada installs millions of feet of copper for gas, the Copper Development Association says its just fine, and it is allowed by the *National Fuel Gas Code Handbook*.

The reason some areas banned copper pipe was because back in the years when gas wasn't "scrubbed" (sulfur removed), it pitted the lines. So unless your area is in the dark ages and uses gas that isn't scrubbed, there shouldn't be a problem. However, when using copper pipe for gas you cannot use just any copper or just any fittings. The pipe has to be flexible (known as "refrigeration copper"), not rigid. Any gauge will do. Solder or compression fittings are not allowed— you must use flare (or other approved) fittings.

Galvanized pipe works better for gas than black iron pipe, though some areas don't allow it. The myth that it isn't used because the zinc will come loose and clog the gas controls is just that, a myth. The problem with black iron pipe is that it rusts, and even galvanized pipe will rust at the threaded joints. This is why neither can be buried, unless the joints are wrapped to keep moisture away from the bare metal threads. Some areas still ban galvanized pipe for gas lines, which is unfortunate because it rusts less than black iron pipe. The big problem with using galvanized pipe for gas is that you can't tell it from a water line. The solution is to paint it yellow and mark it as a gas line.

In addition to the common gas lines, such as copper and iron pipe, you're likely to come across a number of the newer flexible gas lines. There's a trend toward using these flexible lines because they install faster and require fewer fittings because the pipe comes in long rolls. Some of these lines will be corrugated, some will be smooth, some will have a plastic coating over stainless steel, and some will have a plastic coating over copper. All have one thing in common—they are yellow.

Even when rigid pipe is used for gas, it's common to use a short flex line to connect to the gas appliance; some areas require a flex line, others don't. If the house you're inspecting has flexible gas lines to the water heater, simply note that

The flue pipe can run at any vertical angle, but it is not allowed to go up and then back down as has been done with the vent on this water heater.

When running gas in copper, flexible rolled copper and flare fittings should be used. If in any other type of copper or fitting is used, write it up.

Black iron pipe is commonly used as a gas fitting, but it tends to rust. The rust here was caused by the installer using a soap/water mixture to test for leaks.

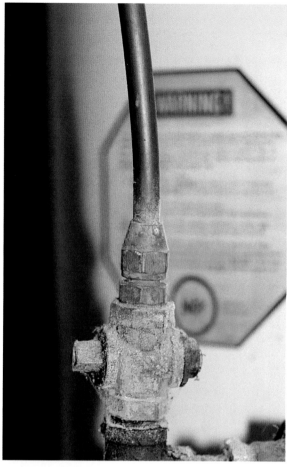

Every gas appliance needs a cutoff valve. Just because you don't see a handle, doesn't mean one isn't there; this type of valve is turned on and off with an adjustable wrench.

Automatic gas appliances need a dirt leg. Gas enters from above and then makes a right-angle turn to get to the appliance. Any debris in the line will fall straight down into the capped nipple instead of going into the appliance.

they exist but do not touch them. If you touch a flexible line, there's always the possibility that you'll create a leak (for the same reason, you shouldn't move any gas appliance). Some flexible connectors that connect the main run pipe to the appliance have been know to corrode, and moving the pipe or appliance can break through the corrosion and start a gas leak. If there are connections, use the sniffer to check for leaks.

Required fittings Every gas water heater requires a cutoff valve so the gas can be turned off for servicing the heater. In areas that are earthquake prone, flex connectors from the fixed gas

pipe to the water heater are sometimes required as well as a chain around the heater that is anchored to a solid wall. Be sure the gas line is not hooked directly into the heater control module. It must go through a dirt leg first. A dirt leg is a combination of fittings arranged so that dirt or debris in the gas line cannot get into the control module. The gas line enters vertically from above and then goes into a T-fitting. The gas has to make an immediate right turn in the T to get to the appliance. Any trash in the lines goes straight down through the T into a nipple with a cap on it. Some installers who don't understand how dirt legs work put them in upside down,

The Down and Dirty on Dirt Legs

It can get confusing trying to figure out why one gas appliance is required to have a dirt leg and another is not. In the past, gas was "manufactured" on site with fossil fuel products. This was considered a wet gas because it had a lot of moisture inside, and there was a need to have a drip leg (a trap just like a dirt leg) to collect the moisture.

Though a few areas still use wet gas, most went over to LP and natural gas that was piped in from long distances away (considered dry gas). For these gases, a drip leg is not required. But the reason to have a dirt leg has never changed—to catch metal shavings and debris that still might be in the pipe. However, some local areas don't require a dirt leg either.

The bottom line is that you need a dirt leg when the manufacturer and/or the local gas company requires it. (The reference is *National*

Fuel Gas Code Handbook, p. 52.) As a general rule, all gas water heaters and furnaces require a dirt leg because they are automatic devices. If there is an off switch, such as on a gas stove or dryer, then the rule of thumb is that they are not required to have a dirt leg. However, be aware that the appliance manufacturer can overrule the gas code. For example, some gas log fireplaces are required by their manufacturer to have a dirt leg.

Should you write up on an old installation (for example, a system that was installed in pre-code years) that has no dirt leg but has been working fine for years? I would note the absence of a dirt leg only—and then recommend doing nothing. In other words, if it's not broke, don't fix it. But if it is a new installation, one that went in when dirt legs were required, I would write it up as an area of concern.

with the pipe going up, so be on the lookout for this mistake.

Checking the location Gas water heaters cannot be located just anywhere. For example, they should not be installed under stairs or in an enclosed area. As in the garage, a water heater in a basement must be at least 18 in. off the floor if any flammables are stored in the area. Better yet, move the flammables out of the area.

Electric water heaters

All electric water heaters need to be grounded, without exception. If the house is old and has never been rewired, chances are the water heater is not grounded. I write it up every time. If a defective element opens or a wire touches the

If the house under inspection has old wiring (as shown here), you can count on the water heater not being grounded. There is no grandfather clause here; a water heater must be grounded.

Electric Water Heater Inspection Checkpoints

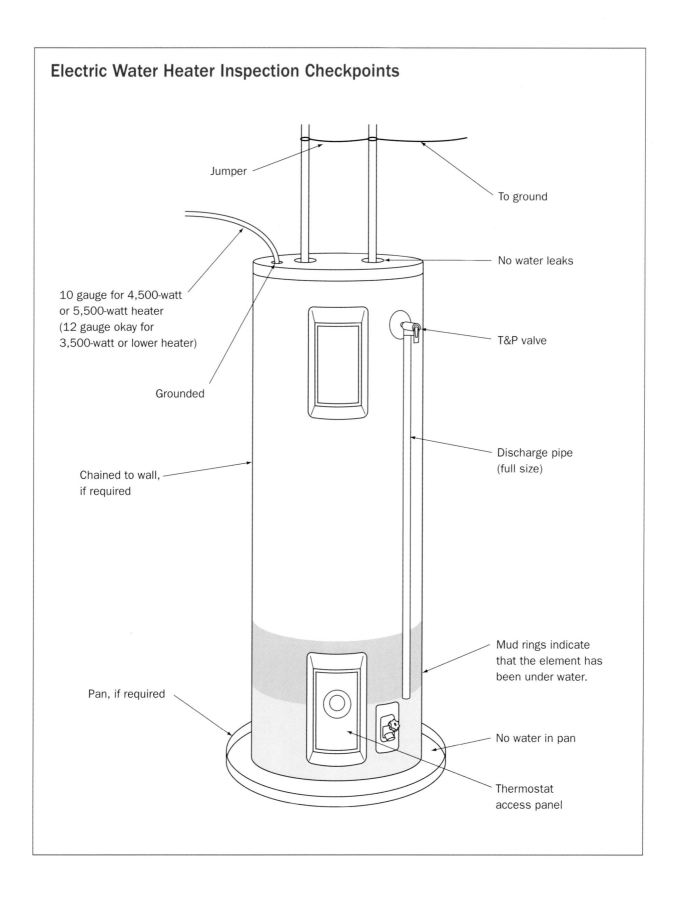

Jumper

To ground

No water leaks

10 gauge for 4,500-watt
or 5,500-watt heater
(12 gauge okay for
3,500-watt or lower heater)

T&P valve

Grounded

Discharge pipe
(full size)

Chained to wall,
if required

Mud rings indicate
that the element has
been under water.

Pan, if required

No water in pan

Thermostat
access panel

Many water heaters are designed to allow the ground wire to exit the splice box and attach onto a special screw, so it's easy for the inspector to spot.

metal jacket, the entire water system can become electrically hot. I've known this to happen many times. Almost every time a complaint comes in from an owner who has gotten a shock off the metal water lines, I can guarantee that there is an electrical problem with the water heater and the metal water lines are not grounded.

A properly grounded water heater is not difficult to spot. The heater is normally grounded via the bare ground wire in modern NM cable, the spiraled metal of old armored cable, or the green wire within rigid conduit or the newer AC conduit. Do not automatically assume that just because a new cable has a plastic jacket it is grounded: NM cable is still made both ways, with and without ground wires. I've also seen quite a few modern cables with the ground wires cut off, leaving the appliance with no ground. If in doubt, you can remove the cover off the splice box that's internal to the water heater to verify that a ground wire is present and connected to the unit.

Most people don't remove the element/ thermostat access during an inspection, but it's a good idea to do so, especially if there are signs of previous flooding. If you see mud stains around the heater where it appears to have been under-water past the element, you need to check the

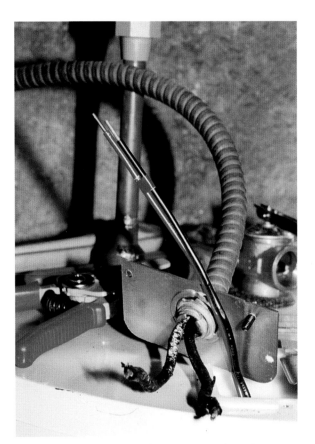

In many older houses, the hot and neutral conductors are housed in armored cable. If the armor is continuous all the way back to the main service panel, the armor is grounding the heater.

This element burned up its wiring and melted down after the heater was engulfed in 2 ft. of water. The house was being sold "as is."

element to verify that it hasn't burned up its wiring. It's common for the element to be ruined after such an occurrence. Turn off the power and remove the bottom cover; if there's a problem with the element, you'll see burned wiring or melted plastic. An element base (where the wires connect) can also be destroyed even if it hasn't been submerged in water, so I always make it a point to remove the cover to check.

You also need to verify that the electric water heater is wired with the proper gauge wire. The typical water heater draws 18 amps to 23 amps (4,500 watts to 5,500 watts). For this wattage, you need 10-gauge wire. Look for "10-2 w/g" printed on the jacket of the cable. Quite often I see these heaters wired with 12-gauge wire. One size smaller element, 3,500 watts, draws around 15 amps, which is quite satisfactory for 12-gauge wire. If you are not sure of the wattage, it should be printed on a factory sticker on the side of the heater.

Dryers

Dryers sometimes stay with the house and other times leave with the homeowner. If the dryer stays, you may need to inspect it (depending on your company's policy). There are four inspection

points for an electric dryer: the appliance hose connection, the vent pipe, the vent exit, and the wiring. On a gas dryer, you need to check for leaks, but only if the gas lines are accessible. Never move a gas dryer to check for gas leaks because you run the risk of damaging the pipe or connections.

The appliance hose connection

It almost seems as though the appliance hose connection is designed to fail on most dryers. The manufacturer typically provides a metal sleeve that tapers down so that the fastener slides off with ease along with the hose. So look behind the dryer to verify that the connection is securely made. If the connection is loose, you'll typically find lint all over the floor and wall.

Vent piping

Vent piping, from dryer to vent exit, is a big problem with electric dryers in all parts of the country. The most common vent problems are the result of using flexible plastic vent hose. Lying on the floor behind the dryer, the hose gets crushed and torn as the dryer is pushed back and forth against the wall. Installers also tend to wind it in all directions (up/down, left/right, and even in circles), which slows down the airflow and allows lint to accumulate in the hose (a potential fire hazard). Despite these problems, many areas still allow plastic flex hose for electric dryers. But for gas dryers there is no debate: plastic hose has never been approved. Gas dryers need metal venting, either flex or solid.

The length of the vent hose is another area of concern. Ideally, the dryer will vent to the outside with only a minimal length of hose, but you cannot flatly condemn a long run of the dryer vent—even runs up to 40 ft. Typically, local jurisdictions have tried to limit the amount of total footage and the number of bends, but this is not realistic. The allowed length of the vent line is determined by the power of the dryer exhaust fan (some are so strong that the manufacturer allows exhaust lines exceeding 40 ft.); and as an inspector, you have no way of knowing that piece of information. If the manufacturer's installation instructions are available, then the figure listed for the maximum length of hose is the one you have to go by.

You may not be able to condemn, but you can criticize, indicating that the dryer vent line *may* be excessive with an abnormal number of turns. The vent shouldn't be run in circles and it should have a minimum number of bends to get outside. Common sense should be used when determining how to support the pipe. Flammable materials shouldn't be used (I've seen vent lines tied up with pantyhose), and the supports shouldn't be so far apart that the line sags between them.

The vent exit

Check where the dryer vent terminates. It has to vent outside. One of the most common problems is a vent that goes nowhere, just blowing moisture and lint-laden air into the room. Just as bad is a vent that terminates in a water bucket, as shown in the photo on p. 170. Available at hardware stores everywhere, water buckets are advertised as devices that allow the dryer heat to remain within the room. Although the product does conserve the heat, it also keeps all the moisture in the room, which rots the wood and shorts out electrical appliances. I've seen basements with water buckets that have made water heaters sweat and malfunction, rusted out furnaces, and put mold and mildew over everything—extremely unhealthy as well as detrimental to the appliances. In my opinion, this type of venting device should be banned.

Also look for vent lines fed into wall and ceiling cavities, and into crawl spaces and attics. These put excessive moisture in the air, rot out all wood in the area, and cover everything with flammable lint. If the vent lines are not open for inspection, you should indicate so in your report. On the outside of the building, be sure to check the exhaust port (or weather hood). Make sure it

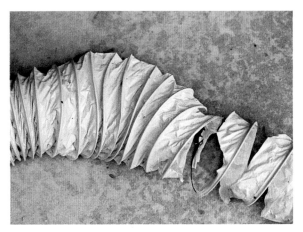

Flexible, plastic dryer vent hose typically gets crushed and shredded.

There are a couple of problems here: Pantyhose is not an approved material for supporting a hot dryer vent, and plastic tape should not be used to hold dryer vent pipe together.

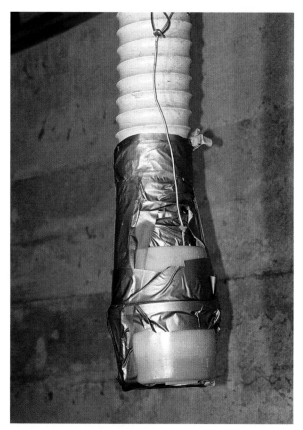

A dryer vent that terminates in a water bucket sends hundreds of gallons of unwanted moisture into the basement. People install them because they want to conserve the heat from the dryer; but in doing so, they rot wood, fill the basement with unhealthy mold spores and mildew, and cause electrical items to malfunction.

Clothes Dryer Checklist

☐ Appliance hose connection secure

☐ Approved vent hose installed and in good condition

☐ Vent terminates outside

☐ Outside exhaust port functional and in good condition

☐ Dryer grounded

☐ Wired with 10-gauge wire

☐ No gas leaks (gas dryer)

Dryer Fire

Any restriction within the vent hose (whether it's a crushed hose, one that's excessively long or wound in all directions, or one that has its weather hood jammed shut) results in reduced airflow and lint buildup. This in turn causes overheating by preventing a fast drying action. When this happens, the high-temperature limit safety switch within the dryer has to cycle on and off repeatedly to control the excessive heat buildup. Most high-temperature limit switches were never designed to cycle on and off continuously; therefore, such action can cause premature failure. The Consumer Products Safety Commission estimates that there are 24,000 clothes dryer fires every year in the United States, which amounts to almost $100,000,000 in estimated property damage. Therefore, it's imperative to check the dryer venting carefully.

isn't broken and that the inside flapper plate is functional.

Dryer wiring

Electric dryers are both 120 volt and 240 volt—that is, they use both voltages at the same time. Almost all dryers have their frames wired to the return neutral of the 120-volt circuit. In other words the frame is hot. This was code to 1996. Code or not, it's not a good thing to have if the owner is standing in a puddle of water on a wet concrete floor. If this is the situation, I suggest the dryer be rewired to take the frame out of the neutral and to ground it. This means running a four-wire circuit to replace the existing three wire. This is not required—just common sense.

Check the gauge of cable that runs to the electric dryer. If it is wired with 12-gauge wire, the wire is too small. It should be 10 gauge. If the cable feeding the dryer is NM cable with only two hot conductors (black and white), it is wired with the wrong type of wire to meet modern codes (but it is normally grandfathered in and never written up). New code demands that the dryer be fed with three insulated conductors and a ground, so SEC cable can no longer be used. For new installations, the cable should have "10-3 NMB w/g" printed on its jacket.

Clothes Washers

As with clothes dryers, washers often leave the house with the seller. If the washer stays, however, certain checks must be made. First and foremost, manufacturers require their washers to be grounded, and it is quite dangerous if this is ignored (as often occurs with washers installed in an old basement). There is no grandfather exemption. Even if the washer is going with the seller, the new owners will need to know if they'll have to add a grounded outlet to operate their washer safely.

Older houses with ungrounded wiring may be using a cheater plug or the ground terminal may be broken off the washer plug. Either way, write it up. Actual operation of the washer to verify its

condition may be out of the jurisdiction of the inspector. If you do run the washer through its cycles, verify that the washer's flexible hose is inside the vertical drain pipe before you start or you will flood the floor. This is a mistake you don't make twice.

Washer Hoses and Valves

If the washer is staying, you'll need to comment on the washer hoses and valves. The standard black hoses typical of a washer hookup are not approved for use as permanent water lines; over time, hoses left pressurized will blister and ultimately explode. Washer hoses should be used

Black washing-machine hoses such as these are typical in almost every household, but they are not approved for use as permanent water lines.

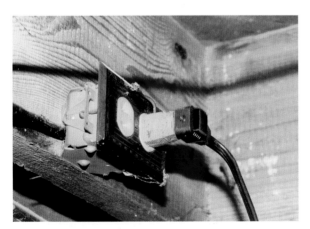

This grounded cord is from a clothes washer in a basement. It is using a cheater plug to connect into the old two-conductor cable. The cheater plug only allows the washer to be plugged in. The washer is not grounded, although it is required to be so by the manufacturer.

This is the reason washer hoses are not listed as water lines and cannot be left pressurized. If pressurized, this hose could explode at any moment.

like a garden hose: You turn the valves on to fill the washer and then turn them back off again. But very few people do this because most washer valves are hard to turn on and off and they're often located behind the washer where they're hard to reach. The solution is to install approved hoses—these have a stainless-steel braid around them and are approved for use as water lines.

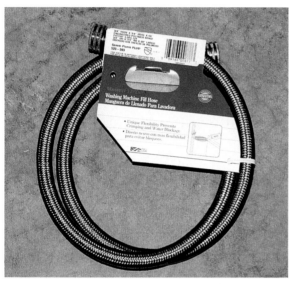

Washer hoses approved to be kept pressurized all the time are recognizable by their stainless-steel braid.

Washer drain

Whether the washer is going or staying, the drain line the washer discharge hose drops into should be inspected (if it is visible). The washer standpipe needs to be 2 in. in diameter to take the full amount of water some washers throw out during the spin cycle, though I've seen washer installation instructions that indicate that 1½ in. is acceptable. I wouldn't write it up if the standpipe is less than 2 in. in diameter, but I would indicate on the report form that this might be an area of concern if a washer is going to be used. The standpipe should be at least 18 in. tall, with a maximum height of around 30 in. (though I've never written any house up for having a standpipe that's too tall).

The trap is normally on the same floor as the washer, but I don't write it up if the washer is on the first floor and the drain is just below it in the ceiling joists of the basement; this configuration allows easy access to the trap. The most ridiculous washer drain hookup I ever saw was a washer in a basement that had to feed into a drain 7 ft. overhead. The standpipe height, limited by the ceiling immediately above the drain, was only 6 in. For

Most washer manufacturers request a 2-in.-diameter standpipe rather than a 1½-in. pipe because it will take more water faster and back up less. This standpipe is 2-in. PVC; the vertical pipe to the left is its vent.

Clothes Washer Checklist

- ☐ Washer grounded
- ☐ Approved washer hoses installed
- ☐ Standpipe of approved diameter installed
- ☐ Standpipe at least 18 in. high
- ☐ Trap in washer pipe (if in concrete slab)

some strange reason the county inspector said that this installation was acceptable.

In some basements, it's possible that you'll find the washer pipe sticking out of the concrete floor. In this case, you'll need to know if there's a trap in the slab. To find out, I drop a tiny rock into the pipe. If I hear a splash, I know the trap is there so I don't write it up. Sometimes the washer drain dumps into a laundry tub and uses its trap; this is acceptable. But I do recommend that the laundry tub, if made from lightweight fiberglass or plastic, be anchored to the wall or floor to keep it from breaking loose from the drain line and trap underneath it. If the washer drain flows out to the backyard, it doesn't require a trap (unless you want to keep the bugs out).

Water Conditioners

If the house under inspection has a water conditioner (installed at the main water line where it comes into the house), simply note that the system exists. Do not test a water conditioner. You are not qualified to determine whether they work or not; if you do run the conditioner, you run the risk of liability if anything goes wrong. Water conditioners can drain wells, get stuck in recharge, place iron or chemicals throughout the system, and cause other problems you don't want to be responsible for.

One thing you do need to check, however, is the water conditioner's drain system. Most conditioners send their backwash water into the house drain system, and you must verify that the small drain line is not plumbed directly into the house drain lines. They must drain indirectly into the lines through an air gap so that any backwash of the drain line cannot flow into the house's water system through the conditioner. (For more on conditioner drain line discharge hookups, see "Cross-Connections" on p. 248).

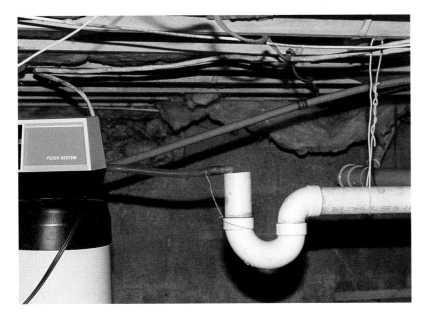

This water conditioner discharge line is installed incorrectly. It does not have the required minimum 1-in. gap between the overflow point and the discharge hose. If the sewer line backs up, the sewage could be siphoned into the water conditioner and from there into the house water supply.

Chapter 9

HEATING AND COOLING SYSTEMS

GENERAL INSPECTION

GAS BURNERS

OIL BURNERS

ELECTRIC FORCED-AIR
FURNACES

ELECTRIC WATER
FURNACES

ELECTRIC BASEBOARDS

WOOD-BURNING STOVES
AND FIREPLACES

HEAT PUMPS AND
AIR CONDITIONERS

GEOTHERMAL HEATING

The purpose of this chapter is not to make you an expert on heating and cooling systems. The heating/cooling trade is a complicated one, and it takes years of training to learn it. Indeed, it is not uncommon for a heating/cooling specialist to be brought in along with a home inspector for an in-depth inspection of the heating system (the buyer pays for both). However, a home inspector does need to have enough knowledge to be able to recognize obvious problems that can be brought to the attention of a professional if needed.

The three bywords for heating/cooling inspection are *smell, look,* and *listen*. Sometimes you can smell a problem before you can see or hear it: Gas and fuel oil leaks are obvious examples. As you approach the system, step back and take an overall look before you start inspecting individual components. From this wide-lens view, obvious problems will show up, such as a missing safety switch, an incorrectly installed dirt leg, or a flue pipe that's too close to combustible materials. The old adage "Can't see the forest for the trees" is sometimes applicable when you're checking a heating system. Finally, don't get so caught up in the visual inspection that you don't take time to listen. For example, if fire is starved of oxygen, it makes a peculiar sound, as do bearings just before they seize up.

General Inspection

Before looking at the basic systems for heating and cooling a house, let's consider a couple of potential problems with individual components that are often overlooked. These include backdrafting and problems with ductwork, filters, and flues.

Ductwork

If the heating and cooling system is forced air, chances are that it has ductwork to distribute it. There are several checks for the duct besides making sure it isn't falling apart. One of the most important is also one of the most ignored: Is it electrically hot? An example will illustrate this.

A do-it-yourselfer friend of mine put his house on the market. During my inspection, he mentioned a "minor" problem with the heating system—in particular, with the ductwork. It seems that, after dark, the ductwork would occasionally light up like a Christmas tree as he walked across the floor. I checked the duct at the furnace and noted a couple of loose sections that had black burn marks where they fitted together—as I moved the sections of ductwork, they arced with electricity. I had seen this alleged minor problem before. The seller was lucky to be alive, and he was about to transfer the problem to a new owner—who might not be so lucky.

The problem was not with the wiring of the furnace but with neutral current flowing through the ductwork. It can come from almost anywhere, but the most common cause is mis-wired sub-panels—neutrals and grounds sharing a common bus. This brings us to the first check of a heating system: measuring for electrically hot ductwork. Here's how to do it. If you are in the crawl space under the house, take a voltage measurement with a multimeter from the metal duct to the moist earth a couple inches down. (If the ductwork is in the basement, measure from the duct to any ground point—such as in a grounded receptacle.) You should get a reading of 0 volts (though you could get a few volts of stray current, which is not a problem). If the reading is above 20 volts, make a note that the duct should be grounded. If you get anything above 50 volts, there's a hot-wire fault to the duct: Stay away from it, it could jump to 120 volts or 240 volts very easily. When you write this in your report, add an exclamation point.

It is not a code requirement to ground the ductwork (although it is recommended), and most inspectors don't add it to their list of checks until they've been "bit." Take my advice and add grounded ductwork to your list of things to check before you have an electric experience.

This is typical of the ductwork you can expect to find during a basement heating inspection. The large rectangular duct is used for the main line runs, and the smaller circular ducts are used for individual feeds to specific rooms or registers.

Checking for "Hot" Ductwork

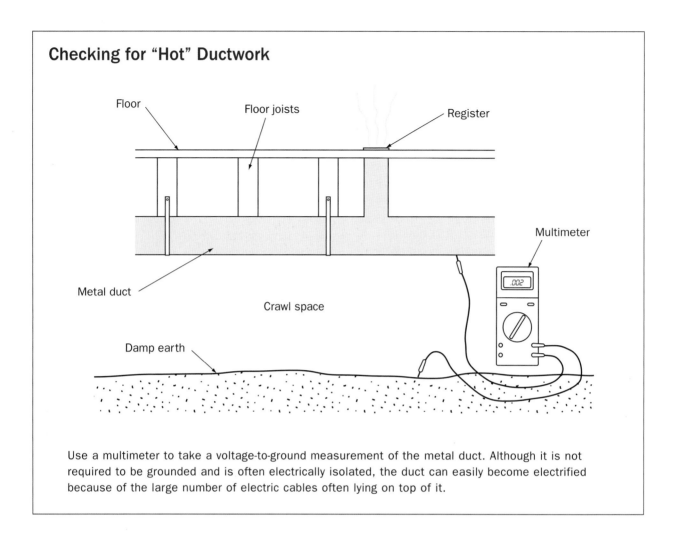

Use a multimeter to take a voltage-to-ground measurement of the metal duct. Although it is not required to be grounded and is often electrically isolated, the duct can easily become electrified because of the large number of electric cables often lying on top of it.

More common duct checks are to observe air flows, observe a heat source in each finished room, and make sure there is no open return vent within 10 ft. of a burner flame. Last, when the fan turns on, be sure to listen for "oil canning." This is the metallic popping sound of a slight dimpling of the duct when the fan tries to pull in more air than the system can supply—thus it sucks the duct sides in. In other words, the system is not balanced.

Flue pipe

The flue pipe is the round duct that takes the exhaust gas from the heating unit out of the house—or, more commonly, to an old chimney. Most flue pipe that is installed for heating is single-wall, class C pipe. Because it is single-wall pipe, it needs to be kept at least 6 in. from all flammable materials (including wood) as it is routed to a brick, stone, or block chimney. Long sections (which should be avoided if possible) need to be supported every 3 ft. or 4 ft. so they don't fall apart. Class C flue pipe is friction-fitted together by having one end slightly smaller than the other; check for any sections that have pulled apart.

Sending the metal flue into an old masonry chimney flue can lead to problems that only an alert inspector will catch. Installers sometimes assume that the flue will draw well when ducted into an old brick or stone flue, but this is not always the case. The inside of the old flue may be a maze of broken and disintegrated brick, accumulated debris, and bird's nests that impede the flow of gases and cool them too quickly. This causes the gas to condense and eat away the galvanized flue where it enters the chimney.

Although you can't look inside the chimney, you can see if the flue pipe is corroded and in poor condition where it enters the chimney. If so, make a note of it on your inspection form. If there's a clean-out door at the bottom of the chimney, make sure it's tightly closed to prevent carbon monoxide fumes from entering the building. If you see holes or wide cracks in the masonry flue, write it up. Besides impeding the flow of gases up the flue, they can also allow carbon monoxide to enter the house.

Also check for a second appliance vent into the chimney. Normally, it is a code violation to vent two different types of gases into the same flue—such as wood and gas (in some areas, both oil and gas may be allowed). If the wood-burning stove is vented into one flue, the gas furnace cannot be in the same one—this is the most common violation I come across in this area. Also check for abandoned vent openings—for example, an old flue that was used to vent a wood-burning stove that is no longer in use. The old opening needs to be sealed—which in most cases means it should be bricked off, not just have a bucket stuck into it or a pie plate placed over it.

Filters

Part of any heating/cooling inspection of a forced-air duct system is to find and inspect the air filter. It may be mounted horizontally or vertically. Location depends on the manufacturer and type of system, but look for the filter first in a slot between the return-air duct and the blower. Slide the filter out and hold it up to a bright light. If the filter is impregnated with dirt and dust to the point that no light shines through, recommend that it be replaced. A clogged filter reduces the amount of air that can be blown into the house, making the system run longer than it should to get the house warm. Be sure to reinstall the filter

This gas-operated forced-air furnace vents into a masonry chimney behind. Check that the sections of flue pipe are secure and that long runs of pipe are supported with straps.

If you can't see through an air filter when you hold it up to the light, it needs to be replaced.

Safety Switches

Whether oil or gas, furnace or boiler, there should be an electrical safety switch (also known as a main switch, kill switch, or panic switch) close to the heating unit so that power can be disconnected in the event of simple maintenance or an emergency. It's also a good idea to recommend (and it is required in some areas) a second kill switch at the head of the basement stairs. That way, if there's a fire in the heating unit you won't have to run down the stairs and reach into the fire to kill the power or go to the service panel to throw the breaker.

correctly: If it is a standard cardboard-framed filter, look for an arrow on the frame that indicates the air-flow direction.

Backdrafting

Any heating system that uses fire and a flue/chimney can backdraft. Backdrafting occurs when the combustion gases that would normally rise through the flue and exit the house reverse themselves and flow back into the building instead.

There are a number of causes of backdrafting, including high air pressure outside the house, low air pressure inside the house, improper appliance operation, and something as simple as a cold flue. For example, if a draft of air comes down the valley and blows down on your house it will overcome the tendency for heated gas to rise and blow it back into the house; most of us have seen this happen to a fireplace. But not all causes of backdrafting are natural. If a large living-area-to-attic fan is turned on, for example, it takes the air from the living area and blows it up and into the attic and outside the house. This puts the living area into negative pressure—outside air will now want to come into the living area to bring the

house back to normal pressure. And the furnace flue is just another hole through which air can be pulled in.

It is difficult and sometimes impossible to check for nature-induced backdrafting, because the condition will probably be intermittent—such as a high-blowing wind from a specific direction. For human-caused problems, you might attempt a negative pressure test by turning on whatever appliance, if any, you suspect might create a backdraft, such as the attic blower mentioned above. If the backdraft is significant and the flue is sealed (with no flow inducers), you will see the flames in the combustion chamber bend backward and swirl around as the backdraft comes down the flue. If the flue is not sealed but has a draft inducer, a designed-in air intake on the flue to induce draft, you can check there as well.

General Heating Checklist

- [ ] Ductwork not falling apart
- [ ] Ductwork grounded
- [ ] 6-in. clearance to flammables for class C flue pipe
- [ ] Flue pipe supported if needed
- [ ] Flue-pipe connections not pulled apart
- [ ] Flue not corroded where it enters masonry flue
- [ ] Chimney clean-out door closed and tight
- [ ] All non-used flue duct openings into chimney sealed
- [ ] No cracks and holes in old masonry flue
- [ ] No mixing of gases in flue or chimney
- [ ] Filter not clogged
- [ ] Check for backdrafting

Backdrafting

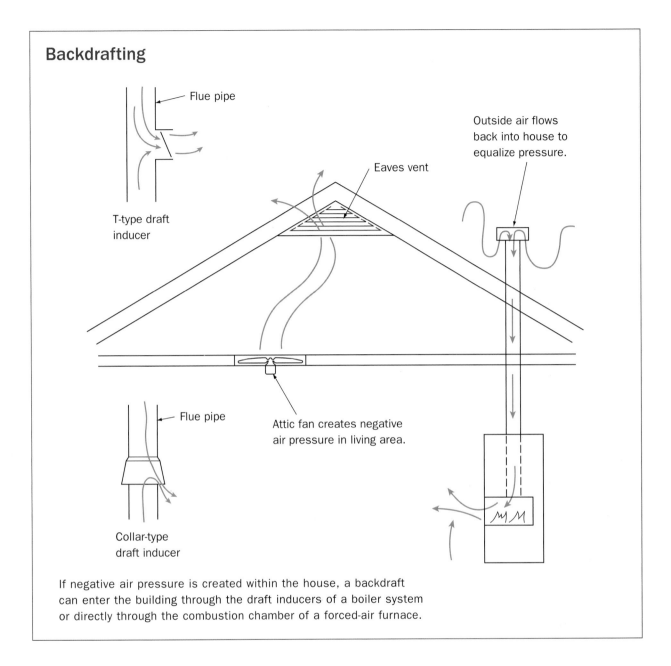

Flue pipe

T-type draft inducer

Eaves vent

Outside air flows back into house to equalize pressure.

Flue pipe

Attic fan creates negative air pressure in living area.

Collar-type draft inducer

If negative air pressure is created within the house, a backdraft can enter the building through the draft inducers of a boiler system or directly through the combustion chamber of a forced-air furnace.

Another test to try is the moisture-on-glass trick. Any time combustion air flows into a room as opposed to flowing up the chimney, it carries with it the suspended moisture in the heated air. This moisture is what you are trying to verify. Hold a piece of flat glass (a mirror) or even your curved plastic eyeglasses where you think the air might be reversing itself from exiting the flue and flowing back into the room—for example, right in front of the draft diverter, furnace-door panel louvers, inspection hole, or at the smokestack draft door. The combustion air, being high in moisture, will fog the glass. If you have one, a draft checker can be used to detect backdrafting.

A more official test uses a fancy piece of test gear that costs about $75, called a digital manometer, available from Dyer Instruments (Magnehelic) in Michigan City, Indiana. A tube

Old Heating Systems

If you go into the basement of an old house and find a giant furnace that looks like it has octopus legs coming off the top, you're looking at a gravity-feed warm air furnace—a very inefficient way to heat a house. It basically has no moving parts. Slightly less ancient systems added a blower to move the air better. There is nothing to check here; just recommend a new furnace and duct system.

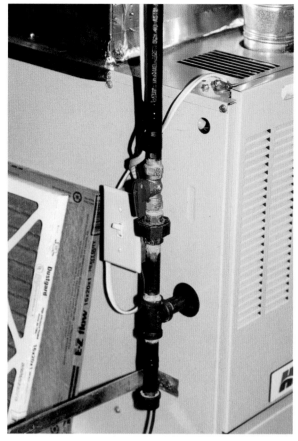

Check to see that there is an electrical safety switch close to the furnace, a gas cutoff valve, and a correctly installed dirt leg.

goes outside the house to sample outside air pressure and then the unit reads the inside air pressure. If the pressure around the furnace/boiler is lower than the outside pressure when the air handler of the unit is on and all of the appliances that can blow air out of the house are on (dryer, bath fan, kitchen fan, etc.), you can assume that backdrafting will occur. Because of the time it takes to do the test (about 15 minutes), you should charge extra for it.

Gas Burners

Oil and gas forced-air systems, which both heat air that is blown via ductwork through the house, are two of the most popular heating systems in North America. With the advantages of a constant supply of fuel, clean burning, and ease of maintenance, gas is the preferred heating system in many areas.

As you approach a gas furnace, there are a number of general checks you can make before you fire up the system. First, do you smell gas? If you don't, you can continue the inspection. If you do, you have a choice: Leave or try to find the source of the leak. Do you see water on the floor? This indicates that the system is a gas boiler and that there's a major crack in the chamber

holding the water (the heat exchanger). Don't fire up this system: The owners need a new furnace.

If the unit is sitting on a concrete floor, check to see if the bottom is rusted out, perhaps as a result of occasional flooding. Check that the flue system, which takes the combustion air out of the room, is intact. If sections are missing or falling apart, make a note of it and do not turn the system on.

There should be an electrical safety switch (or "kill" switch) and a gas cutoff valve close to the unit. Most gas appliances, including gas furnaces, are also required by their manufacturer to have a dirt leg, a combination of fittings arranged so that dirt or debris in the gas line cannot get into the

Gas Burner Checkpoints

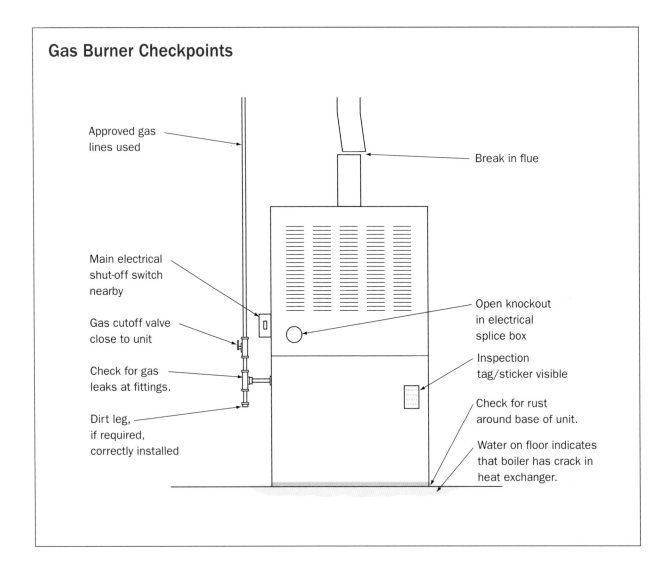

Approved gas lines used

Break in flue

Main electrical shut-off switch nearby

Open knockout in electrical splice box

Gas cutoff valve close to unit

Inspection tag/sticker visible

Check for gas leaks at fittings.

Check for rust around base of unit.

Dirt leg, if required, correctly installed

Water on floor indicates that boiler has crack in heat exchanger.

control module (see p. 165). Check that the dirt leg, if required, is present and installed correctly, with a T placed on the vertical gas line, a short nipple with a cap below it, and a feed to the furnace control from the center of the T (as shown in the drawing above). Some areas may require a flex connector from the rigid pipe to the furnace because of the possibility of earthquakes. If so, make sure it is there and log it if not.

Check that the correct gas lines are run to the furnace. Until recently, black-iron pipe and flexible copper were the most common, but yellow flexible lines are fast becoming the preferred type of pipe. It's interesting to note that some people,

even a few inspectors, maintain that you shouldn't use flexible copper with gas because the pipe will corrode. This may have been true at one time in certain areas of the country because of contaminates in the gas that were not removed, but it's no longer true. However, rigid copper with sweated or compression fittings is not allowed for gas lines.

Check for gas leaks at the fittings. It's common to find gas leaks where the gas line goes into the control module and at the pipe connections adjacent to it. I recommend using a Bacharach tester (or "gas sniffer") to check for leaks. In addition, you'll need a carbon monoxide detector

A Bacharach "Leakator" is the author's preferred tool for checking for leaks in gas lines. An alarm sounds if gas is detected.

(see p. 122) for checking at the registers and along vent lines.

There are a couple more inspection points before you move on to inspect the furnace's combustion chamber. First, are there any knockouts open in the electrical splice box? This happens when someone changed his or her mind about where to bring in the power cable and left the original hole open. The knockout should be plugged so that inquisitive fingers cannot go exploring the wiring. Also check to see if there is an inspection tag or sticker on or near the furnace. If not make note that the last inspection date is unknown. (Gas furnaces require cleaning every few years to stay at top efficiency.) Finally, remember my "smell, look, and listen" advice at the start of this chapter. Do you *hear* anything wrong with the furnace? For example, if the unit is running, does the flame sound smooth and continuous or loud and intermittent, which indicates a lack of oxygen in the air. Do you hear a loud grinding noise like the bearings going out in the blower?

Once you've completed the smell, look, and listen test of the exterior of the unit, you can move on to inspect the combustion chamber. The basics of a gas burner are quite simple. The gas enters a large aluminum box directly in front of the furnace, called a combination control valve or

module. All controls emanate from this box. The pilot (if it has one—electronic ignition systems will not) will get its gas from the small pipe leaving the module, and the furnace will get its gas from the big one. There will be a second little pipe, called a thermocouple tube, that has its opposite end sticking into the pilot flame. The heat from the flame produces a voltage within the thermocouple, which controls a gas valve inside the module. If the pilot flame goes out, the absence of the thermocouple voltage shuts the gas off. If the thermocouple has been bent out of place and is not in the flame of the pilot, the system will shut down. Don't try to fix it, just write it up.

The thermocouple has a high failure rate, and you should verify that it is in working condition. If the gas burner is already in operation or works when you turn up the thermostat, you can assume it is working properly. If the system is down and your company allows you to fire up the system, you can attempt a test. Push the manual control knob, light the pilot, and wait the required 60 seconds for the flame to heat up the thermocouple and produce enough voltage to keep the control module valve open; if you let go of the knob, the flame should stay lit if the thermocouple works. If the pilot light keeps going out every time you release the manual control knob, the thermocouple is faulty.

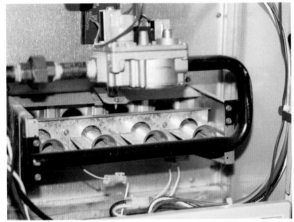

With the front panel removed, the inner workings of this gas furnace are revealed. The aluminum box in the center of the unit is the control module; gas enters via the pipe on the left and exits via the black pipe on the right and circles down to the four burners. On this furnace you can see into the combustion chamber through the four large holes around the burners. If air comes out of these holes when you turn on the air handler, the heat-exchange system is defective.

When the gas leaves the module it goes to a manifold to be distributed between several long tubes, called burner tubes, that tee into it. At the head of the tube are air shutters, where air is mixed with gas for ignition. Inside the combustion chamber, if the furnace is running, tiny flames can be seen all in a row coming from holes in the burner tubes. If you can observe the chamber while the burners are on (most new gas burners have everything totally sealed and you

Pilot Light Caution

Pushing down the manual control knob on a gas furnace bypasses the internal cutoff valve within the module. This means gas is coming out of the pilot tube, whether there's a flame or not. If you wait too long to light the pilot, there will be an abundance of gas around the pilot tube and as you strike a match there'll be an explosion. This has happened to many an experienced gas maintenance person—and some have gotten hurt. Therefore, always have a lit flame at the end of the pilot tube when you push the manual control knob down. If you smell any gas around the gas burner, do not attempt to light the pilot. If you see flames coming from any place other than the pilot and burner, shut the system down.

can't see anything except through a tiny inspection hole), use the light of the flame to look over the tubes and verify that they are intact—not broken or a mass of corrosion. Look for accumulations of rust lying on the burners and blocking the little flame holes. Is there a mass of corrosion covering the metal chamber, separating off in layers and ready to fall?

If you can see into the combustion chamber, look for both large and hairline cracks in the metal chamber itself. Also look for areas that appear to be "etched," caused by acids forming in the wet combustion air and eating away at the metal, and creating holes; some holes will be tiny, others could be 1 in. or 2 in. long. At this time, you can turn on the blower only and put your hand near any suspicious areas to see if you feel any air coming through, which indicates a faulty heat exchanger. Note any soot marks around the outside of the burner area, along the sides of the unit, or even on the access panel. This is an indication of bad air adjustment, blocked burners,

Thermostat Bypass

Some method is needed to turn on a furnace (or any other heating system) in the summer so you can check the system. The thermostat isn't going to want to turn the system on because the room is already hot. There are at least two ways to get around that problem. If the system is a simple two-wire, low-voltage thermostat, all you need is a jumper (two alligator clips and a short piece of wire) to short across the furnace thermostat contacts (two screws at the furnace) to turn it on. If the wall thermostat is a multiwire system, you might try holding something cold against it to convince it that it is wintertime. A small frozen block of ice or a bag of ice cubes will normally do the trick.

These two items—a jumper made from two alligator clips and a short piece of wire and a freeze brick—can be used to turn on almost any heating system in the summer.

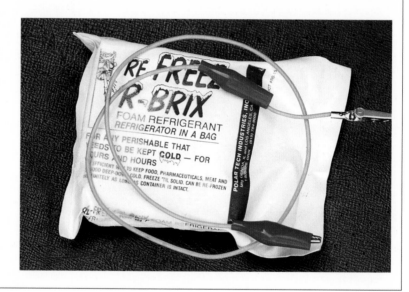

flame rollout from a defective burner, or a bad heat-exchange system. Some furnaces have a flame shield that is supposed to prevent this from happening, but it is occasionally left off by the maintenance person.

If the system is not on, throw the kill switch so it cannot come on and shine a flashlight inside the chamber so you can check its condition. If you don't have enough access to verify any of the above conditions, simply indicate so on the form. For the new ultra-high-efficiency gas burners that may have heat exchangers that are not accessible, the only way to ensure that the unit is functioning properly is to do a carbon monoxide check at the heat registers.

This section on inspecting a gas burner is lengthy; but, overall, all that is outlined is a preliminary check of the heating system. You check for obvious problems, but you adjust nothing and fix nothing. There are many other checks and lots of other controls that can be done for a "complete" systems check, such as checking whether the expansion tank is waterlogged. In my opinion, you don't have time for this; for a complete systems check, the owners need to bring in a furnace specialist. Exactly how many items you have time to check will be up to you or your company's policy. If you found any problems at all in the heating system, including the absence of a tag indicating the last date of service, recommend calling in a furnace specialist.

Grounding gas lines

Grounding of gas lines is a controversial subject. Officially, the gas lines are grounded through the equipment grounding conductor of the electrical hook-up. However, this doesn't cover nonelectrical gas appliances, like a gas water heater and appliances that have the old two-wire hookup.

The National Electrical Code (NEC) requires solid metal gas lines to be connected into the house grounding system. The connection is treated the same as with a water line—by putting a clamp on the pipe and taking a ground wire back to the service panel or ground rod. This connection, however, is sometimes overruled by the local gas company, who, more often than not, stick a ground rod out in the lawn adjacent to their gas meter and run a wire between the two. This is in direct violation of the NEC. You cannot have two grounding systems in the same house.

Gas Boilers

As with any type of boiler, gas boilers will have a water-feed system. If the water system is off (completely shut down with no water pressure), it is not up to you to feed in the water, adjust the water pressure, watch the settings, and do whatever is necessary to get the system going properly. If it is down, leave it alone and note on the form, "Boiler not running and cannot be inspected."

If there is water to the system, there should be a water pressure gauge. Note the pressure—it should be around 12 psi. If it exceeds 30 psi, make a note. This is about the only additional check I make for boilers, other than the obvious one of checking for leaking water lines.

Gas Burner Checklist

Outside

- [ ] Gas leaks
- [ ] Water on the floor
- [ ] Bottom rusted out
- [ ] Flue pipe intact
- [ ] Electrical safety switch nearby
- [ ] Gas cutoff valve nearby
- [ ] Dirt leg present and correctly installed
- [ ] Flex connector from rigid pipe to the furnace, if required
- [ ] Approved gas lines used
- [ ] Gas leaks at fittings
- [ ] Open knockouts in electrical splice box
- [ ] Inspection tag on/near furnace

Inside the unit

- [ ] Thermocouple working
- [ ] Burner tubes intact (not broken) and not corroded
- [ ] Rust and debris lying on the burner tubes
- [ ] Major or minor cracks in heat exchange system
- [ ] Acidic corrosion holes in heat exchange system
- [ ] Black soot marks on furnace coming from the combustion chamber
- [ ] Excessive rust in burner chamber
- [ ] Carbon monoxide check at registers, if needed

This isolated grounding of a gas line is not allowed by the NEC. Note also the ground rod connector, which is not approved for outside use.

Vent-Pipe Problems

From the 1970s on, fairly efficient furnaces, called condensing furnaces and pulse-combustion furnaces, came onto the market. With increased efficiency came lower flue temperatures that allowed the venting of exhaust gases horizontally out the basement wall via high-temperature plastic vent (HTPV) pipe. Immediately after came vent failures and the recall of the vent pipe. Although not all plastic venting is affected, the inspector needs to check any plastic vent pipe for cracks, places where the pipe has pulled apart from its fittings, and discoloration. After the visual check, the pipe needs to be sniffed, using a carbon monoxide checker, for any escaping flue gases.

Such a system is not only useless but also dangerous. If a hot wire touches the metal gas line, the current flow must have a low-resistance path back to the panel for the breaker to kick—that's the purpose of a ground wire or bond. If you ground the pipe to earth (other than to the house ground rod), the current has to flow through the earth to get back to the house ground rod and from there to the main panel. The earth acts as a high resistance, and not enough current can flow to kick the breaker. The result is that the gas line stays hot, ready to electrocute anyone who touches it.

This grounding issue puts the inspector in a quandary: The NEC says one thing; the gas company may say another. I have no solution for this other than to tell the customer the truth—the gas company's system, or perhaps the building contractor's system, doesn't work. If I find improper grounding of gas lines, I write it up. One thing that everyone does agree on is that metal gas lines are never to be used as a grounding electrode or ground rod. One final note on gas-line grounding: You cannot ground a metal gas line by grounding it to a metal water line.

Oil Burners

Oil burners came into residential use right after World War II as an advance over coal furnaces. The oil to power the burner is stored in a large tank either above ground or below ground. Between the tank and the burner, there is an oil filter and a shutoff valve, which can be at the tank itself or at the oil pump. In my area, the oil tanks are normally above ground and outside, so I check them while I am inspecting the exterior. Obviously, there are no checks for a buried tank.

Check that the oil tank is stable and not falling over. Look for rusted-through support legs or legs that are buckling or sinking in the ground. Also check that there's a fuel filter and shutoff valve somewhere in the line and that neither is leaking. And rap on the tank's bottom with your knuckle to see if there's fuel in the tank; a hollow sound indicates that the tank is empty. This is not an official check, but if the system doesn't start up it may be for lack of fuel.

As with a gas burner, the oil burner inspection starts with the smell, look, and listen tests. When you step into the basement, do you smell any fuel oil? Do you see anything wrong, such as fuel on the floor, soot around the furnace, disassembled ducts, flues that are falling apart, or flammable materials stored too close to the furnace? Spilt fuel and flue problems make the system too dangerous to operate. If you think it's safe to inspect the unit, go ahead (but first make sure that there's a kill switch close by that you can throw if you sense anything wrong). Otherwise, remember that you won't be the first inspector to walk away and write up an oil burner as unfit to run.

Buried Fuel Tanks

Most buyers will want to know if there are any buried fuel oil, propane, or gas tanks on the property. No tank is perfect—all will rust through sooner or later. Unless the tank is coated with epoxy or a similar material, its typical life expectancy is about 30 years. There is no test for belowground tanks—which is the problem and why the buyer needs to know if such a tank exists. If the tank is buried, write it up in your report because the new owner will be assuming responsibility for any problems.

An oil burner is quite a complicated piece of machinery. The oil first flows into an oil pump, normally mounted to the left of the circulator motor, which in turn is always mounted dead center bottom of the system. The pump pressurizes the oil to about 100 psi and sends it through a tiny hole in a nozzle deep inside the

A typical oil burner. The oil line comes in to the left of the furnace just above the floor, followed by the cutoff valve and then the oil filter. Check for oil leaks, which are visible as stains on the floor.

Oil Burner Checklist

- [ ] Oil tank stable and in good condition
- [ ] Fuel filter and shutoff valve present and not leaking fuel
- [ ] Excess fuel oil smell
- [ ] Fuel oil on floor
- [ ] Ducts and flue intact and not falling apart
- [ ] Kill switch nearby
- [ ] Grinding noises of bad bearings
- [ ] Draft regulator functioning (if present)
- [ ] Resets stay in
- [ ] Maintenance tag on/near furnace

unit that sprays an oil mist into the combustion chamber. Electrodes placed near the nozzle send 10,000 volts arcing through the mist and igniting it. Once fired, it is self-sustaining. The combustion chamber is not open and needs a supply of air to sustain the flame. This air comes form a blower mounted and run by the same motor that runs the oil pump.

Although the machine is complicated, the checks are few. Shine a light into the inspection hole and look for disintegrating refractory lining and pooled oil (do not start the unit up if you find either). Once the oil burner is up and running, if it wasn't already when you got there, listen for any loud grinding noises or squealing noises that could indicate a bad bearing in the motor and blower fan. You will also hear the circulator running and the fire roaring from within the combustion chamber. The combustion chamber is not as easily accessible as in most gas burners, so there's nothing to check inside it. With the system running, the draft regulator (or "barometric damper") cut into the exhaust flue should swing open 1 in. or 2 in. If it stays permanently open or closed, it is adjusted incorrectly; write it up.

If the furnace doesn't run and you know there is oil and the breaker is on, check the resets. There is normally a reset button in a control box immediately over the blower fan. There is another at the flue, called a stack heat sensor, a primary control that cuts off the power if the temperature gets too high (as in a flue fire). Never press a reset button more than twice—it must be kicking off for a reason; write it up. Look for a maintenance tag to verify when the unit was last serviced. If none is visible, make note of it and mention to the owners that it may be time for service.

Electric Forced-Air Furnaces

Electric furnaces are popular in many areas because they are not only economical to purchase but also fast and easy to install. One cable run, one wiring connection, and the house has heat. Their most significant disadvantage is the same as with all furnaces—the entire unit has to kick on just to heat one room.

An electric furnace is essentially one giant electric heater with a blower. Electric furnaces come in all sizes and configurations, both flush mounted and surface mounted. Some electric furnaces use ductwork to distribute the heated air, others blow directly into the room. Being of forced-air design, electric furnaces draw cool air into a grill at the unit itself or through ductwork from a distant location. As the air is pulled in, it passes across elements that electricity has heated red hot. The blower sends the heated air across the room or into ducts to travel to the various heat registers throughout the house.

Most electric furnaces are fed via 240 volts. Some feed from a single large breaker—80 amps to 100 amps, for example. Other designs break the feed down into two double-pole breakers of lesser amperage. Look for these breakers in the main service panel if you have to turn the system on to test it.

Before you turn the furnace on, check the filter, which should be on either the front or the side of the unit. It should slide right out or be

A flush-mounted electric furnace. The grill network pulls in cold air; the filter is horizontal between the upper and the lower sections. The bottom section (shown with its cover removed at right) houses the blower and electrical components.

pinned against the louvers of the return air grill. The filter needs to be replaced if you can't see through it when you hold it up to the light.

The ultimate test for the furnace is simply to turn the thermostat up and see if heat comes out of the registers. However, electric furnaces work somewhat differently than most furnaces. Because they draw a significant amount of electricity, the electrical load is staggered. This means you won't get the full current draw and, therefore, won't get the full amount of heat the moment the system kicks on. Practically, this means you must wait a few moments if you are measuring the temperature with a temperature gauge or just with your hand. Once the unit is running, make sure you test it long enough (5 to 15 minutes) to be sure the breakers are going to hold and not kick off. If the unit pulls too much current or the breakers start going bad, they will cut the current from the furnace with a resounding click as they turn off. You may reset the breaker once and try it again— but never twice. Write it up.

Electric Forced-Air Furnace Checklist

- [ ] Furnace turns on, produces heat, and turns back off again
- [ ] Filter not clogged
- [ ] Breakers hold and do not kick off

Electric Water Furnaces

As the name implies, an electric water furnace is a boiler that uses electricity rather than oil or gas to heat water. Instead of the typical large boiler that sits on the floor and takes up a lot of room, an electric boiler is a small box that mounts on the wall with two large water pipes (cold in, hot out) and a circulator to push the water through. Heated water circulates to various parts of the house and is removed in each room via horizontal baseboard radiators that are mounted just above the floor.

The wall-mounted box contains relays and water heating elements. Once the system is turned on, you should see each light click on in sequence as the load is applied, just as with an electric forced-air furnace. To verify that the system is working, simply feel the outgoing water pipe—it should be hot. There may be thermostats controlling solenoid valves that allow the heated water to circulate to each room. To check these, simply turn the thermostats up and you should feel the pipes going to the rooms start to get hot.

Electric Baseboards

Electric baseboard heaters are very popular for contractors on a tight budget and for do-it-yourselfers. They are quick to install and relatively inexpensive to buy. I prefer baseboards to electric boilers because there is a thermostatically controlled independent unit in each room; if one fails you still have heat in other parts of the house. But it's rare to have problems with baseboard heaters because they have few moving parts.

Baseboard heat is controlled by a thermostat that can be mounted on the heater itself or on

Electric Water Furnace Checklist

- ☐ Boiler kicks on and produces heat
- ☐ Element lights come on in sequence
- ☐ Outgoing water pipe gets hot
- ☐ If individual room thermostats are used, their respective pipes heat up as their thermostat is turned up

An electric water furnace does the same job as an oil or gas furnace but takes up considerably less room. The unit is thermostatically operated; you should see a red light turn on every few minutes as the elements come on one by one.

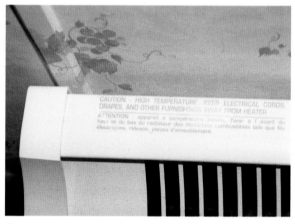

Electric baseboard heaters are a fairly common source of heating, but their warnings are often ignored. A closeup look at the label on the left side of the heater tells the inspector what to check for. This heater is a better design than most—a grill stops cords and drapes from falling onto the hot elements.

the wall. Most baseboards are 240 volts, which means they have two hot input feeders, called legs, both of which must connect to the heater element to produce heat. Thermostats can be either single pole or double pole. The inspector should know the difference between the two.

A single-pole thermostat has one leg permanently wired to the heater and the second controlled by the thermostat. This means that when the thermostat has opened the circuit and there is no heat, power is still on one leg of the element. This thermostat will have a high and a low and perhaps even a gradient scale, but it will not have an off position. This means that you cannot turn off a baseboard heater that uses a single-pole thermostat. You can turn it down low, but if you want it to never turn on when the

room gets cold, you must throw the circuit breaker that gives it its power. This is important to know and log because if the new buyer wants the heat turned off in some rooms while others are left on, it will be impossible to do if they are on the same circuit; if you throw the breaker to kill the power in one room, you kill the power to all on the same circuit.

A double-pole thermostat has two legs controlled by the thermostat, which means that when the thermostat is turned off, all the voltage is completely removed from the heating element. But, more important, this thermostat will have a listed off position. You do not have to kill the power to the baseboard to keep the thermostat from turning the heat on.

Receptacle Placement with Electric Baseboards

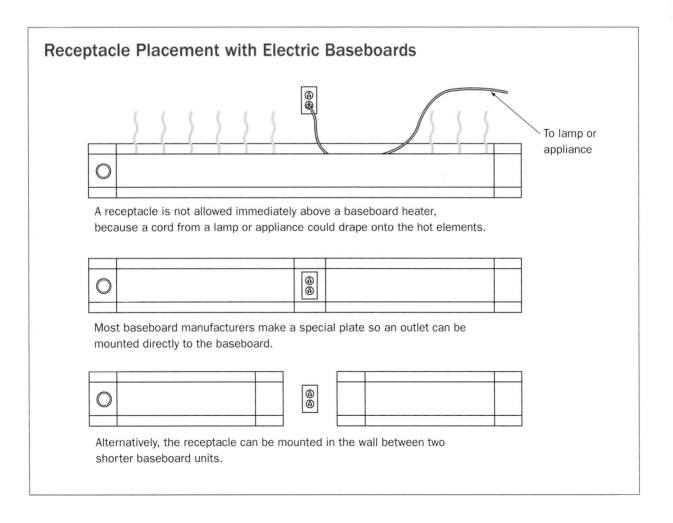

A receptacle is not allowed immediately above a baseboard heater, because a cord from a lamp or appliance could drape onto the hot elements.

Most baseboard manufacturers make a special plate so an outlet can be mounted directly to the baseboard.

Alternatively, the receptacle can be mounted in the wall between two shorter baseboard units.

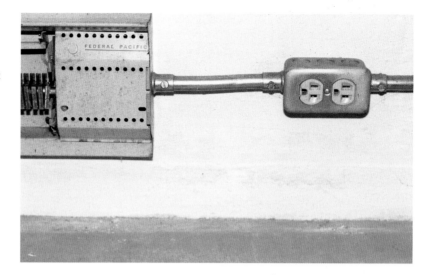

There are two problems here. First, the cover is missing from the baseboard heater. Second, the receptacle is in the same electrical line as the baseboard. It's highly likely that it is on the heater circuit, which is against code.

As with in-heater thermostats, wall-mounted thermostats can also be single or double pole. Single-pole thermostats, however, are no longer allowed as a wall mount by code, so you should see fewer of these. As with the baseboard unit, look for the off position to tell them apart. I never write anything up on this unless I know the house has just been built.

To test the baseboard heater during the inspection process, turn up the thermostat. You'll hear a muffled click and the crackling sound of the elements heating up. If the baseboards have not been used in some while, you'll quite likely smell dust, cobwebs, and dirt burning off the units' elements. If you can't get the heaters to turn on, check the breakers—it's common for the owners to keep the breakers off, especially if there is no off switch on the thermostat.

Observe the position of the baseboard heater relative to the wall receptacles. You're not allowed to have a receptacle above a heater, although I've seen them pass inspections time and time again. Such a location allows the cord of a light fixture or appliance to loop into the heater elements and fry. Other times the heat from the elements will harden and crack the line cord—and as the insulation cracks and breaks off, it will expose the hot conductors. Instead of being located above

Electric Baseboard Checklist

- [ ] Single-pole or double-pole thermostat
- [ ] Baseboard heaters turn on and produce heat
- [ ] No receptacles over baseboard
- [ ] Receptacles within baseboard not on baseboard circuit

the heater, the receptacles are supposed to be either between two heaters or integrated into the heater frame (see the drawing on p. 191). Most baseboard heater manufacturers sell special end sections that allow a receptacle to be mounted within the frame assembly. You are not, however, allowed to wire the receptacle into the heater circuit. You must bring in a separate cable. To test this, turn the breaker off that powers the baseboard unit and test the receptacle with a plug-in tester—you should still have power. If you don't (but you do have power when the breaker is on), write it up. This is a significant wiring error.

Wood-Burning Stoves and Fireplaces

Wood-burning stoves and fireplaces are generally not considered a primary heat source. However, many homeowners have succumbed to the old-time lure of one or the other—some for the looks, others for the free heat. But along with the attraction comes a fire hazard, and it's up to the home inspector to verify that the zeal of the installer to have free heat has not pre-empted the requirement for safety.

Wood-burning stoves

Most home fires caused by wood-burning stoves are the result of improper installation (for example, having flammable materials too close to the stove) or inadequate maintenance (for example, ignoring a flue pipe that has come apart). Local jurisdictions usually have their own set of rules and regulations for dealing with wood-burning stoves. In addition, the manufacturer's installations need to be followed; but remember these are minimum clearances. If in doubt, refer to the National Fire Protection Association (NFPA) standards on clearances for wood-burning stoves.

In an ideal installation, the stove will be surrounded by rock or masonry on the sides and bottom, with plenty of room overhead and a short piece of horizontal flue pipe to the chimney. Note that clearances can be pre-empted if the manufacture has a UL listing for closer clearances—for example, some woodstoves have built-in heat shields.

Typically, wood-burning stoves need at least a 36-in. clearance from a combustible wall. Don't forget that studs, drapes, carpets, throw rugs, and wooden mantels are all flammable and are not allowed within this clearance. Materials such as sheet metal, brick, or mineral-wool batts may be used to protect the combustible wall from the heat of the woodstove. The material should be

The ideal installation for a wood-burning stove is in a location surrounded by rock or masonry on three sides and the bottom, with no flammable materials nearby.

spaced 1 in. out from the combustible wall to allow air to circulate between the wall and the protective materials. Jacketed woodstoves allow closer clearances to combustibles. However, you won't know the exact clearances unless you have the manufacturer's installation manual.

Clearance above a woodstove can normally be reduced to a minimum of 12 in. if a nonflammable shield is placed a minimum of 1 in. off the flammable surface. The shield should be at least 22 gauge and must also continue vertically until there is at least a 36-in. clearance to the stove. The legs of the stove should extend the firebox at least 6 in. off the floor.

The stove should be sitting on a nonflammable floor; however, there are a couple of exceptions.

On a wood-burning fireplace, check for any major cracks in the masonry and verify that the damper works and the flue has a liner.

Stoves with legs or pedestals providing 2 in. to 6 in. of ventilated open space beneath the fire chamber or base may be installed on combustible floors protected by 4 in. of hollow masonry, laid to provide air circulation, and covered with 24-gauge sheet metal. If there is more than 6 in. of ventilated open space beneath the fire chamber, a stove may be placed on a combustible floor protected by a solid brick, concrete, or stone masonry unit at least 2 in. thick. The floor protection should extend at least 18 in. on all sides of the stove.

The flue pipe from the stove to the chimney should be kept as short as possible and have a slight increase of slope (approximately 1/4 in. to the foot). It should never be sloped down to enter the chimney. The crimped end of the flue pipe should fit into the stove collar to prevent creosote from dripping to the floor. Sections of flue pipe should be screwed together, not just friction fitted, and, obviously, the pipe should not be falling apart. Make note of any creosote you see dripping from the pipe. Flue clearance to flammables should be a minimum of three times the flue diameter. For example, a 6-in. flue pipe needs an 18-in clearance to flammables. The flue pipe should be sealed where it enters the chimney,

with no large gaps, so that gases cannot re-enter the room. Class B double-wall pipe should never be used as a flue pipe.

The clearance of the metal flue pipe in the chimney should be at least 2 in. from flammables (unless greater clearance is required by local code or the manufacturer). If the house is old, it's rare that the metal chimney flue is not touching, or extremely close to, something flammable. It's also rare that an old masonry chimney is without cracks or disintegrating brick. Knowing this, ask the homeowner if the chimney has been inspected recently (not just cleaned, but inspected). Ask for the inspection report; if it is unavailable, write the chimney up as an area of concern. There should be no major cracks in the chimney, no flue holes left open, and the clean-out door should be tightly closed.

Every stove must have a way to control the air entering it or have a stovepipe damper (a round plate with holes in it that pivots inside the stovepipe and is turned by rod that runs through it). By controlling the air intake or gas exit via the damper, you can control combustion. And if the combustion gets out of hand, as in a flue fire, it can be stopped by cutting off the air or turning the pie-shaped damper sideways to block the flue pipe.

The typical bare-metal, wood-burning stove is a simple box with a flue pipe out the top or back. However, with the addition of catalytic converters to increase the heat output, things have become a little more complicated. A catalytic converter is a ceramic, honeycombed combuster coated with a special metal that reacts to the stove gases as they pass through to give the stove an afterburner effect by superheating the flue gases. However, the converter must be kept free of ash as much as possible to work properly and has a life span of only about five years. If the woodstove has a catalytic converter, note the age of the converter (there should be a maintenance tag nearby); if you can't determine how old the converter is, simply note that it may need cleaning or replacing.

Fireplaces and chimneys

Fireplaces are generally considered to be extremely inefficient heat sources, but that doesn't deter many homeowners from wanting them in their houses. There are two basic types of fireplaces: masonry and metal insert. The first is a brick (sometimes rock) and mortar fireplace, and the latter is a prefab unit with masonry surrounding it. Both types are quick and easy to inspect.

Begin by stepping back and looking at the fireplace from a distance. Check for any major cracks in the masonry surrounding the firebox. Hairline cracks can be ignored, but larger cracks may be settling cracks caused as the heavy masonry shifts its footer; write these up. Now for the dirty part: Using a strong flashlight and wearing some gloves and protective goggles, look up into the flue and operate the damper to verify that it works. Then look beyond the damper as best you can to verify that the flue has a liner.

Chimneys have to be lined to provide a smooth, unbroken passage for the smoke to rise and leave the house. It is this unbroken barrier that keeps the flames and gases from entering the house and causing sickness, death, or fire. However, the lining has a habit of cracking as it ages

What's the Difference between a Chimney and a Flue?

A chimney is not the same as a flue. The chimney is the visible outside structure—the rock, block, slate, or brick. The flue is the internal shaft that vents the gases (the smoke) produced from the fire to the outside. The terms *liner* and *flue* are normally used interchangeably, although the flue is technically the air space inside the liner. It is this flue or liner that must be unbroken from the heat source—be it a woodstove, oil burner, or fireplace—to the outside air. If it is broken or cracked, gases and flames can breach the flue and get inside the house.

and from the intense heat of the fire in the chimney. The basic problem with a liner inspection is that, owing to its inaccessible location and the creosote buildup within, you really cannot see if there is a crack or missing mortar somewhere that could, on the very next day after inspection, pass a spark of flame and burn the house down.

Most chimneys that are unlined were built before the 1950s. If the chimney looks old and you cannot see a liner extending out the top of the chimney, there is a good chance there is no liner. Most unlined chimneys are made from stone, block, and common brick—not fire brick. If a fire occurs in this type of construction, the flames could easily spread to the house structure.

Because you do not have x-ray vision, you cannot see if there are any internal problems within the chimney. But you can inspect the exterior of the chimney while you are doing your walk-around of the house exterior. Problems on the outside of the chimney are a good indication that there may be problems on the inside. First, observe the condition of the masonry: Is it solid

Chimney Fire Checkpoints

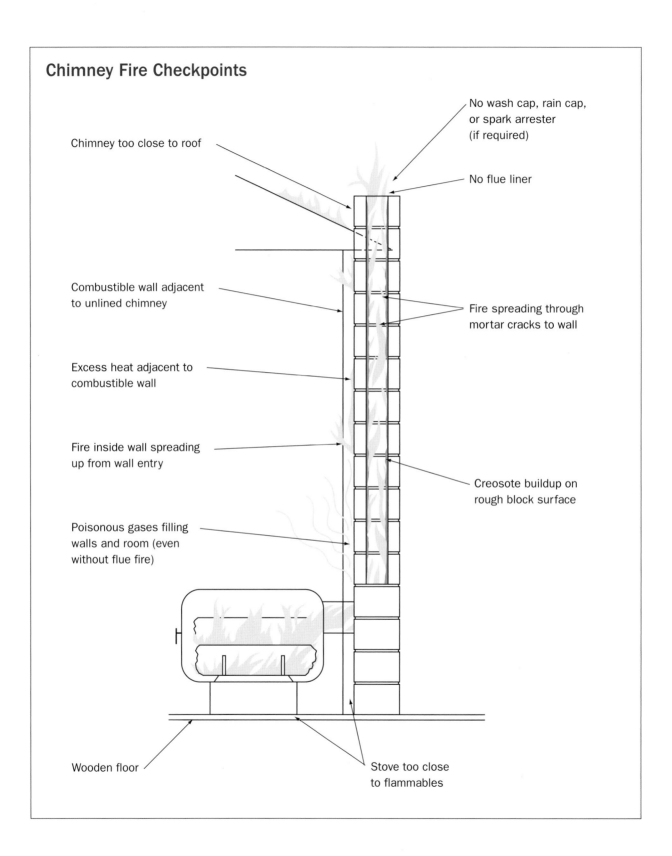

Chimney too close to roof

No wash cap, rain cap, or spark arrester (if required)

No flue liner

Combustible wall adjacent to unlined chimney

Fire spreading through mortar cracks to wall

Excess heat adjacent to combustible wall

Fire inside wall spreading up from wall entry

Creosote buildup on rough block surface

Poisonous gases filling walls and room (even without flue fire)

Wooden floor

Stove too close to flammables

A tale of two chimneys. The chimney above left is from a modern fireplace with two flues. Note the caps and grills. The installation below left is ready to fall over: There is no visible flue liner, the mortar is disintegrating, the bricks are falling out, and the flashing looks a little worse for wear.

or disintegrating? Is the chimney still snugged up against the house structure or has it pulled away? Look for creosote stains leaking out from the mortar joints, which indicates that there is a break in the flue liner. If the flue liner is metal and parts of it are visible, check that it is not falling apart and that it is not warped or discolored, which could indicate that there has been a flue fire.

If the owner is present when you do your inspection, ask if there has ever been a flue fire. When chimney fires occur, the temperature can reach 2,000°F, which can disintegrate mortar, crack tiles, and cause liners to crack or collapse. Sometimes it is a chimney fire that creates the gaps; a later fire can then penetrate and ignite the

house. Signs of a previous fire include puffy, rainbow-colored creosote, a distorted rain cap, creosote flakes on the roof around the flue, and smoke stains around mortar joint cracks.

In addition to the liner within the chimney, some jurisdictions may require a wash cap on the chimney where the flue exits. This is a 2-in.-thick concrete cap that prevents rain from entering the chimney. Similarly, a flat metal chimney cap may be required to seal unused chimneys. In dry areas of the country, a grill network, known as a spark arrester, may be required on top of the chimney to prevent large sparks from leaving the chimney and flying in the air to set fire to the woods beyond.

Gas Log Fireplaces

Gas log fireplaces may be fueled by natural gas or propane and be either vented or unvented. Vented means that the combustion gases vent to the outside. Unvented means that the exhaust gases stay in the house (approved for BTUs up to around 30,000). The appeal of the latter is that they are essentially 100% efficient. But the controversy with unvented gas fireplaces is that the house becomes the flue. In theory, there are safety devices built into the units that are supposed to cut the unit off if anything goes wrong. But, allegedly, people have been harmed by carbon monoxide. The long- and short-term affects, include memory loss, severe muscular pain, headaches, and tiredness.

The inspector may be asked to comment on the benefits of vented versus unvented models, but I'd recommend that you don't voice an opinion on the matter. Simply note on the form that the heater is vented or unvented. An exception would be if the local area has banned unvented heaters; then you should note on the form that the unvented heater is in violation. Similarly, make note if you know that the heater model is not approved for an unvented installation (too many BTUs). Also note the presence or absence of a carbon monoxide detector; if absent, recommend that one be installed. Finally, check the gas pipe coming into the heater. As with most gas water heaters, there should be a cutoff valve and a dirt leg.

Most gas log manufacturers require their fireplaces to have a gas cutoff valve and a dirt leg. This unit is unvented.

Heat Pumps and Air Conditioners

A heat pump is a unique device. Most heating systems create heat from a burning fuel and then have a blower system or circulator to transfer it to the rest of the building. A heat pump doesn't burn a fuel, it transfers heat from the outside to the inside for heating purposes and then does just the reverse for cooling purposes. Heat-pump efficiencies decline the colder the outside air becomes, which is why most units in cold climates will have electric furnace coils incorporated into the system as emergency backup.

There are two units to check—an indoor unit that's coupled with a forced-air system and an outdoor unit, called a heat exchanger, that also has a blower. In the heat mode, the outdoor unit pulls air across the coils, heat is extracted from the air and transferred to the refrigerant, the

This outside unit is frosted over—note that the heat pump is not working properly.

The heat pump outside unit should be wired with water-tight flexible conduit. Rigid conduit cannot take the vibration and will eventually crack or break.

compressor compresses the refrigerant to extract the heat and sends it into the indoor unit. Which is how you tell if the system is working—one of the two copper lines should be warm after it runs for a while. The fluid goes through the coils of the indoor unit and a blower sends the air to be heated across the hot coils. In the air-conditioning mode, the process is simply reversed.

The outside unit is the most vulnerable, because it has to operate in all kinds of weather. The first thing to note is where the unit is located. It should not be directly in the sun for most of the day, and it should not be placed

directly under the drip edge of a house (without guttering) in freezing climates—the dripping water can freeze the blades to the grill. Sometimes homeowners get carried away with plantings around the unit; make sure that there are no bushes blocking the unit's side air intake for at least 1 ft. and that there are no trees overhanging the unit for at least 5 ft. and no debris falling into its grilled top. Walk around the unit to make sure there is no physical damage—people have been know to run lawn mowers into them. Also check that the unit is mounted level on a concrete slab. The outside unit should be raised at least 6 in. off the ground in moderate snowfall areas and 12 in. in heavy snowfall areas.

Working tests are quick and easy. First, check to see whether the entire outside unit is frosted over. Don't waste your time trying to troubleshoot the problem, simply note that the unit needs servicing. Look down into the grill with the fan off, and observe whether the coils are frosted over; again, make note if they are. When the unit

Heat Pump Checkpoints (in Air-Conditioner Mode)

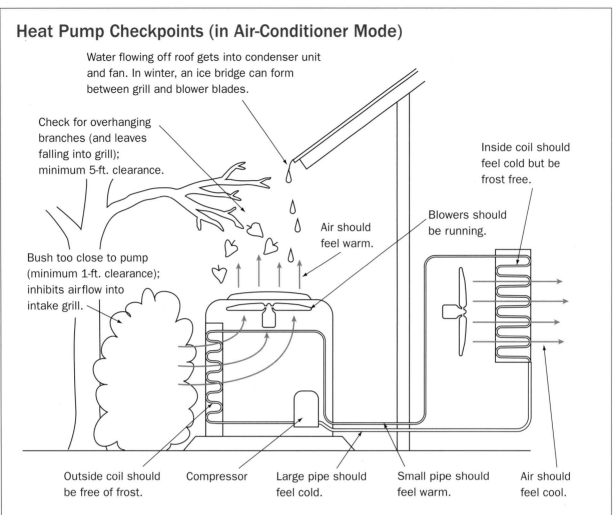

Water flowing off roof gets into condenser unit and fan. In winter, an ice bridge can form between grill and blower blades.

Check for overhanging branches (and leaves falling into grill); minimum 5-ft. clearance.

Inside coil should feel cold but be frost free.

Bush too close to pump (minimum 1-ft. clearance); inhibits airflow into intake grill.

Air should feel warm.

Blowers should be running.

Outside coil should be free of frost.

Compressor

Large pipe should feel cold.

Small pipe should feel warm.

Air should feel cool.

During the heat cycle, the two copper pipes going into the house will feel the same as during air-conditioning, but the functions of the two coils will reverse. The inside coil becomes the condensing coil, taking in cold air and blowing out hot air, and the outside coil becomes the evaporator coil.

turns on, look down into the grill from above—the fan should be turning and blowing air into your face. Check the two copper pipes that run from the outside unit to the inside. In air-conditioner mode, the large insulated copper pipe should feel cold and the small bare copper pipe should be warm. Knowing that the two copper pipes will always have opposite temperatures, you can easily tell if the rest of the system is working.

Also check the electrical hookup. Every modern outside unit needs a manual cutoff switch for maintenance. The switch does not have to be

fused, because its only purpose is to disconnect. However, the amperage of the overcurrent protection in the main panel should match that indicated on the inspection plate of the unit.

The two copper lines from the outside unit continue into the house to the inside unit. Do the same temperature test there, checking that the large pipe is cold and the small one warm. In the cooling mode, the cooling coils will produce condensate (water), which is supposed to drain to an internal pan and follow a small line outside or into a drain with an air gap (see "Cross-

Always look for the heat pump condensate line and trace it to its drain.

Connections" p. 248). Make sure that wherever the condensate drain terminates, there is a 1-in. air gap between the end of the pipe and whatever it drains into (many simply drain outside onto the ground). Condensate drains have a habit of clogging up, which is why some drip pan designs have an auxiliary drain. If used, these should be two independent pipes for their complete run, so that if one clogs up, the other is free to work. These are rarely installed, however. If one pipe is connected to another or if it just sticks up into the air, you can write it up if you want. Whether a trap is required is controversial; however, most systems require a trap if the fan pulls air across the coil.

As you did on the outside unit, look at the coils to see if they are frosted over (write it up if they are) and if the fan is turning. In heat mode, the ultimate check is for heat coming through the registers. In the air-conditioner mode, of course, cool air should be coming from the registers.

One additional check inside the house is the heat pump's backup heat strip. Most heat pumps have backup electrical heating elements that come on when the outside air has gotten too cold for the unit to effectively extract heat from it. To test the heat strip, turn the thermostat up to where it says emergency heat; a tiny light in the thermostat should come on and you should note a dramatic increase of heat coming through the registers. A second check is to watch the utility meter—it should turn considerably faster when the elements are engaged.

Heat Pump Checklist

Outside unit

☐ Unit is not in the direct sun for long periods of time

☐ Unit is not placed under a drip edge without guttering in freezing climates

☐ No physical damage

☐ Unit is mounted secure, level, and above snowfall height

☐ No brush blocking intake

☐ Grill clear of leaves and limbs

☐ Trees not overhanging unit

☐ Cutoff switch present

☐ Overcurrent device matches that recommended on unit's inspection plate

☐ Unit frosted over

☐ Coils frosted over

☐ Fan turns freely when unit is in operation

☐ After the system has been on for at least 15 minutes, there is a cold pipe (the large one) and a warm pipe (the small one)

Inside unit

☐ One pipe warm and the other cold

☐ Auxiliary condensate drain not connected to primary drain

☐ Condensate drain has 1-in. air gap

☐ Frost visible on coils

☐ Fan turns

☐ Backup heat strips work

Most units with compressors have design temperature limits. For example, most manufacturers don't want you to run their units on air-conditioner in the winter or on heater in the summer. Tricking the thermostat to make the unit run when it shouldn't is done at your own risk. Make note that the air-conditioner or heater mode couldn't be tested because of the season.

Packaged Heat Pump Systems

Most heat pump systems are called split systems because they are half in the house and half out. If the entire system is together as one unit, it is called a packaged system. Mounted outside, it connects to the house via two duct systems—one to send air into the house, and the other as a return. Other than checking for physical damage and making sure the ducts are intact, the only check to verify the system is working is to feel the hot or cold air coming out of the registers. Also make sure the unit is level, that the intake grill is relatively clean, and that the grill on top is free of debris.

On a packaged, all-in-one heat pump system, there are no copper lines to check for hot and cold. To test, turn the unit on and see if warm or cold air comes out of the registers.

Geothermal Heating

Also called a ground-source system or a water-to-air heat pump, a geothermal system is a heating and cooling system that uses the energy of the earth to heat a house in winter and cool it in summer. As with all heat pumps, the system simply transfers energy from one place to another. A few feet below the earth's surface, the air and water stay at an almost constant temperature. Using that as a reference point, you can take heat from water, then circulate the cold water back into the ground and let contact with the earth bring the temperature back up again. You can do the same if you make the water hotter—circulate it back into the earth and it goes back to its original temperature. In other words you are using the earth as one gigantic heat sink. Unlike heat pump systems, which have part of the system in the house and part out, the entire geothermal unit is inside. One big advantage geothermal systems have over air-to-air heat pumps is that they provide warmer air in the winter.

Before you test the unit you need some information from the owner. First, is the system open or closed? A closed system recirculates the same water over and over again through one long pipe buried in the ground. If it is closed, did the owners use antifreeze? And, if so, was it a food-grade formula? Ask and look for a notification tag. An open system uses fresh water all the time—such as a pump pulling water in from a pond. Second, whether the system is open or closed, you'll need to know what type of subsystem is in use. For example, an open system could bring water in from a pond or river, run it through the system, then dump it. Make note where the water is dumped. A closed system might have 1,000 ft. of horizontally buried pipe 3 ft. underground or just a few hundred feet going vertically into one or more wells and then back to the heat pump.

Of all the heating/cooling systems, the geothermal may give the inspector the most problems, because it is one of the least common systems. However, the tests are relatively simple, such as a filter that needs to be checked and an inspection tag so you can log the last maintenance check.

Geothermal System Checklist

- ☐ Air filter not clogged
- ☐ Food-grade antifreeze
- ☐ Note where open system dumps its water
- ☐ Inspection tag close by, recording date of last maintenance check
- ☐ Unit gives warm air/cold air (depending on mode) when thermostat is adjusted
- ☐ Water rushing through pipes, air blower on
- ☐ Water on floor (indicating bad heat exchanger or broken water pipe)
- ☐ Gauge temperature differential
- ☐ Flow at 2 gpm per ton minimum

On a geothermal heat pump, check that the incoming and outgoing water lines (the two lines on the right) are not leaking. (Photo courtesy of Geothermal Heat Pump Consortium, Inc.)

The ultimate test, of course, is simply to adjust the thermostat and see what happens. Like air-to-air heat pumps, the output will be warm air, not hot. You can use you hand or insert a temperature probe into the heating register to get the temperature of the air. If the system has been off for a while, let it run 10 to 15 minutes before checking the heat (if the duct is cold it will take a few minutes for the duct to heat up enough to be able to feel warm air coming out the register). While you are waiting, walk over to the heat pump and listen. You should hear the water rushing through the pipes and the air blower should be on. Also look on the floor: If there is water flowing out, either the heat exchanger is cracked or a water line is broken.

Some geothermal systems have temperature gauges in the water lines going into the unit. If gauges are present, compare incoming water temperature to outgoing water temperature. You should note a few degrees difference in temperature between the two. For example, in heat mode you might see that the incoming water temperature is 52°F. The outgoing water temperature would then be 46°F to 50°F, depending on how fast the water is going through the unit. Some units will also have a flowmeter in series with the loop to register the number of gallons per minute (gpm) being pumped through the system. Typically, you want 3 gpm per nominal ton of capacity (with an absolute minimum of 2 gpm).

Like most heat pumps, a water-to-air pump will occasionally incorporate an electric heat strip. To test the heat strip, turn the thermostat up to emergency heat (how this is done depends on the thermostat) or raise it 5°F. You should feel hotter air coming out of the registers, and the utility meter should be turning a lot faster. Be aware that some thermostats have a built-in delay for the heat strips.

Chapter 10

THE KITCHEN, BATHROOM, AND OTHER ROOMS

THE KITCHEN

THE BATHROOM

BEDROOMS AND HALLWAYS

A few years ago I was inspecting a house that never seemed to sell. Once inside, I knew why: The kitchen was a disaster zone. The floor was so wet that the vinyl was bubbling up in front of the kick space under the sink cabinet. I was afraid to look under the sink to see where all the water had come from; the bottom of the cabinet had to be completely rotted out. With more than a little trepidation, I turned on the faucet—and got sprayed for my effort. The water didn't go into the sink but shot straight forward out of a rusted-out spout that had, until then, been patched with epoxy.

All would still have been fine, with only a wet shirt to complain about, but the faucet wouldn't turn off. So I then had to open the under-sink doors to turn off the water. No luck, the doors were glued shut. While using one hand to attempt to divert the spraying water into the sink bowl, I glanced around and saw a mop and bucket within arm's reach. With my free hand, I grabbed the bucket and shoved it down over the faucet so the water spray would be deflected into the sink. But it was only a temporary reprieve. The sink drain was backing up, and before long water would be overflowing onto the kitchen floor. I flew down the basement stairs to look for the main water shutoff valve. It took a while, but I finally found it behind a mountain of boxes ready for the movers.

I turned the valve, but it was a broken old gate valve; the stem had rusted through, and you could turn the valve forever and never it shut off. By this time, water was flowing down the stairs. I went over to the main service panel and searched for the pump breaker. Nothing was marked. In desperation, I threw the main. Eventually, the water stopped, after the water pressure tank had dumped its last 10 gal. onto the kitchen floor. I knew then why there was a mop and a bucket so conveniently near the sink—it had been left by the last inspector.

The kitchen and bath are the two most used—and consequently most abused—rooms in a typical house. Within these rooms, you'll find myriad plumbing, electrical, and mechanical devices, along with rotted cabinet bottoms and warped floors, all of which need to be inspected. In my experience, many inspectors don't do as thorough an inspection in the kitchen and bathroom as they should, either because they don't know what to look for or simply because of the large number of items that must be inspected. This chapter will give you a set procedure not only for inspecting each room but also for inspecting each area within the room, so that all areas get covered equally well.

The Kitchen

For most people, the kitchen is the showpiece of the house. How a kitchen looks and works can often make or break a sale. If the kitchen is not in top operating condition, the new owner will want to know, so it's important not to pass lightly over the kitchen and miss obvious problems. Rather than just walking into the kitchen and haphazardly looking for problems, I use a set system of inspection to make sure I don't overlook anything. I begin at the kitchen sink and work from there.

The kitchen sink

The kitchen sink inspection can be broken down into five separate steps: the faucet, the sink itself, the basket strainer, the drain line, and miscellaneous leaks.

Kitchen faucet The first thing many prospective home buyers do the moment they enter the kitchen is to walk over and turn on the kitchen faucet. The faucet is the heart of the kitchen, and it's where you should begin your inspection. First, observe the finish on the faucet: Is it smooth or pitted with corrosion and losing its finish? Next, swivel the spout left and right. Each kitchen faucet will have some type of swivel joint that is prone to corrode and bind. Feel for a metal-to-metal grind as opposed to a smooth turn.

Put a couple of paper towels under the kitchen sink drain lines (you'll see why in a minute) and turn both the hot and cold faucets on full. Very gently tilt the spout a hair to the side to check for a leak around the spout/base assembly. Observe any leaks around the handles, and, of course, check for a drip from the spout. Was it dripping before you turned it on? Does it drip after you turn it off?

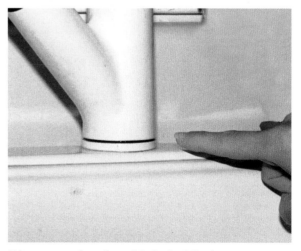

It is common for a faucet to leak at the base as water flows through it.

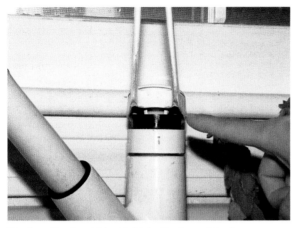

The handle should be tight to the faucet body; it shouldn't flop around or shut itself off, and it shouldn't leak.

The ever-illusive drip—the bane of all faucets, the source of endless frustration to homeowners, and one of the things that keeps plumbers in business.

Weak faucet spray indicates low water pressure throughout the house. If house pressure is satisfactory, the cause might be debris in the diverter valve inside the faucet body. Don't try to fix it; just log it on the report form.

At the head of a faucet/sprayer combo there's a rocker switch; one position is spray and the other is full flow. Test the faucet in both positions with varying water pressure by adjusting the handle.

Check the faucet sprayer (if there is one). It's possible that the sprayer is purely decorative and isn't plumbed to anything. Sometimes the bypass mechanism within the faucet doesn't work. It takes a certain amount of water pressure for it to engage; if the house system doesn't supply the needed pressure, it won't work. Alternatively, if the pressure is minimal, the spray will be weak.

Some newer faucets have a sprayer that uses an extension hose as the sprayer spout. At the head of the spout there's a switch that rocks from front to back to change from full flow to spray. The early versions of this type of faucet have a "machine-gun" problem when switched to spray. The check valve within the faucet or immediately below it vibrates, creating chatter that sounds like an M-16 on full automatic. The faucet will

Kitchen Faucet Checkpoints

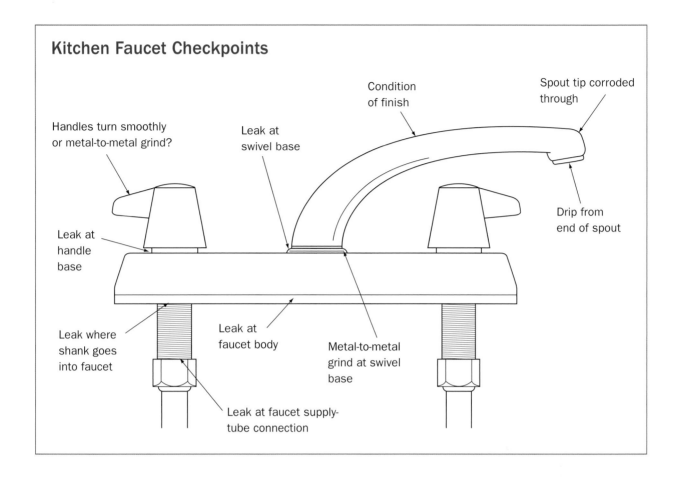

Handles turn smoothly or metal-to-metal grind?

Leak at swivel base

Condition of finish

Spout tip corroded through

Leak at handle base

Drip from end of spout

Leak where shank goes into faucet

Leak at faucet body

Metal-to-metal grind at swivel base

Leak at faucet supply-tube connection

probably not machine-gun in all positions, so vary the water flow with the handle while keeping it in the spray position to check for the noise. (Note that with old-fashioned two-handled faucets, you'll hear a similar sound if the water seal inside the handle gets loose enough to vibrate.)

Check the condition of the handles. How do they feel as you turn them on and off? Is the motion smooth or is there a metal-to-metal grinding, which indicates that the faucet is worn out? One manufacturer designed all its two-handled faucets (kitchen, lavatory, and tub) with a weak "stop" position. That is, the little plastic piece that stops the handle would easily break if the handle was turned a little too far. You'll know this faucet design if you come to it—the water will turn on and off, but the handle turns in a never-ending circle. Write it up.

Observe the water flow out of the spout. Acid water can corrode the end of a metal spout within a few years. Instead of making a 90-degree turn and flowing into the sink, some of the water sprays straight ahead out of a hole in the end of the spout. Don't worry about overlooking this defect; your shirt will be wet. A close inspection of the spout end might show where someone tried to use epoxy, silicon, or even tape (I've seen them all) to try to cover the hole. Also note whether the water flow is good; if not, unscrew the aerator to see if it is filled with debris. Check the relative water flow on the cold and hot side. It's possible that either one has pipes or valves that are corroded and filled with rust, causing lower flow in one line than the other.

Turn the water on and off fast—and listen. What you are listening for is "water hammer,"

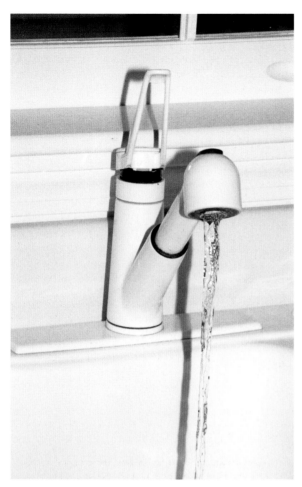

Check the water flow on the hot and cold side. A single-handled faucet will need to be on and positioned dead center to allow both hot and cold to work.

Kitchen Faucet Checklist

- ☐ Faucet finish not corroded
- ☐ Spout and handles swivel without grinding metal
- ☐ No leaks around handles and spout
- ☐ Sprayer works, has sufficient pressure, doesn't machine-gun
- ☐ Good flow of water from spout
- ☐ No water hammer
- ☐ Pressure not significantly reduced by lavatory sink running or toilet flushing
- ☐ Faucet not leaking under sink

which occurs when water flows rapidly in one direction and then smashes into the pipes when the faucet turns off. This happens only in very fast-closing valves and in metal pipes, like galvanized or copper. If you hear it, write it up. Water hammer is not only annoying but also damaging to the pipes.

With the water running, turn on another faucet in the house to determine if there is a significant (half or more) loss of water pressure and volume in the kitchen faucet. This is usually the result of having installed water lines that have too small of a diameter (½ in. or less) throughout the house. If this problem exists, the new owners will either have to live with the low flow or replace all the small-diameter water lines with ¾-in. pipe—an expensive proposition.

The final faucet check is done under the sink. With the water still running, check to see if the faucet is leaking water through its body and dripping under the sink. Because the water will run down the supply tubes and drip from the lowest point, it will look as though the leak were coming from somewhere else (like a supply valve). Always check for the source of leaks higher than where you see the drip. To find the source, follow the moisture up until there is no more wetness.

Kitchen sink After the faucet, the next check is the kitchen sink itself. First, observe the condition of the sink. Different types of sinks deteriorate in different ways. For example, an enamel-on-steel sink can have its enamel break off in large sections or in small chips. Stainless-steel sinks will stain (regardless of what the manufacturers will have you believe), especially the cheap ones, which also have a habit of denting because the metal is thin. Cast-iron sinks can lose their coating—especially if a hot pan is put in a cold sink. Make note of any major cracks or chips in the sink, but don't worry about

Whatever the material (this one is stainless steel), check all sinks for damage such as dents, chips, gouges, loss of coating, and discoloration.

hairline cracks, which may be visible but don't leak. Also, check that the sink is firmly attached and not leaking around the edges.

Basket strainer Along with the problems of cheap sinks come the problems of cheap basket strainers. A really good strainer can cost more than the sink itself, so it's no wonder that few get installed. Cheap strainers leak under the sink where the strainer lock nut tightens against the bowl. Sometimes the problem is the strainer itself, other times it's the sealant that's at fault. The plumber's putty, which is supposed to provide a watertight seal, has hardened and cracked. In addition, on some all-plastic strainers you simply can't get the nut tight enough to seal properly.

To check for leaks, insert the strainer baskets and fill both bowls half-full with water—then check under the sink. Open the doors under the sink and run your finger along the circular rubber seals where the bowls of the strainers go through the sinks; if one of them is wet, there's a leak. While you have water in the sinks, check to see if the strainer baskets keep the water in the sink bowls.

Drain line After checking the baskets, remove the strainers and let all the water out of both bowls. Again, you are checking several things at

Strainers are prone to leak. They're invariably installed with plumber's putty, which hardens and cracks. The plastic ones seem more prone to leaks than the metal ones; and, not surprisingly, high-quality metal strainers, like this one, tend to leak less than bottom-line units.

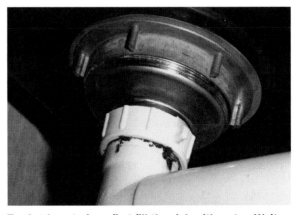

To check a strainer, first fill the sink with water. Wait a few minutes, and then check under the sink to see if any water is coming through where the large flange seals against the bottom of the bowl.

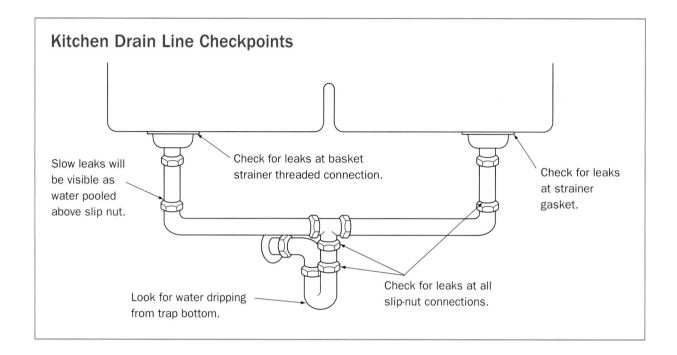

Kitchen Drain Line Checkpoints

Slow leaks will be visible as water pooled above slip nut.

Check for leaks at basket strainer threaded connection.

Check for leaks at strainer gasket.

Look for water dripping from trap bottom.

Check for leaks at all slip-nut connections.

once. The first check is the most obvious—how fast the sinks drain. The water should drain within a minute or less. If it drains slowly (or not at all), there's a blockage in the trap or drain line. The most common reason for a slow kitchen drain is that there's not enough slope in the drain line. Today's pipe, made from plastic, will soften as hot water travels slowly down the drain line. If the pipe supports are too far apart (and most are, even if they follow the code), the pipe will start to bend down between supports. The food debris in the kitchen drain water will settle in the low spots, eventually causing the water to back up and filling the entire pipe full of debris. A test for this is to rap the pipe bottom with something heavy (like a pair of lineman's pliers). If the pipe is full, you'll hear a dull, thud as opposed to a hollow sound.

If there's a problem with the slope, it gets worse if the drain pipe is too small—by which I mean 1¼-in. or 1½-in. pipe. Although both sizes are allowed by code in most areas, a 2-in. pipe would be a better standard, judging by the number of pipes I've seen fill up with debris.

As the water flows down the drain, the next check is to listen for a *glug, glug, glug* sound,

indicating that there are air bubbles coming up the line. This is a vent problem or, more often than not, both a vent problem and a partial drain line (or main sewer) blockage problem. When you did your exterior inspection, you should have seen a kitchen vent protruding through the roof. If so, was there anything clogging the end of the vent? If not, was there a kitchen vent in the attic tapping into the main vent? (Also acceptable is an automatic or mechanical vent underneath the kitchen sink immediately behind the trap.) If a 1¼-in. or 1½-in. drain line is more than 8 ft. from a larger pipe and there is no obvious vent, write it up as an area of concern.

Check for leaks in the drain line under the sink. Serious leaks will be obvious. To check for slower leaks, feel for any dampness in the paper towels that you put under the pipes when you were inspecting the faucet. The most common leak area is at the slip connections in the thin-wall pipe under the sink (see the drawing above). If there's a dishwasher, run the dishwasher and verify that there's no leak where its discharge pipe connects to the under-sink drain line.

Miscellaneous leaks Not all water leaks under the sink come from the drain lines. Other things that can leak include the water pressure lines, the supply-tube valve handle, the supply tube-to-valve connection, and the supply tube-to-faucet connection. I had one service call where I spotted a large pool of water on an unfinished basement floor. Looking up I could see where water was traveling along an overhead wall for about 20 ft. I went upstairs and found the hidden leak—a dripping valve handle under the kitchen sink.

The trouble with under-sink valves (also known as "stops") is that they tend to leak once adjusted, which is why I don't recommend that an inspector turn on a valve. If you must (for example, to pressurize the lines or an appliance for testing), be sure to turn the valve back off and to check constantly for leaks around the handle–valve body interface while you're in the kitchen.

Kitchen countertop

There are many different types of countertops, but the inspection is basically the same regardless of material. All you need to do is check for the obvious—is the countertop coming apart or is it in good condition? Gaps between the sink lip and the countertop are common, but one area that's often overlooked is the section of countertop between the back of the sink and the wall. This area can rot because of leaky faucets and bad countertop design. Some designs allow water to pool right behind the faucet. If this happens and the water gets into the wood under the laminate or tile, the wood will rot. Pressed board is especially vulnerable to rot, because it absorbs water like a sponge. The test is easy—press down on the wood to see if it is spongy, or gently lift the spout and see if the entire countertop moves with it. One other thing to look for is large, round discolored areas on the countertop, which indicate that hot pots have been set on a counter that cannot take excessive heat.

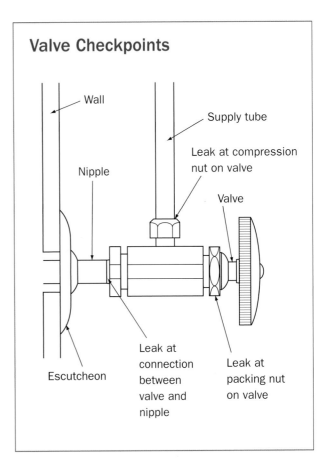

Valve Checkpoints

Wall

Supply tube

Leak at compression nut on valve

Nipple

Valve

Escutcheon

Leak at connection between valve and nipple

Leak at packing nut on valve

Kitchen Sink, Counter, and Cabinets Checklist

- ☐ Sink in good condition and securely attached
- ☐ Basket strainers hold water and are not leaking under the sink
- ☐ Sink drains reasonably fast with no gurgling
- ☐ Under-sink drains not leaking
- ☐ No leaks from under-sink water lines and valves
- ☐ Kitchen counter, cabinets, and floor in good condition

Kitchen cabinets and floor

Check kitchen cabinets for broken, warped, or ill-fitting doors and for missing knobs. I usually pull out and close a couple of drawers to verify that they don't bind and that their slider mechanisms are still intact. Never underestimate the ability of some people to cut corners. I inspected one house in which the builder, a do-it-yourselfer, made the kitchen cabinets so narrow that a single dinner plate couldn't lie flat within the cabinet.

Obviously, the under-sink cabinet and adjacent cabinets are the most prone to water damage from leaky pipes, so pay particular attention to them. Water can damage the kitchen floor as well as the cabinets. Look for sagging areas immediately under the sink cabinet and around the refrigerator and dishwasher, where slow leaks may have been rotting the flooring for years.

Kitchen electrical system

In many homes, there are more receptacles and switches in the kitchen than in any other room. To further complicate matters, the kitchen also has more circuits than any other room. Most people are aware that the kitchen needs two small appliance circuits along the countertop and that the rest of the general-purpose receptacles in the

kitchen and dining area can share those circuits. However, this applies only to newer homes; older homes may have only one kitchen circuit. Rather than trying to determine the year the house was built and whether it should or should not have two kitchen circuits, simply note what it does have and go on with the next inspection.

To find out whether a kitchen has one or two circuits, first check the service panel, which should list the number of kitchen circuits. If nothing is listed, or if you don't trust what's written on the panel, you can easily tell by throwing circuit breakers and seeing which receptacles lose power (try the GFCI breakers first). Rather than wasting time continually walking back and forth from panel to kitchen, one fast-and-easy method is to plug a radio into the countertop circuits, turn it up loud, and throw the breakers off and back on one by one. As soon as the music stops, leave that breaker off and go back into the kitchen and see if any of the countertop receptacles still have power. If any do, you have two circuits. Throw the breaker back on.

Don't be fooled into thinking that there are two kitchen circuits simply because there are two GFCI receptacles along the kitchen counter. The installer could have wired both receptacles from

Make sure the cabinet doors open and close properly; don't forget to check the shelves inside.

One GFCI for Kitchen and Bath

It's possible that, to save a little money, the person who wired the house used one GFCI to power both the kitchen countertop receptacles *and* the bathroom receptacles. Check this out when you're inspecting the kitchen. If the bath receptacles lose their power when you're testing the kitchen receptacles, this is the problem. A single GFCI for the receptacles in both the kitchen and bath was never allowed, and it needs to be brought to the attention of the buyer.

Receptacles come in several different styles in the kitchen. This one is ungrounded and should be written up.

one feeder. The only way to really tell is to start throwing breakers.

Countertop receptacles There are four scenarios you might come across when inspecting the kitchen receptacles. First, the old-fashioned two-prong ungrounded receptacles, which will be common in older homes. There's nothing to worry about with these receptacles, because they are grandfathered in because of their age. However, the new owners need to know they are ungrounded in case they have a lot of modern grounded appliances that they want to plug in. Simply note on the report, "Kitchen receptacles: 2-prong, ungrounded."

The second scenario is the common duplex three-prong grounded receptacle. If these are wired properly, there's nothing to find fault with, but be sure the grounding part is not an illusion. A favorite trick of do-it-yourselfers is to leave old ungrounded cable in the wall to feed the old ungrounded receptacles and then to bring in a new grounded cable to feed the new grounded receptacles. If the installer left it at that, there might not be a problem—you can see which receptacles are grounded and which are not by the number of prongs they have. But some installers remove the old ungrounded receptacles and install three-prong grounded ones, without

rewiring. Write this up. You are not allowed to have an ungrounded cable terminating in a grounded receptacle (unless the ungrounded cable has ground-fault protection; see below). This problem will be found when you use your plug-in checker (see p. 14)—the ungrounded indicator light will come on.

There is a further complication: If the installer has run a "bootleg ground" from the ground terminal of the receptacle to the neutral terminal, the plug-in checker won't detect it (see the photo on p. 214). Other than visual inspection, the only way a bootleg ground can be found is if the inspector uses a special plug-analyzer checker called a SureTest Digital Circuit Analyzer (see p. 14). In this case, its display will glow "FG" for false ground.

The third kitchen receptacle scenario is the common duplex three-prong receptacle fed by a ground-fault breaker. As with the previous scenario, check that the three-prong receptacles are

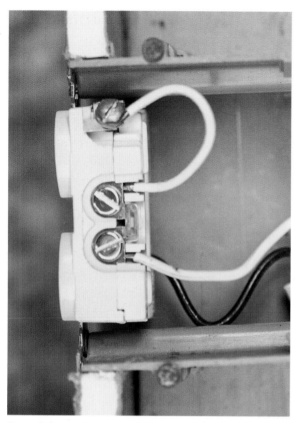

Sometimes an installer will jump a wire from the neutral to the ground (known as a "bootleg" ground) in an attempt to fool the tester into thinking the receptacle is grounded. The standard three-bulb tester does not pick this up, but the SureTest analyzer will indicate "false ground."

really grounded. To verify that the ground-fault protection system works, use the button on your tester to simulate a ground fault. You should hear a loud click as the reset button on the GFCI breaker pops out. If you don't hear the click, make note of it on your report.

The fourth scenario is GFCI receptacles in the kitchen. Here the power is brought into the line terminals of the ground-fault receptacle. All other countertop receptacles feed off the load terminals to obtain ground-fault protection. In older houses, you might still find ungrounded receptacles along the countertop feeding off the GFCI receptacle; this is okay. In fact, GFCI receptacles are allowed to feed (off their load terminals)

ungrounded three-prong receptacles, as long as the receptacles are labeled ungrounded and GFCI protected.

It's important to verify that any ground fault receptacles along the countertop are working properly. Insert the GFCI plug-in tester into the receptacle and push the tester's test button. The GFCI should trip. Once tripped, note how many receptacles are not working. Find the second GFCI that protects the kitchen counter appliances and check it as well with the tester. Verify the additional number of receptacles that lost power. There should be no receptacle on the counter that has power if the house was built under the newest codes. If the protected receptacle doesn't lose its power, the GFCI protection circuitry is not working. This happens more often than you might think; make note of it.

Kitchen wall circuits Almost all major kitchen appliances are required to be grounded by the manufacturer—there is no grandfather clause. Pay particular attention to a refrigerator plugged into a kitchen wall circuit. In an attempt to ground the appliance, the owners may be using a cheater plug. Such items normally do not ground, they simply allow one to plug in the appliance without first breaking off its ground lug. This is an instant write up. If the receptacle is a two prong and there is no cheater plug, someone has broken the ground lug off the refrigerator plug (otherwise it wouldn't fit in the outlet); write it up. If the outlet is a three prong, use an analyzer and verify that it is grounded.

Normally, the refrigerator shouldn't be on a GFCI circuit. Code does not prohibit it, nor does it suggest it, common sense simply tells you it shouldn't be. GFCIs are sensitive and sometimes trip when they shouldn't; no one wants to lose an entire refrigerator full of food because of a tripped ground fault.

The refrigerator outlet may be the only wall outlet in the kitchen. If there are others—for example, for a clock, gas range, and garbage disposal—use the SureTest analyzer and verify that they are wired correctly. However, use the same

This refrigerator plug is a perfect example of why cheater plugs should not be used. The grounding clip on the cheater plug has broken off and the weight of the cord is pulling the plug out of the wall, exposing the hot and neutral conductors. In addition, you are not supposed to operate the appliance ungrounded—the adapter only allows the appliance to be plugged in; it does not ground it.

Kitchen and Dining Room Overcurrent Protection

The breaker or fuse protecting the kitchen and dining area circuits should be 20 amps. Although 15-amp protection is not necessarily wrong if the wiring is pre-code and the wire is 14 gauge, the new owners need to know that they may have problems if they load the circuit up with new appliances. For example, a 15-amp circuit cannot hold a toaster and a large microwave at the same time without popping the breaker.

The problem you typically encounter in the kitchen is not underfusing but overfusing. As the house gained more appliances, more current was needed to power them. Eventually, the fuses blew. Rather than run new circuits to split up the load, the owners increased the size of the fuse to 30 amps. Most old houses will have 30-amp fuses in all the kitchen circuits, even though they were designed for only 15 amps or 20 amps. This is a fire hazard, and it is vitally important for the inspector to find these overfused circuits and note them on the report.

grounding logic as with the refrigerator: If the appliance has a grounded plug, the appliance must be grounded—no exceptions.

Kitchen lighting circuits There needs to be some type of switched lighting in the kitchen and dining area; check that the switch and light are working properly. If there is more than one entrance, the lighting could, but doesn't have to be, on a three-way or four-way switching circuit.

In today's kitchens, the lighting is not supposed to be on the same circuit as the kitchen/dining receptacles. If the house is new and you want an easy way to verify this, simply throw the

two breakers that go to the kitchen/dining receptacles. Then check the kitchen/dining lights to see if they still work. If they don't, the electrician has wired the two together; this is not allowed. This happens very easily because the light switch and receptacle are sometimes in the same above-counter box. It's much easier for an electrician to power the switch with a little jumper from the receptacle hot leg than to bring in a new feeder—I know, I've been tempted.

Don't take logical switching for granted: by that I mean having a switch that controls the

A GFCI Primer

It's common knowledge that GFCI means "ground-fault circuit interrupter" and that circuits that use these devices, whether circuit-breaker type or receptacle type, are considered ground-fault protected. It's also commonly known that if you have a tool plugged into a GFCI circuit and the tool malfunctions while you're standing on a wet floor or lawn, you won't be electrocuted. This is all well and true—but there's a little more to it than that.

For example, most people don't realize that a GFCI doesn't need a ground connection to work. GFCIs were developed to provide protection from ground faults (hot wire shorting through you to the earth). They do this by comparing outgoing current to incoming current: The current going to the load via the hot wire must be equal to the current coming back from the load via the neutral. If the two currents are unequal, then the missing current must be going somewhere—probably through you to ground. Once the GFCI detects this it will immediately open the circuit. Thus the outlet will lose its electrical power. So why the ground connection on the receptacle GFCI if it isn't needed? To provide the same protection that all grounded receptacles do—to place the frame of the appliance at ground or zero-volt potential.

Another fact that many people (including some inspectors) aren't aware of is that it is possible to be using a GFCI receptacle and still be electrocuted. If you are standing on an insulator (such as a dry wood floor) so that the sensing device within the ground-fault receptacle or breaker cannot sense any current going to ground, the unit will not trip. If the current that goes through you returns to the neutral circuit, the hot current through the sensing device will equal the neutral current coming back. As long as the two are equal, the device won't trip.

Ground-fault devices come in two different configurations. The first looks like a breaker with a test button and is located in the service panel. The more common ground-fault device looks like a receptacle with two buttons: test and reset. The latter device has a history of a short life span in many locales.

GFCI breakers must be wired properly. When making the initial check in the panel make sure the circuit neutral is connected to the breaker, not the panel (where a neutral normally goes). Also verify that the wire gauge to the breaker matches the overcurrent protection—14-gauge for 15 amps, 12-gauge for 20 amps. Unfortunately, there is no way to check the proper wiring of a GFCI receptacle. Although common errors like reversed polarity and perhaps a missing wire will show up on the bulb indicators of the plug-in tester, the most important problem—reversed line and load (backward wiring)—will not. Aware of this problem, manufacturers now produce GFCI receptacles that won't work if they're wired backward.

Unless someone recently installed them, older houses won't have any GFCI protection, because such protection did not exist when the house was built. In addition, codes are constantly evolving for this concern. For many years, ground-fault protection was required only on receptacles within 6 ft. of the sink. Now, ground-fault protection is required on all receptacles along the countertop in new houses. The inspector's job is simply to note if the GFCIs exist and if they are in working condition, noting whether they are providing their life-saving protection.

How a GFCI Receptacle Works

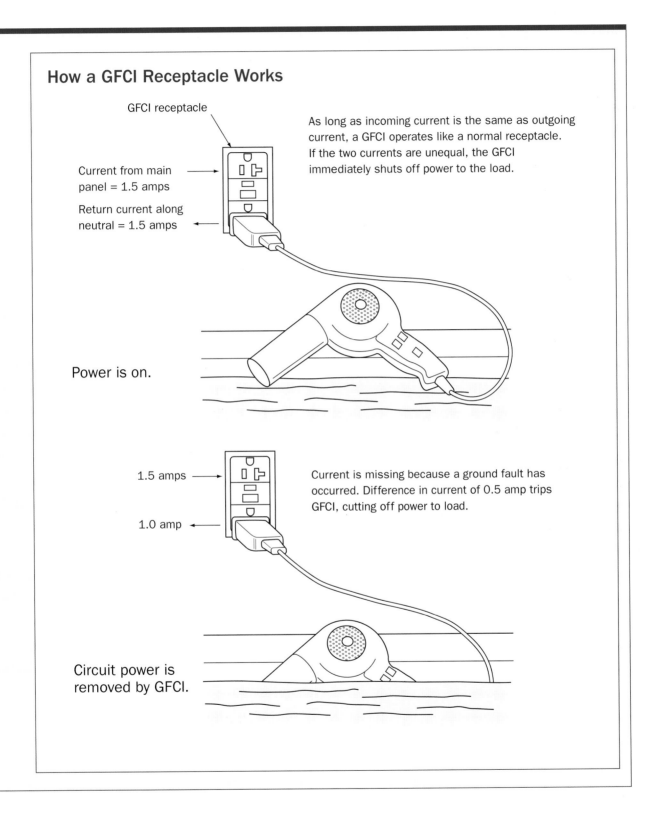

GFCI receptacle

Current from main
panel = 1.5 amps

Return current along
neutral = 1.5 amps

As long as incoming current is the same as outgoing
current, a GFCI operates like a normal receptacle.
If the two currents are unequal, the GFCI
immediately shuts off power to the load.

Power is on.

1.5 amps

1.0 amp

Current is missing because a ground fault has
occurred. Difference in current of 0.5 amp trips
GFCI, cutting off power to load.

Circuit power is
removed by GFCI.

Checking Three- and Four-Way Switching Circuits

If the house you're inspecting has three- (or four-) way switching circuits, you must verify that they work. It takes three (or four) throws of the switch to do this.

Checking a Three-Way Switch

1. Assuming the light is off, throw one switch. The light should go on. Leave the switch in the on position. The light should be a steady glow, not intermittent. If it goes dim and bright, make note of it. The problem could be caused by a number things, including a bad switch, a bad splice, a bad light receptacle, or a loose bulb.

2. Throw the other switch. The light should go off.

3. Throw the first switch again and it should go back on.

Checking a Four-Way Switch

1. Perform the same test as for the three-way switch.

2. Throw the four-way switch. The light should do the opposite of whatever it was doing before the switch was thrown. If the breaker kicks, the light is wired incorrectly.

lights in a logical place. One house I inspected had the overhead dining room light controlled by a switch in the bedroom. If the house you're inspecting has such an illogical setup, make note of it. The new owner will either have to put up with it or have pay to have it rewired. In any case, the new owner should know about it ahead of time.

Problems always arise when the electrician installs a four-gang (or more) switch; no one seems to remember which switch is which. Mark this on your report. Draw a four-gang switch and

above each switch indicate what it controls. The new owner will appreciate it. But don't spend a lot of time hunting down what controls what—if it isn't obvious, write it up.

If the kitchen has under-cabinet lighting, check it as well. If it doesn't come on, check for individual switches on the lights themselves that may be in the circuit. There may also be over-sink lighting to check.

Kitchen appliances

Some inspection companies include a check of kitchen appliances as part of their standard inspection; others do not. If you are inspecting appliances, here's what to look for.

Garbage disposal Check the disposal by throwing the switch on with water flowing through the disposal. If the disposal hums as opposed to making the usual grinding noise, it's locked. Don't bother to unlock it, just write it up. If the disposal makes a loud squealing noise the bearings are going out; a metallic banging sound could mean that an eating utensil is caught in the disposal. If the disposal doesn't work at all, the overload has probably kicked out; don't reset it, just write it up.

Dishwasher The dishwasher should have been checked for leaks earlier when you were testing for under-sink leaks. Make sure water is getting into the unit (you should hear it pump out any residual water and start filling), that it fills and shuts off, and that it discharges water. Also check for leaks around the door seal (water will be dripping around the door).

Stove The stove may or may not stay with the building when the house is sold. If you need to check the stove, simply turn the switches on and verify that all elements (or gas burners) are working. I normally don't worry about the clock and timer switch. I do note whether the stove is a three- or four-wire appliance in case the buyer wants to upgrade to the new codes. Since 1996, it has been required that one remove the stove's frame from the neutral return and ground it like

Verify that the fan and light above the stove work and that the housing is securely attached. On this stove fan, the screws for the housing have pulled loose on the right side.

most appliances. If you're inspecting a gas stove, check for leaks around the fittings with a gas sniffer (if you have access to the gas line).

Above the stove, there should be a light and fan housing. Verify that both fan and light work by turning on the switches on the front of the fan housing. Also make sure that the housing is firmly attached. If the fan uses a carbon filter, check that it is not clogged with grease.

Refrigerator Typically, the refrigerator stays with the house when the sellers move. Obvious checks are to verify that the inside is cold and that the freezer freezes. (You may have to turn the breaker on for the fridge if the seller has shut off the power.) A not-so-obvious thing to check is the seal around the door. To check for a tight seal, put a lighted flashlight inside the fridge. If you can see the light through the seal, the seal is bad.

Other appliances Portable microwaves will likely leave with the seller, but large built-in units typically stay. Check that the microwave works by boiling a cup of water. If the kitchen has instant hot and/or cold water appliances, check them simply by using them. Note the handles: They have a nasty habit of gumming up and sticking. If these appliances are unplugged under the sink, I would advise asking before you plug them back

Kitchen/Dining Room Electrical Checklist

- [ ] Check number of circuits
- [ ] GFCI protection present and working
- [ ] Grounds present on three-prong receptacles
- [ ] Receptacles fed from GFCIs are labeled "GFCI protected"
- [ ] Adequate number of receptacles on counter and around room
- [ ] No overfusing at panel
- [ ] Lighting and switching works
- [ ] Lighting not on receptacle circuit on new houses
- [ ] Logical placement of switches

in—they might be unplugged for a reason other than just saving electricity.

Two other appliances you might also find in the kitchen are a washing machine and clothes dryer. Detailed inspections for these two appliances can be found in chapter 8.

The Bathroom

In a typical bathroom inspection, the inspector will check the toilet, the sink, and the tub/shower. Although the condition and proper operation of these three fixtures are key parts of a functioning bathroom, it's equally important to check for signs of moisture damage.

Moisture damage

Obvious moisture damage and the general condition of the bath are the first things I note when I enter the bathroom. Look for streaks down the paint where water has run after condensing on the walls. Peeling wallpaper or wet drywall is another sign of excess moisture. Taken to its extreme, the walls and ceilings will be rotted through.

The most common causes of moisture damage in a bathroom are not having an exhaust fan in the room, having too small a fan, or not using the fan. Most code jurisdictions do not require a fan if there is an operable window in the room—something that doesn't make a lot of sense given that no one's going to open a window to vent the moisture out of a steamy bathroom in the middle of winter. Many fans don't get used because the contractor installed a cheap model that makes so much noise the owners can't stand to run it. Turn the fan on when you go in the bathroom; if it's unusually loud—like the metal-to-metal sound of bad bearings—write it up. And if there is no fan, simply write "no fan" on the report form.

If there is a fan or light in the shower or tub enclosure, it has to be GFCI protected. Press the test button on the bath GFCI and throw any GFCI breakers. If the fan still works, write it up. The fan also needs to be listed for wet enclosures, but there is no way to check for that unless you remove the cover and look inside.

Some baths have a moisture problem even with a fan installed; this is invariably because the fan is too small for the size of bathroom it's trying to ventilate. If the fan is on but moisture is running down the mirror in little rivers, the fan is either too small or its discharge pipe is blocked.

If possible, try to locate where the fan exhaust discharges from the house—it should discharge through ductwork to the exterior. I know of one contractor who always cheats on the bathroom fan installation. If I want to know if that contractor built the house I'm inspecting, all I have to do is to open the fan cover and see where it exhausts to. If it goes nowhere, I know he built

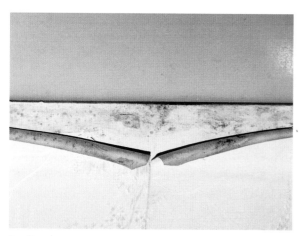

Peeling wallpaper is a sure sign of excessive moisture in the bathroom. Check that there's an exhaust fan installed and that it runs.

Every bathroom without a window that can be opened is required to have an exhaust fan. The cover for this one is missing.

the house. He has the habit of leaving out the ductwork and burying the fan housing under several layers of attic insulation. When the fan is turned on, it hums like a normal fan—but it blows out no moisture, no air—nothing. On one job I inspected, the contractor sent the moist exhaust air between the two overhead joists where the unit's exhaust port came out, causing condensation problems in the attic.

Another possible source of moisture damage in the bathroom is water getting in around the tub/shower faucet. If the plumber didn't make a watertight seal around the faucet handles and spout that protrude through the tub or shower wall, the drywall behind it will rot. Many times the problem is so severe that the tile around the faucet handles is falling off the wall, because the drywall it was glued to has rotted away. Make sure you check this area carefully, because it is a common problem and is expensive for the new owner to repair. In tiled tub/showers, also check for cracked and missing grout between tiles and grout that is stained with mildew.

Some of the worst moisture damage I've seen in bathrooms is at the tub and floor interface. Water comes around the shower curtain or door and flows right onto the floor. If the floor covering extends under the tub, there shouldn't be a problem, but some contractors stop the vinyl at the edge of the tub. This allows the water that leaks around the curtain or shower door to get to the wood floor underneath, and the rot begins. With your foot, press hard on the floor adjacent to the tub to see if it deflects downward, indicating rot underneath.

Another sign of excessive moisture in a bathroom is corrosion of metal fixtures. Baseboard heaters are especially prone to rust, and hanging light fixtures come in second. Look closely at the fixture's surface for pitting and corrosion. Some lights are made so cheaply nowadays that even a small amount of moisture can ruin them.

Check for gaps around the faucets in the tub/shower, which allow water to pour into the openings and rot the drywall behind. It's unlikely that you'll find many examples worse than this one.

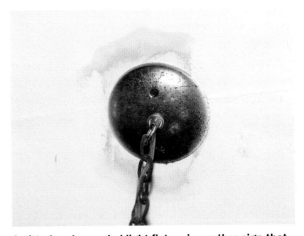

A pitted and corroded light fixture is another sign that there is excess moisture in the bathroom.

Checking for tub/shower leaks

To check for leaks in the supply pipes to the tub/shower faucets, first look for the plumbing access panel, which should be mounted in the wall immediately behind the faucet handles. If there is no access panel, make a note of it on the report: Whoever owns the house when the faucet needs replacing will have to pay to have the wall torn apart to get to the pipes. Open the panel, turn on the tub faucet, and look for water drips and signs

A split oak toilet seat is a common problem.

of water damage. Run the shower and check for any water dripping from above. This is also a good time to check for leaks around the shower door seals.

Be sure to check that the shower-head support is not loose. The shower head screws into a special angled chrome pipe, which in turn screws into an adapter called a winged elbow. Some do-it-yourselfers don't know how to use a winged elbow and let the angled connection float in the wall, which means the shower head is not secure. At best, this makes for loose connections and at worst you can actually break a pipe. I make sure that the owners know that the only way to correct the problem is to rip out the wall behind it, mount a board inside the wall immediately behind where the shower head pipe enters the wall (across the back from stud to stud), and then mount the winged elbow to it.

Inspecting the toilet

The toilet will need more than the cursory glance that many inspectors give it. First, check for cracks or breaks in the tank and bowl. The crack might be hairline or a major break—both should be written up, because the new owner needs to know that the unit could break or start leaking at

Always check the water level in the toilet tank. This one is up to the overflow tube and has been overflow-ing for some time, judging by the level of the dark stain inside the tank.

any time. Also check for cracks in the toilet lid and seat. Then look closely at the toilet shutoff valve and supply tube for any signs of a slow leak. Don't confuse moisture condensation on the pipes and tank with a leak. Wipe away the water and check again.

One of the most common problems is a toilet that runs, meaning that the water doesn't shut off completely after it has filled the tank. Take the lid off the tank and check to see if the water is up to the overflow tube, which indicates that the refill mechanism isn't cutting off. While you have the tank lid off—listen. Many times, if the water

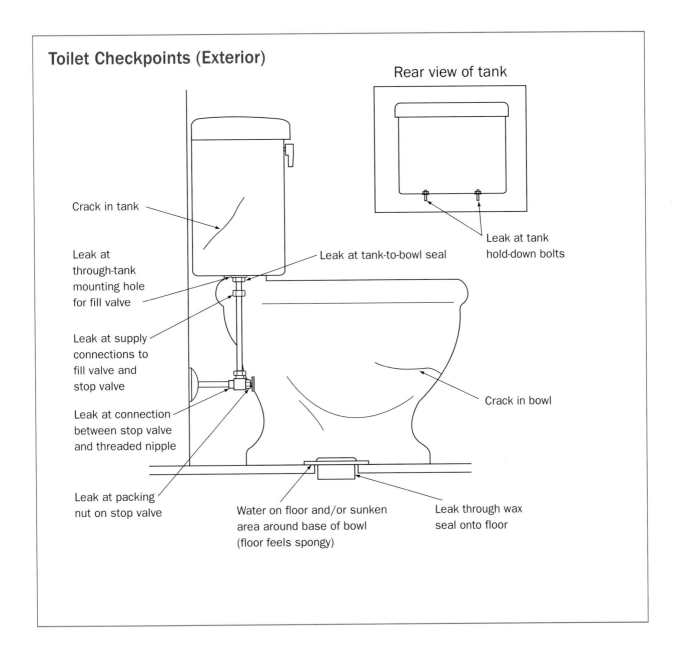

Toilet Checkpoints (Exterior)

Rear view of tank

Crack in tank

Leak at through-tank mounting hole for fill valve

Leak at supply connections to fill valve and stop valve

Leak at connection between stop valve and threaded nipple

Leak at packing nut on stop valve

Leak at tank-to-bowl seal

Leak at tank hold-down bolts

Crack in bowl

Water on floor and/or sunken area around base of bowl (floor feels spongy)

Leak through wax seal onto floor

release seal is leaking, you can hear the water flowing out from under the rubber seal. If in doubt, you can put food coloring in the tank and see if any bleeds through into the bowl.

Next, press the handle down to verify that the toilet flushes properly. Once all the water has left the tank, watch and listen as the tank and bowl refill. It should be reasonably quiet—not sound like a machine gun or a high-pitched scream— and the tank and bowl should fill reasonably fast.

If there is a red, slimy coating over everything within the tank, this is iron bacteria; make note of this because it clogs and stains the plumbing. Replace the tank lid gently—porcelain breaks easily.

Check how secure the toilet base is to the floor. Gently try to move the toilet side to side to verify that it's tight against the floor (loose toilets leak sewer gas—do you smell anything in the room?). When you flushed the toilet did you see water

The Problem with S-Traps

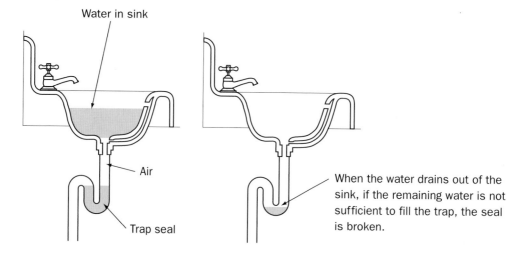

Water in sink

Air

Trap seal

When the water drains out of the sink, if the remaining water is not sufficient to fill the trap, the seal is broken.

S-traps are no longer allowed because water can drain too forcefully, pushing and pulling the trap dry. The loss of the water seal allows sewer gases to backflow into the house.

run out from the toilet base onto the floor, which indicates a bad seal? If the toilet rocks, it could mean the bolts are not tight, the flange is broken, or the floor is rotted. Check to see if the floor is spongy around the toilet from all the leaks, indicating that the floor has rotted out.

If there's water on the floor behind the toilet it doesn't necessarily mean that the bowl is leaking around the wax seal. By far the most common source of water around the toilet is condensation. This alone is sometimes enough to rot the floor. Another couple of potential leak sources are at the tank itself: at the tank hold-down bolts and at the tank-to-bowl seal. If the leak is at the former location, you'll see water dripping from the bolt threads under the tank. (If you think the drip of water on the bolts might be condensation, put some food coloring in the tank and see if the drip changes color.) If the leak is at the tank-to-bowl seal, you'll see water pooling at the back of the bowl shelf.

The lavatory sink

The lavatory sink, or vanity, will need to go through the same thorough inspection that you gave the kitchen sink (see p. 205): faucet, drain, and water-line leaks; countertop; rotted out cabinet; and so on. Verify that the stopper works, that the sink can hold water, and that the sink drains reasonably fast. One of the most common problems you'll encounter in older bathrooms will be S-traps used in lieu of P-traps. The former are no longer allowed because of their tendency to siphon and allow sewer gas to enter the house. Although they don't need to be replaced in older houses, the inspector must list that an S-trap exists. If the house is new, I always write it up— the S-trap should not have passed code.

If there's a wall-hung sink in the bathroom, you need to check that it's tight to the wall. Wall hungs tend to pull away from the wall if they are not securely fastened to the interior framing. As a

S-traps are not allowed in new housing, but they can be grandfathered into old houses. The inspector should, however, make note on the form that the S-trap is in place so the buyer will not be surprised by the odor of sewer gas in the room.

Wall-hung sinks have a tendency to pull away from the wall, causing the front of the sink to tilt down lower than the back.

Bathroom Checklist

- [ ] No moisture damage to room or metal fixtures
- [ ] Exhaust fan works and is not noisy
- [ ] Fan discharge exits house
- [ ] Tiles secure to walls
- [ ] Missing, mildew-stained, or cracked grout
- [ ] Floor deflects around tub indicating rot
- [ ] No leaks behind access panel
- [ ] Shower head supported
- [ ] No cracks in toilet tank, bowl, seat, or lid
- [ ] No leaks in water lines, cutoff valve, or tank hold-down bolts
- [ ] Toilet does not run
- [ ] Toilet flushes properly and does not machine-gun
- [ ] Toilet secure to floor; floor not rotted
- [ ] Pop-up drain on lavatory sink works
- [ ] Lavatory sink and faucet checked as for kitchen (see p. 205)
- [ ] No S-traps
- [ ] Wall-hung sink secure, drains not leaking
- [ ] Pedestal sink secure, drains not leaking
- [ ] Outlet GFCI protected

result, the front of the sink tilts toward the floor, leaving a large gap between the back of the sink and the wall. This, in turn, can cause the drain and supply lines to move, increasing the potential for leaks.

The bowl of a pedestal sink is attached to the wall and sits on a stand for additional support. Check to make sure the installation is secure and doesn't move around. The plumbing, especially the P-trap, is partially hidden. To check for leaks, you'll have to peak around the back and perhaps shine a light in.

You'll likely find an electrical outlet close to the sink; it should be ground-fault protected. Older houses may not have such protection, and it is not required by code, unless the bathroom is renovated. Because the danger of being electrocuted is just as real in an old house as in a new one, I always write it up if there is no GFCI. Another outlet to look for is one installed in older medicine cabinets. This one is never ground-fault protected—always write it up.

Spas and Whirlpools

Spas and whirlpools can be located inside a house or out. To test either, you need to be able to fill the unit (at least to above the water ports) to see if it works. However, if the outside unit is filled with leaves and debris, don't bother. Just write up what you see. As you run water into the inside unit, remember that you are mixing the new fresh water with that of the stale water that is inside the pump and water lines of the unit. Legionnaire's disease may be spread through stagnant water, so I advise you to keep your hands out of the water (or rinse your hands and arms with an antiseptic mouthwash when you're done). You may see little black flakes in the water during the test. These are the dried up debris, minerals, and water that has clung to the sides of the pipes and is now breaking loose and floating around. Make note that the tub needs to have its water system cleaned and sanitized.

The power that feeds the spa or whirlpool has to go through some type of ground-fault protection. Some manufacturers build the ground-fault breaker into the electronics at the tub controls. Other manufacturers make the installer put one in via the breaker in the panel. A 50-amp double-pole GFCI is common. Such breakers are expensive, and many times when they fail they are not replaced. The most common problem for the heated units is a bad element tripping the ground-fault circuit. The element gets a hairline crack and bleeds some current to ground through the water. If you flip the breaker on and it flips itself back off, this is probably the problem. The inspector must verify that a ground-fault breaker is in place and working. Finally, check that the tub motor and controls are located where they can be maintained.

The black flakes floating in the whirlpool's water are the dried-up debris, minerals, and water that accumulated in the pump lines when the tub was not being used. This tub will need to be disinfected before it can be used.

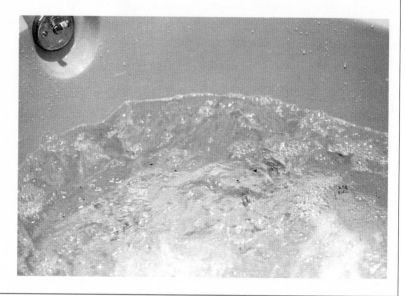

Bedrooms and Hallways

Once you've inspected the kitchen and bathroom, a large part of your room-by-room inspection of the house is done, but you still need to make note of the condition of the other rooms of the house and of the hallways that connect them.

Bedrooms

The first thing I do when I open the door and walk into a bedroom (or any other room of the house), is check that the door latches and un-latches properly. Then I look behind the door for any hole in the wall that the handle might have caused.

Once in the room, check the condition of the floor, walls, ceiling, and trim. You're looking for out-of-level and sagging floors; loose floorboards; major cracks in the wall and ceiling surface; and missing, broken, or loose trim. Any problems with the finished walls should be obvious. Drywall may have holes, nails popping out, settling cracks, or some badly taped joints showing through. Plaster walls may be cracked, disinte-grating, or have missing or loose sections. If the walls are painted, check for peeling paint; look up at the ceiling and note any discoloration from water leaks. If the walls are papered, check the seams, which is the first place wallpaper begins to peel off the wall.

Thin wall paneling may have been installed without any backing support (such as drywall). Rap on the paneling and listen for a solid sound to verify that the support is present. Often, if the wall has only thin paneling, you'll notice it warp-ing between the studs and you may see small holes in the wall where it has been bumped.

You've already checked the condition of the windows on your inspection of the exterior (see p. 75). Once inside, check whether windows open and close (you don't need to check every window, just a representative sample) and whether the window latches are operable. Check for the ob-vious: cracked and broken glass and condensation rot in the windowsill.

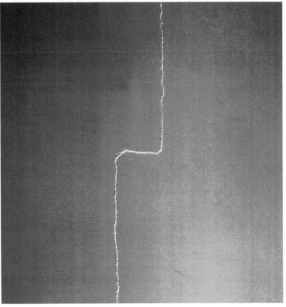

Check for cracks at drywall seams above doorways.

Checking the Receptacles

Check all receptacles with a plug-in tester. In particular, note the ground light on the tester. If the receptacle is a grounded receptacle and it doesn't have a ground, write it up—this is not allowed. People have a habit of placing grounded receptacles on old ungrounded wiring, thinking everything is all right. An exception to the grounding rule is that non-grounded three-prong receptacles are allowed as long as they are protected by a GFCI and have "no ground" written on the receptacle. If a two-prong duplex receptacle is protected by a GFCI upstream, it needs to have "GFCI protected" written on it.

Also check the receptacles for proper polarity. If the plug-in tester indicates reverse polarity—that is, the hot and neutral wires are switched at the receptacle—record the problem.

Bedroom windows are supposed to serve as emergency exits in the event of fire. Verify that the window opening meets the minimum size requirement and that the sill to floor distance is within your jurisdiction's standards for use as an emergency exit.

A bedroom must have either a switched overhead light or a switched outlet. If there is no overhead light, leave the light switch off and check all receptacles for wiring problems (see "Checking the Receptacles"). If furniture is in the way, follow your company's policy of whether you are to move it. As you check the receptacles, note which ones have only half a duplex working. These should be the switched receptacles. Throw the switch on and note if the power returns. If it doesn't, write it up. There may be an overhead paddle fan and light in the bedroom. Don't worry about checking all three speeds—just see that it turns on and doesn't wobble significantly.

Hallways

The hallway inspection is a quick one. Check for obvious problems like loose floorboards, peeling paint, and cheap paneling that's coming loose. Otherwise, you just need to check for switching and lighting.

Three-way switching is a must for most home buyers. Note whether the hall has three-way switching and verify that it works (see the sidebar on p. 218). Also check that the switch itself is in good condition—it should feel firm and not flop back and forth (which indicates that the switch is on its last legs). You should hear no arcing, and the light should not be intermittent. Wiggle the switch a little; if the light blinks on and off, it is bad. If there is no light at all, the bulb, of course, could be broken or burned out. But that's not your problem; simply write it up as not working.

Most halls should have an outlet. Don't concern yourself with code requirements. Just note if one exists, and don't forget to use your plug-in tester to verify that it is grounded and wired properly.

Bedroom and Hallway Checklist

- [ ] Doors open and latch properly
- [ ] No hole in wall behind door
- [ ] Floors, walls, ceiling in good condition
- [ ] Windows open, close, and latch
- [ ] Bedroom window can be emergency exit if required
- [ ] If habitable, room has switch lighting
- [ ] Receptacles work and are wired properly
- [ ] Hall has outlet and three-way switched lighting

Chapter 11

WATER SUPPLY AND SEPTIC

THE WATER SOURCE

SEPTIC TANKS

No one wants a house without adequate water or water pressure, which is why inspection of the water supply is high on the priority list of both the buyer and inspector. For all its importance though, a water pressure and volume check is fast and simple—at least for city dwellers. Homeowners who get water from a utility shouldn't have any problems with either volume or pressure, as long as the house's water lines (and the line from meter to house) are of adequate diameter. Rural water-supply systems, with wells, pumps, and tanks, are a bit more complex.

Similarly, waste disposal (through sewers) in urban areas is pretty straightforward for the homeowner, whereas septic systems in rural areas can be problematic. Checking septic systems, however, is not something that I recommend you get into. Within the time constraints allowed, it's impossible for an inspector to adequately check whether the system is functioning properly. Indeed, sometimes it's even impossible to verify that a septic system exists. A neighbor of mine paid an engineering firm to check to see if he had a septic tank and, if he did, that it was functioning properly. They said he did, and it was. Some time later I was doing a bit of backhoe work in his yard and cut through a clay-tile line heading to the creek behind the house, which turned out to be his sewer line. There was no septic tank—the house was dumping the sewage directly into the creek. Therefore, unless you want be sued, I don't recommend that you include checking septic systems in your battery of tests.

The Water Source

In the city, water is taken for granted, but not so in the country. With no utility to supply un-limited water at continuous high pressure, rural dwellers depend on a well or spring, and they often have to live with limited water volume and pressure. The first thing for the inspector to do is to list the water source.

This cistern is located above ground level to prevent surface water from entering and contaminating the 1,000-gal. tank. A submersible pump inside the tank (not visible) sends the spring water to the house.

Spring-fed house

The earliest settlers built their houses close to a spring or creek, and some homeowners still prefer a spring-fed source over utility water or even well water. Springs provide a fresh, cold source of water, but they are easily contaminated.

If the house you're inspecting is fed by a spring, a few questions to the owner can go a long way in getting information for the buyer. First, is the water pumped into the house or gravity fed? Springs can be tapped directly in three ways: by putting a large tank over a source, by having nothing more than a pipe sticking into the source that drains the water into a large collecting tank or cistern, or by having a pipe feed the source to a small tank that feeds its overflow to a large collecting tank.

Regardless of the system, you need some information about the cistern. The basic rule of thumb is that you can have a small cistern (25 gal. to 100 gal.) as long as there is plenty of water coming into the spring box. Conversely, if there's only a small amount of water flowing into the box, you need a large cistern. Ask how often (if at all) the cistern needs to be cleaned—many fill up with sand and silt. One important check is look at the area around the spring box to determine if it is being contaminated by runoff from the surrounding fields. If there's a pasture or crop field that drains into the area around the box, and especially over the spring box or cistern, I

Water Source Checklist

- [ ] City water
- [ ] Well
- [ ] Hand dug
- [ ] Machine drilled
- [ ] Spring:
  - [ ] With pump
  - [ ] Gravity fed

make note that it might be an area of concern because the spring may be contaminated.

I usually don't try to verify the spring "recharge" (the rate of water flow back into the tank after water has been drawn out), but it can be done. If you have access to the overflow pipe (the pipe that takes the excess water inside the tank away from the tank), you can hold a gallon jug under the pipe and time how long it takes to fill. If the pump is not running and the tank has no cracks in it, the overflow water is equal to the recharge water.

Wells

The earliest wells were shallow, hand-dug wells that tapped into water close to the surface. You still find some houses with hand-dug wells, which can be of any diameter and are usually lined with rocks. These wells can be anywhere—I've seen them in basements and under the front porch. There's little to check with a hand-dug well; you already know that it's shallow and easily contaminated because it collects water near and on the surface. If the current owner is present for the inspection, I'll typically ask if there are any problems with water pressure and volume.

As technology developed, deep wells that took a pipe straight down into the bedrock became the norm. For this type of drill, a hole is drilled through the dirt, and the casing (a plastic or metal pipe around 6 in. in diameter) is pushed into the vertical hole and pounded into the bedrock. Machine-drilled wells are typically 50 ft. to 500 ft. deep, depending on the water level of the area. (An artesian well provides an almost unlimited, high-pressure water source, which has been tapped and is flowing out of the top of the well casing.)

The two most frequently asked questions about a drilled well are How deep is it? and How powerful is the pump? There's no test for either, but it's a good idea to ask the owner and record his or her answers on your form (if the owner doesn't know, make a note of that too). If the pump is a three-wire pump, the horsepower may be noted

The well casing should extend at least 12 in. aboveground. Check to see that the well cap is on, the casing is not broken, and the wire to the pump is in conduit.

on the control box (typically mounted next to the water-pressure tank).

The only part of a drilled well you'll be able to see (if any) is the aboveground casing, or well pipe. The casing should extend about 1 ft. out of the ground to keep dirt and surface water out of the well. The top end of the casing should have a cap; some areas require this cap to be watertight, others don't. Either way, verify that the cap is installed and secure. If the upper end of the well casing does not extend above the ground, you need to indicate it on your report. This is an important point; if the well pipe is cut off belowground, there's a strong possibility that the seal installed where the cut pipe ends may leak, allowing surface water to enter and contaminate the well.

If the well casing terminates in an underground pit or tank there's no less risk of contamination. The pit or tank can flood and contaminate the well if the well seal leaks. The worst case I've seen was a well that was contaminated with chlordane every time it rained. The area around the house was sprayed

Problems with Belowground Well Casings

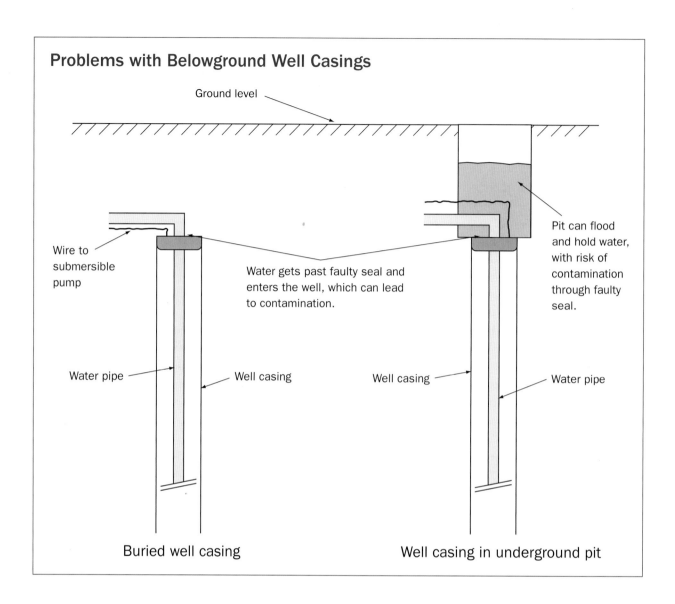

Ground level

Wire to submersible pump

Water gets past faulty seal and enters the well, which can lead to contamination.

Pit can flood and hold water, with risk of contamination through faulty seal.

Water pipe

Well casing

Well casing

Water pipe

Buried well casing

Well casing in underground pit

Well Casing Checklist

☐ Upper end of the casing extends above ground

☐ Well cap installed and secure

☐ Wires (if present) are protected in conduit

☐ Well casing grouted (if local area requires it)

☐ If plastic, aboveground casing not cracked or broken

with the pesticide (before it was banned), and once it started raining, the runoff around the house would go into a dug hole, at the bottom of which was the well casing with an open seal.

If there's a submersible pump in the well (see p. 237), there will be wires coming up out of the ground next to the casing and going into the well cap. These wires should be protected by conduit of some kind. You'll see any variety of materials used for conduit, but as long as the wires are protected, I don't write it up. Some areas require grout to be poured around the well casing (on new houses) to prevent water from following the outside of the casing underground. Finally, verify

This well casing is in a belowground concrete tank. Note that the yellow pump wire enters the casing via a galvanized elbow, which also allows entrance to water, mice, frogs, and other creatures. Write it up.

that the aboveground casing (if plastic) is not cracked or broken. More than one casing has been hit and damaged by a car bumper.

Water quantity

It's not easy to determine exactly how much water a source has; and, in my opinion, this is not something that an inspector should attempt to do. If the water supply is from a well, it's a fact of life that it's limited by the amount of water that is in the well (the static water level) and by the restrictions of the aquifer (the recharge rate). What's there is what the owners live with—unless they want to spend a lot of money to dig a deeper well, drill an additional well, or add a cistern (a large concrete or polyethylene tank) for storage.

Some home inspection organizations require their inspectors to verify that thousands of gallons are available or instruct them to let the hose run for a certain period of time. A common test that inspectors employ to determine water quantity is to turn the hose on and estimate the amount of flowing water for a specific period of time. However, if the source pulls dry while you're testing it, you run the risk of ruining the pump (if it's a submersible pump) or losing prime (if it's a jet pump). If the water source is a gravity-feed, spring-fed system, you risk creating an air lock (whereby an air bubble gets caught in the line and stops the water flow to the house). Either way, it can be an expensive undertaking because

How Much Water's in the Well?

A typical 6-in. well will hold about 1.6 gal./ft. However, if a well is 200 ft. deep, it doesn't necessarily mean that it has 200 ft. of usable water in it. In fact, it rarely will. The water level within the well, known as the static water level, can be at any depth—for example, 80 ft. down from the surface. And the pump is never at the bottom of the well, which is where all the accumulated debris settles, but is normally 20 ft. off the bottom. That leaves 100 ft. of water in the well, or about 160 gal. of usable water. The water will recharge into the well as it is pumped out, but it comes in slowly via cracks in the rock. The recharge rate is commonly between 1 gal. and 5 gal. per minute; if it's any faster than that, the owners can consider themselves lucky.

you've created a problem that you may have to pay to repair.

I know some home inspectors who use a flow meter in an attempt to indicate how much recharge a well has, but this is a pointless test. The flow meter gives a rating of how much water is flowing through the gauge, but it cannot give you an indication of well recharge. The only

A low-pressure cutoff switch, which cuts power to the pump when pressure falls below 12 psi, is a good indicator that the house you are inspecting has a limited supply of water.

Don't confuse a no-load current-sensing device (left) with a common control box (right). The current-sensing device senses the pump's current and shuts off power when the current falls as the pump pulls dry. The control box is present on all three-wire submersible-pump systems.

practical way to do a recharge test is to measure the static water level in the well using a long tape measure, pump water out of the well for a specific time, measure the static water level again, and then calculate how much water came back into the well to give you the amount of water recharge per minute.

I must reiterate that in my opinion any recharge test is beyond the scope of the inspector. If the buyer wants an accurate estimate of the amount of water available, he or she should contact a reputable well driller or pump expert. What you can do as an inspector is simply ask the present owners if the water source has ever pulled dry and how much water they think they have; log their answer on your report form. In some areas, well drillers are required to file the recharge rate (in gallons per minute) with a local state or county agency, so the buyer may be able to obtain accurate information from this source.

A good indicator of a low-yield system (one with limited gallons per minute) is the presence of a low-pressure cutoff switch or a no-load current-sensing device near the water-pressure tank. The purpose of a low-pressure cutoff switch is to remove the power to the pump if the system pressure falls below 12 psi. It's assumed that if the pressure is that low, the source is pulling dry. Once the device is triggered, it has to be reset manually. A no-load current-sensing device (like a

Pumptec or a Coyote) senses the current flow that the pump draws. When the pump pulls dry, it will pull less current than when it is under a heavy load pumping water. The device will sense the current difference and cut the power to the pump. Power will automatically be returned to the pump a preset time later. Do not confuse the low-yield sensing switch with the three-wire control box that is on all three-wire pump systems.

Water-pressure test

The standard water-pressure test is to screw a water-pressure gauge onto an outside hose bib and turn the hose bib on. You can also test water pressure at a sink faucet, but because there are so many different types of aerators and thread types I find it easiest to check at the outside hose bib. If the water pressure is above whatever the local jurisdiction determines to be too high (usually 75 psi to 80 psi), make note of it on your report form. Many jurisdictions don't have a low water-pressure reference, but experience has shown that if the house is below 30 psi, there will be water-pressure problems, and I recommend writing it up.

Whereas water pressure in the city is relatively stable, in country systems with a pump, pressure is constantly changing as the pump sends water to the water-pressure tank. Therefore, measuring

Use a water-pressure gauge installed on an outside hose bib to test the house's water pressure. Turn the water on and read the dial; anything between 30 psi and 80 psi is acceptable.

The gauge mounted on the T in front of the water-pressure tank gives a direct pressure reading. If the pressure drops to 0 psi for a second or two just before the pump cuts in (as shown here), there's a problem.

the water pressure at a hose bib tells you what the pressure is at only that specific instant. The fluctuation in water pressure is caused by a pressure switch that has a 20-lb. differential. The system works like this: Water is in the pressure tank waiting to be used. As water is used, the water pressure lowers to a designated amount (known as the cut-in pressure), and the pressure switch turns on to apply power to the pump. The pump brings in more water, which increases the pressure. When the pressure switch determines there is enough pressure (known as the cut-out pressure), it turns the pump off.

Old jet pumps run about 20 lb. cut in and 40 lb. cut out, which is not acceptable to many people. Most modern houses on submersible pumps run about 30 lb. cut in and 50 lb. cut out. You can get greater water pressure by adjusting the pressure switch (I normally set a two-story

house up at 40 lb. cut in, 60 lb. cut out). However, I would not recommend that any home inspector adjust the pressure switch if requested to do so by the owner; suggest instead that the owner bring in a plumber, because the tank air must be adjusted at the same time.

The best way to conduct the water-pressure test on a pump system is to observe the water-pressure gauge at the water-pressure tank; it gives you a direct pressure reading. If the gauge is missing or not working, you'll have to use the hose bib test and verify the low-end pressure and high-end pressure by leaving another hose bib or tub faucet on to cycle the system. Check the gauge when the pump kicks on; if the pressure reading is about 30 lb. or greater, it is okay. If the system cuts out around 20 lb. above that, everything is still okay. If the pressure ever drops to 0 lb., as might happen just before the pump kicks on, the pressure switch is adjusted incorrectly (or there is the wrong amount of air in the tank); write it up. High pressure is rarely a problem in country water systems, but you should still use 75 lb. to 80 lb. as your reference; write up anything above that.

Water volume and water temperature test

It's a familiar problem: You're in the shower and, suddenly, there's a surge of cold (or hot) water. This problem occurs because the water lines cannot supply enough water volume for the number of fixtures being used at one time. I write up any house with a water line less than ½ in. in diameter that feeds two or more fixtures. Less

than ½ in. diameter normally means the pipe cannot handle the volume of more than one fixture at a time—especially if the shower is one of the fixtures. Galvanized pipe can give you volume problems even if the pipe is of a large diameter. Because it tends to rust out on the inside, its inside diameter can get so narrow that it may not be able to supply even a single fixture.

One way to test the water volume is to run the kitchen sink faucet and visually note the water flow. Then turn on the lavatory sink faucet and flush the toilet; if you note a significant reduction in flow, write it up. A better test is to use the shower as a reference for both water volume and water temperature. To do this, turn on the shower

To test the water volume, first turn on the shower (both hot and cold) and note the pressure at the shower head (top). Then flush the toilet and turn on the lavatory faucets (hot and cold). If the shower volume reduces enough to see (above), there's a problem with the water volume.

To test the water temperature, turn on the shower and adjust the temperature to around 105°F (top). Flush the toilet and turn on the cold water faucet at the lavatory sink. If the temperature goes up significantly (by more than about 5°F), report it (above).

Water Pressure, Volume, and Temperature Checklist

- ☐ Water pressure
  - ☐ 30 psi minimum
  - ☐ 75 psi to 80 psi maximum
  - ☐ Drop to 0 psi at low end of cycle
- ☐ No significant drop in water volume when two other fixtures on
- ☐ No significant change in water temperature with two other fixtures on
- ☐ Water temperature no higher than 120°F

and adjust the water temperature to around 105°F (the typical temperature at which people shower). Now flush the toilet and turn on the lavatory faucet to full cold. If the water flow in the shower slows significantly and/or the temperature changes significantly (I use 5°F as a reference), write it up. While you are doing this test, you should also note the maximum water temperature when the hot shower faucet is full on (assuming you have not already done so in the kitchen or

bathroom). Anything over 120°F can present a scalding problem and should be written up.

Pump types

There are two basic types of pumps to bring water into the house—a submersible pump and a jet pump—and the inspector should be able to determine and log which type is being used. A submersible pump is located inside the well or spring. Although you won't be able to see it in a well, you may be able to see it in a spring box. If so, make sure that it's not lying in a bed of mud or debris. A jet pump goes in the basement or covered spring house—you can see it and hear it. Jet pumps will either have a single pipe or dual pipes going into their nose. The single pipe indicates that the well system is shallow, normally 25 ft. or less. A dual-pipe system indicates a deep water system—around 90 ft.

A typical submersible pump will pump 7 gal. to 10 gal. a minute; a jet pump will normally pump a lot less. A jet pump is a less efficient than a submersible pump, because a large portion of the pumped water has to be thrown back into the water to pull more water back in. It works on the principle that a fast-moving water stream will create a vacuum as it is forced into a small hole. It

This submersible pump is located in a spring box. It is sitting on a concrete block to keep debris out of the intake screen located in the middle of the pump. If the pump intake screen is lying in mud or sand, indicate so on your form—it can pull in trash to the house.

Jet Pumps

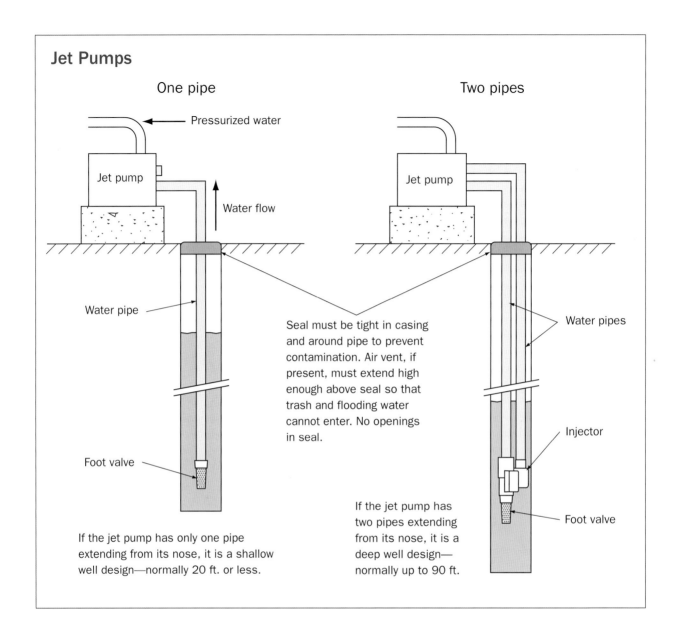

One pipe

Pressurized water

Jet pump

Water flow

Water pipe

Foot valve

If the jet pump has only one pipe extending from its nose, it is a shallow well design—normally 20 ft. or less.

Two pipes

Jet pump

Water pipes

Injector

Foot valve

Seal must be tight in casing and around pipe to prevent contamination. Air vent, if present, must extend high enough above seal so that trash and flooding water cannot enter. No openings in seal.

If the jet pump has two pipes extending from its nose, it is a deep well design—normally up to 90 ft.

is this vacuum that pulls the water in from the spring or well. This is why you always have to prime a jet pump to get it to work. Priming is the act of filling the entire pipe system (and pump) with water. If there is a section within the system that doesn't have water (called an air lock), the system won't pump water.

Besides checking to see whether the pump works, there are a couple of other tests you can make on the pump system (regardless of whether it is a jet or a submersible). First, if the pump turns on for no reason, shuts off a few minutes later, and then turns back on again a few minutes after that, there's a problem. It could be a small hole in the line, a leaking fitting underground, a leaky check valve in a submersible pump, a leaky foot valve in a jet pump, or something as simple as a running toilet. Your job isn't to determine what's causing the problem but simply to note that it exists; note on your form that the pump is running for no apparent reason.

This is a typical jet pump, with a single pipe (galvanized with union) going into the pump's nose, which indicates that it is a shallow well design. Check that there is no water spraying or dripping from the pump where the shaft enters the pump head.

When a jet pump turns on, the motor sound should be quiet and smooth (something like a vacuum cleaner). If you hear a high-pitched scream, it indicates that the bearings are going. If water sprays out from the center of the pump (the area between the pump head and the motor), the seals are gone. Also listen for how long the pump runs; if it runs for only a couple of seconds or if it never seems to shut off, recommend that the owners have it checked out.

If any part of the water system (pump, tank, controls, etc.) is in a buried tank, there are possible water contamination problems (see "Cross-Connections" on p. 248) and components may have rusted out. A closed tank always has moisture in the air. I write it up as an area of concern, because I know how fast the controls can rust and how moisture shortens their lifetime—water and electricity don't mix.

A jet pump has a tapered, one-way check valve (known as a foot valve) at the end of the pipe that extends down into the water. As long as the valve is surrounded by water there is no problem, but if it is in a spring box that has sand and dirt filling in the box, the valve can get buried. Sand

If a water-pressure system is located in tank below-ground, write it up as an area of concern, because of the potential for rusting.

If a jet pump and water source are next to each other, try to look at the bottom of the water pipe where it extends into the water. It should not be sticking in sand or mud. This system has the foot valve in a clear container to keep trash out of the valve end.

Pump Checklist

- [ ] Type of pump:
  - [ ] Submersible (in the water)
  - [ ] Jet (in the basement or spring house)
- [ ] Pump system turns on and off for no reason
- [ ] Pump run time very short or very long
- [ ] Submersible pump lying in a bed of debris in spring box
- [ ] Jet pump makes a high-pitched squeal
- [ ] Leaks around jet pump
- [ ] Jet pump in closed tank
- [ ] Debris around jet-pump foot valve

and dirt can jam the check open and stop the system from pumping water. If you can see into the spring box, make sure the foot valve is not within 4 in. of any dirt or debris (concrete is acceptable); any closer and the trash will be sucked up into the foot valve and damage the system. Write it up and recommend that the spring box be cleaned.

Water-pressure tanks

The purpose of a water-pressure tank is to store the pressurized water that the pump sends into the house. The primary test here is to determine whether the tank is waterlogged—a condition that occurs when the pressurized air that is trapped above the water has dissipated into the water. Without the pressurized air, you start losing the amount of usable water the tank can provide, because it is the pressurized air that pushes the water out of the tank when a faucet is turned on.

There are several different kinds of water-pressure tanks. Originally, the only tanks were galvanized tanks, which work fine as long as air is constantly put into the tank, either by hand or a mechanical device, to make up for the air lost into the water. Eventually, however, the mechanical device fails or someone forgets to shoot air into the tank, and the tank waterlogs. When that happens, the time between the pump's turning on and turning off keeps getting shorter and shorter until the pump cycles on and off so fast that it burns up. So one test for a waterlogged tank is simply to listen for a pump that turns on and off every few seconds.

The old and the new. On the left is an old-style 42-gal. galvanized tank; on the right is its modern-day replacement—a bladder tank. Both yield 5 gal. to 7 gal. of usable water.

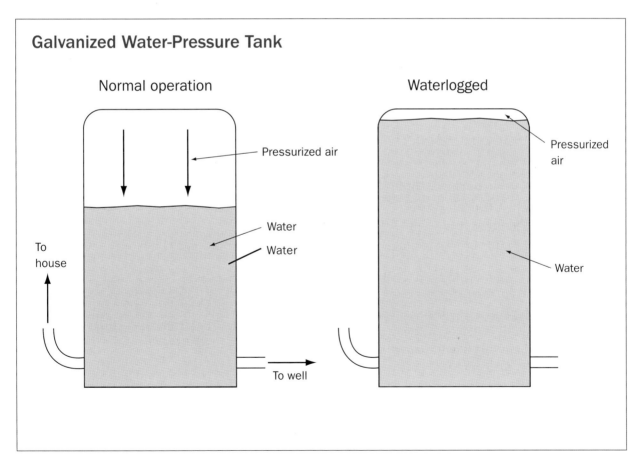

Galvanized Water-Pressure Tank

Normal operation

Pressurized air

To house

Water

Water

To well

Waterlogged

Pressurized air

Water

Bladder Tank

Bladder tank operation eliminates waterlogging.

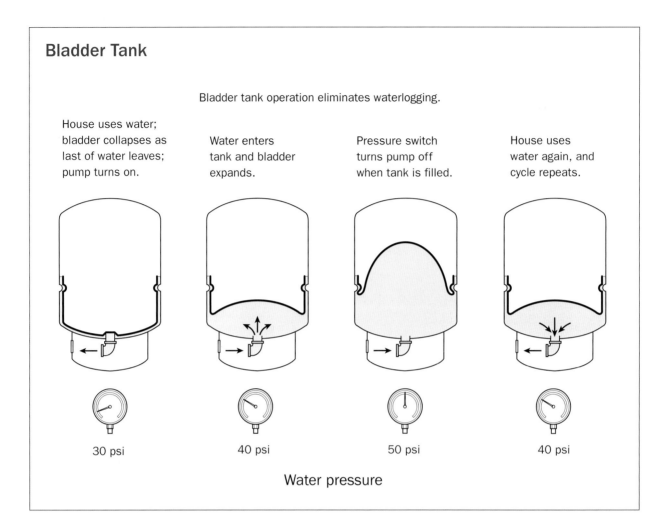

House uses water; bladder collapses as last of water leaves; pump turns on.

Water enters tank and bladder expands.

Pressure switch turns pump off when tank is filled.

House uses water again, and cycle repeats.

30 psi　　　　40 psi　　　　50 psi　　　　40 psi

Water pressure

Another test is to rap on the top of the tank with your knuckle or something metal; if it sounds hollow, everything is fine. Now do the same to the bottom of the tank (which is filled with water); you should hear a dull thud. If you hear a dull thud at both the top and the bottom, the tank is waterlogged. Finally, observe the metal tank: If it is sweating from the top, the tank is waterlogged.

In an attempt to ameliorate the waterlogging problem, design engineers worked overtime to come up with a better water tank; but most of the time they failed. One type used a wafer that floated up and down inside the tank to break the water-air contact; if you find one of these,

chances are good that it will be waterlogged. Unless the wafer tank still has its original sticker, you won't be able to tell what type of tank it is by looking at it, but it will fail the rap test. Another tank to watch for is one labeled CAT (captive air tank). It will also likely fail the rap test.

Today's tanks are designed with a bladder, and they work very well. But many people think they are supposed to shoot air into bladder tanks just as with galvanized tanks; when they do, they rupture the bladder. Other times the bladder splits when excessive water pressure enters the tank (normally above 100 lb.). The bladder can also split because it was poorly designed by the manufacturer.

There are a number of possible tests to determine if the bladder is ruptured and the tank waterlogged. First, you can try the rap test. If the tank top sounds full of water, it probably is. As with a galvanized tank, you can check to see if the tank is sweating from the top, indicating that there is water where there should be air and that the tank is waterlogged. You can also turn the power off to the system and bleed the water out. If there is any water left in the tank to slosh around, the bladder has ruptured. A waterlogged galvanized tank just needs to have some air shot into it, but a waterlogged bladder tank will have to be replaced.

Ultraviolet filters

In some basements, you'll find a stainless-steel unit with a glowing light hanging next to the water-pressure tank. This is an ultraviolet (UV) filter, usually installed because the homeowner suspects there is harmful bacteria in the water (as when pulling from a spring). You should inspect the filter at the same time you inspect the water-pressure tank.

The first thing I do is stand back and look at the overall installation. Add-on systems might have been installed by a licensed plumber, but they might also have been put in place by the homeowner, so expect to find some unusual installations. Observe how the unit is mounted. Is it installed securely to a wall or it just hanging by a thread? Look for obvious problems like water leaks at the threaded connections or improper plumbing connections.

Check that the filter is installed in the correct place. The unit must be plumbed into the main water line before there are any taps to the household fixtures and after the water-pressure tank and all other water-treatment systems (except point-of-use systems, such as might be found at the kitchen sink). In other words, the UV filter needs to go after the neutralizer, iron-removal system, and softener.

Look through the hole on the side of the unit to verify that the bulb is on. The earliest UV units

An ultraviolet filter needs to be securely attached to the wall. Here, the unit's head has pulled loose from the wall and is currently hung by a wire from the PVC drain pipe. Write it up.

UV filters kill bacteria as the water passes through them. Verify that the light is on by looking through the peephole in the side of the unit.

UV Filter Checklist

- ☐ Unit mounted securely
- ☐ No leaks or improper plumbing connections
- ☐ Unit plumbed in before taps to the house fixtures and after major water-conditioning systems
- ☐ Bulb is on
- ☐ Water clear
- ☐ Water softener or cartridge not on bypass
- ☐ Recommend that water be tested by a state-certified lab

were wired to the pressure switch and ran only when the pump was engaged, but this allowed untreated water to enter the house. The light should always be on. Next check how old the bulb is. Most bulbs are rated for 14 months. Look for a tag noting when the bulb was installed or when a new one should be.

For a UV filter to work, it has to shine on the bacteria, which means that the water must be clear and free of debris. Therefore, it is common to have a cartridge filter before the UV filter. If you can see into the cartridge filter housing, check to see if a cartridge is indeed installed. If the water is cloudy at the faucets, write it up. Another problem is hard water—or iron water, which can coat the inside sleeve of the filter and reduce the amount of light getting to the water. The inspector cannot check for this, but it's common to have a water softener immediately before a UV filter to take out the iron and hardness. Check to see if the water softener and/or cartridge is on bypass; if they are not in use, they cannot work, and the UV filter probably isn't working either.

Finally, even if you can't find any problems, always recommend that the new owners have the water tested by a state-certified laboratory. There

is obviously a problem with bacteria or the system wouldn't be there; and there is no way of knowing if the system is working for sure, unless such a check is done. Some lending institutions require a bacteria test before any house can be sold, whether it's in the city or in the country.

Septic Tanks

In urban areas, waste disposal is taken for granted, and all the inspector needs to do is note on the form that waste disposal is through sewers. In rural areas, most homes will have a private disposal system on their property, known as a septic system. This system must be maintained. The theory and practice of a septic tank and system are quite simple. The sewage from the house goes into the tank where bacteria break everything down. The liquid effluent rises to the top and flows into a small distribution box a few feet away. The distribution box has several drain lines leaving from it that take the effluent through pipes to the drain fields. The effluent drains into a gravel bed under slotted drain lines and from there into the earth.

The problem with septic systems is that because they are buried you have no idea that one even exists let alone how well it is working. I know of one house in which the septic tank turned out to be a drum in the ground. Another house had a system put in illegally. And, as mentioned at the start of this chapter, an engineering firm stated that a house had a well-functioning septic system, when sewage was actually being dumped directly into a nearby creek. The bottom line is that, in my opinion, the inspector should not inspect the septic system. It takes too long to find the tank (you have to keep sticking a rod in the ground till you hit the tank), and once you do find it, you have to dig it up and raise a heavy concrete lid to access the tank.

There are, however, a couple things you can watch for. First, is sewage backing up into the

Septic System

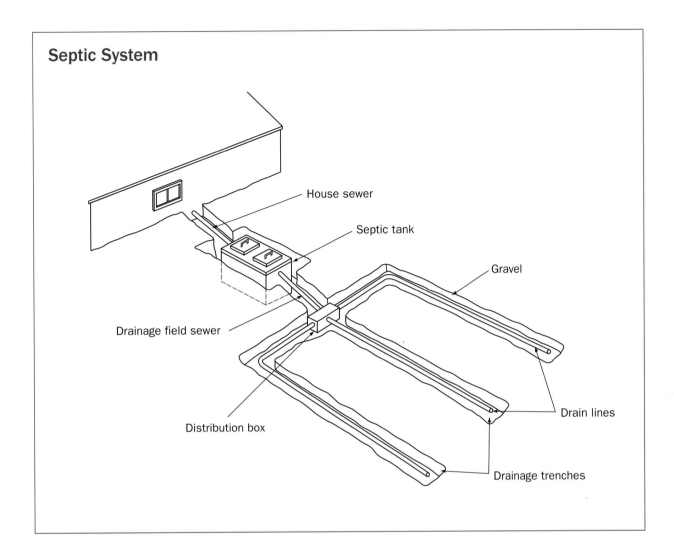

House sewer

Septic tank

Gravel

Drainage field sewer

Distribution box

Drain lines

Drainage trenches

house and, second, do you see or smell water seepage (effluent) on the surface of the ground? You can also ask the owner how long it has been since the tank was pumped; where I live, it's recommended that tanks be pumped every 3 to 5 years.

Sometimes the drain field is uphill from the house. In this case, there needs to be a pumping system to get the effluent to the drain field. If the house has a pumping system, the new owner needs to know, because these systems tend to break down frequently, and there's an alarm system to deal with. With this setup, there will be two buried tanks. The sewage stays in the first tank. The liquid overflows into a second tank, called the effluent tank, which has a pump to force the effluent uphill. This tank normally has an access lid to get to the pump system for maintenance. On older systems, the tanks were completely buried. Note whether the access lid is present.

An effluent pump, set about 1 ft. off the bottom of the tank, pumps the liquid uphill to the drain field. The pump is turned on by a mercury switch (which has a high failure rate, as does the pump itself). Unfortunately, there's no way to test whether the pump or switch is working, but if the pump doesn't work, the effluent rises and triggers

Effluent Tank System

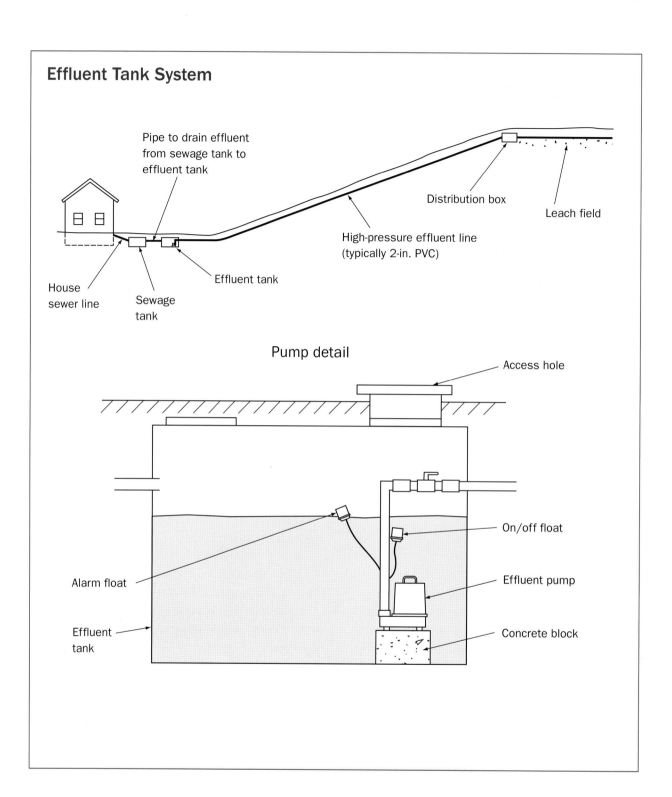

Pipe to drain effluent from sewage tank to effluent tank

Distribution box

Leach field

High-pressure effluent line (typically 2-in. PVC)

House sewer line

Sewage tank

Effluent tank

Pump detail

Access hole

Alarm float

On/off float

Effluent pump

Effluent tank

Concrete block

Waste Disposal Checklist

- [ ] City sewer
- [ ] Septic tank:
    - [ ] Sewage backing up
    - [ ] Effluent seeping aboveground
    - [ ] Date tank was last pumped
- [ ] Septic tank with pumping system:
    - [ ] Does the alarm work?
    - [ ] Lid to effluent tank accessible
- [ ] Dual-pump system
- [ ] Septic chlorination system
    - [ ] System under warranty

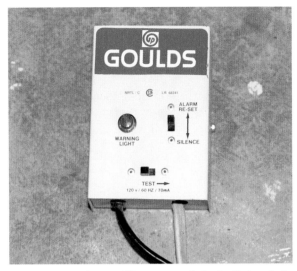

The alarm box for an effluent pump is typically located inside the house at or near the water-pressure tank. Check that the unit is plugged in and that the alarm sounds and flashes when the test switch is thrown.

an alarm. It's the inspector's job to test this alarm to see if it works. No, you don't have to climb into the tank—all you have to do is throw the alarm switch to "alarm" or "test" and watch and listen. The switch is in a small metal box normally located close to the pressure tank. You should see a red light and hear an alarm. If the alarm mechanism is unplugged, it will be up to you to decide whether you want to log it as unplugged and nonfunctioning or plug it in and test it. Sometimes the homeowner has unplugged it just to silence the alarm.

The ultimate pumping system, which is required in some areas, has two pumps located adjacent to each other as well as one or two alarms to test. The logic behind such a design is that if one pump fails, the second can take up the load until the first pump gets fixed. Otherwise, no water can be used in the house until the pump gets replaced.

If you come across something that looks like a series of round lids, you are looking at a system that takes the place of a septic tank—a type of sewage chlorination system. These are used as a last resort—when the land is so low or close to a creek that a septic tank with drain field isn't allowed. This is a miniature water-treatment plant. It takes raw sewage, superchlorinates it, and takes the chlorine back out via a carbon filter and then dumps the treated water into a creek. Don't touch anything on this type of system—don't even raise the lid. At most, you should ask if the system is still under warranty and who is doing the maintenance. In some parts of the country, newer-style sewage systems are being installed. If the house has one of these systems, simply make note of it so the new owners know what they are buying.

Appendix

CROSS-CONNECTIONS

"If I could not be a prince, I would be a plumber." The year was 1871 and the prince of Wales was lying on his deathbed at Londesborough Lodge. Already dead was his groom and his good friend the earl of Chesterfield. A plumber was called in to find if there was a problem with the water. There was. A "cross-connection" was found from the sewage line to the drinking water. In his gratitude for the plumber saving his life, the prince uttered this famous line.

What the prince almost died of was typhoid. One of the ways typhoid can be spread is by sewage contaminated with the bacterium *Salmonella typhi* getting into water used for drinking or washing food and dishes. In other words, it is one of several water-transmitted diseases that can be spread by sloppy plumbing practices created by cross-connections. Knowing what to look for can bring cross-connection problems to light before such tragedies occur, making this often-overlooked inspection one of the most important the home inspector can make.

Exactly what is a cross-connection? Simply put, it is normally construed to be a physical connection from something that contains potable water to something that contains nonpotable water—thus giving you the potential for contamination. The most common cross-connection problems in modern homes bring in sewage, garden fertilizer, insecticides, and herbicides to the drinking-water system. Technically, however, a cross-connection does not have to involve

How the Water Supply Can Become Contaminated

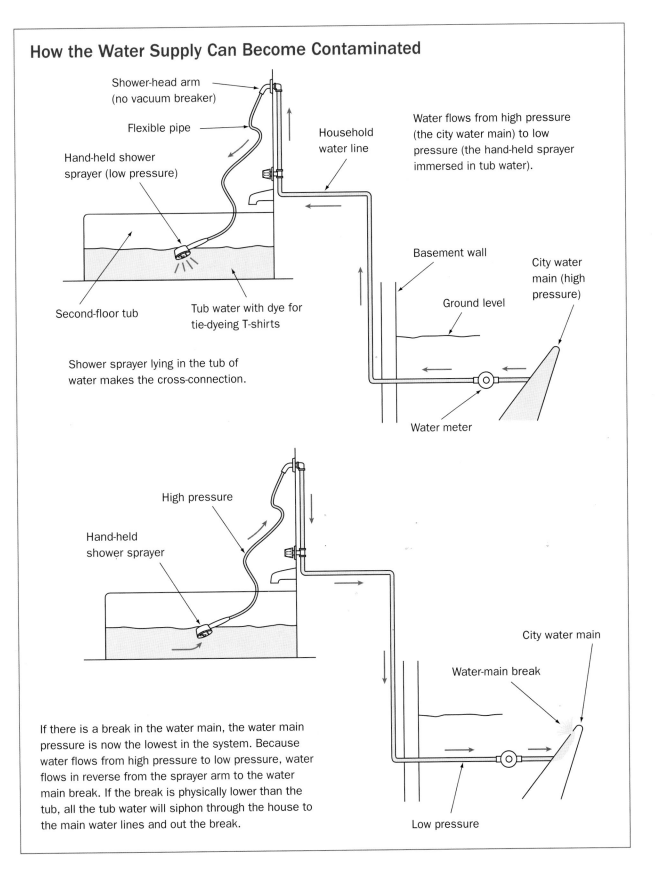

Shower-head arm (no vacuum breaker)

Flexible pipe

Hand-held shower sprayer (low pressure)

Household water line

Water flows from high pressure (the city water main) to low pressure (the hand-held sprayer immersed in tub water).

Basement wall

City water main (high pressure)

Ground level

Second-floor tub

Tub water with dye for tie-dyeing T-shirts

Water meter

Shower sprayer lying in the tub of water makes the cross-connection.

High pressure

Hand-held shower sprayer

City water main

Water-main break

If there is a break in the water main, the water main pressure is now the lowest in the system. Because water flows from high pressure to low pressure, water flows in reverse from the sprayer arm to the water main break. If the break is physically lower than the tub, all the tub water will siphon through the house to the main water lines and out the break.

Low pressure

A dual-check valve, commonly called a backflow preventer, installed on the incoming main water line prevents water in the house lines from flowing back into the well or city water main. Although not required in all areas, the absence of the valve should be listed as an area of concern, because it may allow the city or well water to become contaminated.

potable water. For example, a customer of mine once complained of sewer gas coming out of the underground gutter drain where the rain water was piped away from the house. Upon inspection, I found that the sewer drain crossed over the gutter drain; at the point where they crossed, there was a hole in the sewer pipe and the sewer water was draining down into the slotted, corrugated gutter drainpipe immediately below it.

Normally, two problems have to occur simultaneously before the water supply can become contaminated. First, a physical cross-connection has to exist. Second, a backflow situation has to occur to pull the contaminated water through the cross-connection and into the noncontaminated water. The backflow situation typically occurs when there is a main water-line break within the street or deep in the well. As the in-line water now flows backward toward the break, the reversal of flow (called backflow) creates the pull that can suck the water right out of your house and into the street or well.

If at the same moment someone nearby is spraying pesticide on the garden via a garden hose with a large pesticide container attached to it, the pesticide will start to flow backward. If the main water-line break is physically lower that the person spraying the garden, all the pesticide in the pesticide container will siphon out of the container to the main-line break and contaminate everything along the way—just like gasoline being siphoned from a gas tank. Similarly, if a hand-held shower head is immersed in a tub of water that's being used, for example, to tie-dye a T-shirt, the water will siphon through the water lines if there's a main water-line break (see the drawing on p. 249).

Fortunately, preventing such a catastrophe is quite simple. All the home inspector has to do is to check to make sure that the house under inspection is in compliance with at least one (though preferably both) of the following two rules.

1. First, the house should have a dual-check backflow preventer installed on the main water line. This device allows water to flow in one direction only—into the house, but not out. Some areas require a dual check not only for city water but also for wells, reason being that if the well gets contaminated, so can the entire aquifer system, which could affect hundreds of people.

The backflow preventer has to be a dual-check valve ("dual-check" is normally printed on the unit), not a single check, which is commonly called a check valve. The latter has only one spring-loaded seat, which allows water to go one way only. If rust and debris get into the seat, the valve will allow water to flow both ways. A dual check has two spring-loaded seats, which makes it harder for the valve to malfunction.

I recently learned that inspectors in some areas of the country had no idea that backflow preventers should be installed on the main water line. This was apparently because the local utility was putting them in along with the water meter, and the valves were never visible to be inspected. It's up to the inspector to find out whether backflow preventers are being installed. If they aren't, you should list their absence as an area of concern.

2. The second checkpoint is to make sure that all hose-bib connections, inside and out, have a vacuum breaker, check valve, or similar device to keep contaminated water from entering the house water system; these are called point-of-use devices. Some areas do not require a backflow preventer on the main water line entering the house if point-of-use devices are installed. In my opinion, however, this policy is shortsighted, because most point-of-use devices are portable

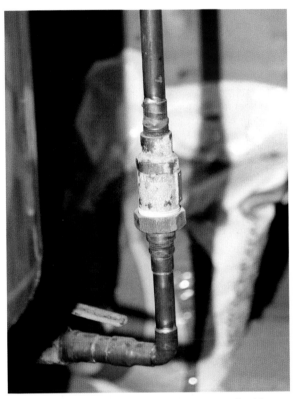

In some areas a dual-check valve is also required in country water systems. Look for the valve between the water-pressure tank and the house water line.

This through-the-wall outside hydrant has a vacuum breaker incorporated as part of the hose bib. The vacuum breaker prevents any water from being pulled back into the hydrant.

and easily removed, which negates the entire safety issue. Also, Julius Ballanco, a well-known code specialist, has shown that hose bibs with integral vacuum breakers can fail after just a few years of use. For best protection against potential cross-connection problems, houses should have both a backflow preventer on the main water line *and* point-of-use protection on individual hose-bib connections.

Common Cross-Connection Points

Now that you know what a cross-connection is and how to check for potential problems, let's take a look at some specific cross-connection points in the home plumbing system. We'll begin in the basement with the condensate lines from a heat pump/air conditioner.

Heat pump/air-conditioner condensate lines

If there's a heat pump in the house you're inspecting, it's important that you trace the condensate drain line that comes out of the pump. The line can be drained away from the building outside or it can run into a drain in the basement. If the latter, you must verify that there is a 1-in. air gap between the hose end and the overflow point of the pipe it goes into. Condensate lines cannot go directly into a sewer or drain line. Any backup within the sewer lines will spill the sewage directly into the condensate tray and cause potential cross-connection problems.

One problem I encountered that was created by a cross-connected heat pump condensate line started out as a complaint about sewer gas entering the house. The owner said that two things had to happen at the same time for the sewer gas smell to permeate the building: Someone had to be taking a shower, and the heat pump had to be on. Indeed, I could smell sewer gas coming out of the floor registers when I simulated these two conditions—it was coming from the duct system. The heat pump condensate line was run through

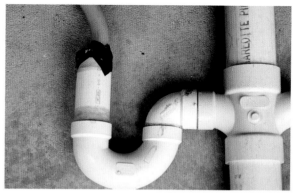

You are not allowed to run a condensate line from a heat pump directly into a sewer or drain line. If the line blocks up, whatever is in the line will back up to the spillover point (the pipe opening just above the trap where the condensate line comes in), which will immerse the opening of the condensate line in the sewage.

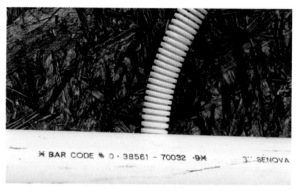

Nor can you drill a hole into the sewer or drain line and insert a condensate line (or any other discharge pipe).

Three lines (one high pressure and two condensate) discharge into a basement floor drain. The only one that is permissible is the copper pipe. The other two, the PVC and the green hose, do not have the required 1-in. gap to the spillover point, which in this case is the top of the floor drain.

This through-the-wall outside hydrant does not have a vacuum breaker and should be listed as an area of concern.

A vacuum breaker can be screwed onto any hydrant or faucet that has a hose-bib connection on its spout.

a small flexible pipe on a long run that went behind the basement furniture, behind the wood pile, and ended up feeding into a PVC P-trap that flowed into a vertical sewer line coming down from the upper floor. The condensate pipe was stuck down into the P-trap, and the opening was taped over. The P-trap had no water in it (the owners never used the air conditioner), so when the shower water displaced the sewer gas in the septic tank, the sewer gas came up the sewer line into the house and was sucked into the heat pump through the dry trap when it turned on.

Outside hose bibs

There are two common outside hose bibs that present potential cross-connection problems: through-the-wall hydrants and yard hydrants. There are other connections, such as those on some water-pressure tanks, boiler drains, and water-heater drains, but these are less commonly used and rarely present a cross-connection problem.

The through-the-wall hydrant is the one you attach an outside hose to when you wash your car, water the garden, or spray insecticides and fertilizers on the lawn. A cross-connection here, along with the absence of any type of backflow preventer, can affect more than a single home. In 1977, an entire town in North Dakota had to ration drinking water brought in from National Guard water trucks while the town's water-distribution system was flushed and disinfected after contamination by DDT. An investigation determined that two residents spraying DDT had made direct cross-connections to their homes. A backflow condition had occurred, sucking the DDT through the home piping systems and out into the town's water-distribution system. This situation is not an exception, almost every town or city has its own horror stories concerning

Freeze Warning with Through-the-Wall Hydrants

Be wary when using and testing through-the-wall outside hydrants—it's possible that you may flood the house. Although the handle is outside, the water actually turns off inside the house, and some water may be left in the copper barrel inside the wall. When installed properly, the water left in the barrel drains to the outside. However, if a hose is left connected to the hydrant, the hydrant cannot drain, resulting in a possible freeze break in the barrel if the weather turns cold.

The water will leak out the break only when the hydrant is turned on. Thus it's possible that you could innocently flood the interior wall or basement the minute you turn on the spigot. To avert this problem, try to feel for a split in the barrel inside the wall. If there's no access to the wall, you obviously can't do this; but if you listen carefully, sometimes you can hear the water spraying out of the break. You should, if possible, ask the homeowner about such a problem before you turn the hose bib on.

Installing a screw-on vacuum breaker on an outside hose bib to prevent backflow can also cause freezing problems. A typical vacuum breaker has a plastic pull-down collar around it. In the down position, the collar seals the water within the hydrant (as it must do to act as a vacuum breaker), and water flows out the end of the hose bib. Once the handle is turned off, however, the water that remains in the barrel does not automatically drain. Left as is, the hydrant will freeze and break in cold climates. To drain the hydrant manually, you need to pull up on the plastic collar to expose the drain slots. (Always make sure the collar is in the down position when you turn the hydrant on or you'll be sprayed with water.)

If the previous user did not release the water from the hydrant, the hydrant barrel could already be ruptured, and you could flood the house, crawl space, or basement when you turn the handle on. The bottom line is that you should always ask the homeowner if he or she knows of a problem with the hose bib before you turn it on; failing that, check for a split inside the wall and listen for the sound of spraying water.

From on to off. When the hydrant is turned off, water remains within the barrel of the hydrant inside the house wall, because the add-on vacuum breaker does not allow it to drain. In cold climates, freezing temperatures cause the water to freeze and split the hydrant. To drain the water still in the hydrant, you must raise the black plastic collar beyond the O-ring seal. Once open, it takes only a few seconds to drain. Pull the collar back down over the O-ring to reseal the vacuum breaker.

cross-connections. When new construction occurs, building inspectors are supposed to make sure that through-the-wall hydrants have built-in vacuum-breaker systems, but this requirement is not always enforced.

The yard hydrant is one of the most commonly ignored cross-connection points. This is the one that has its lower end buried in the ground out next to the barn to supply water to the horses or installed in the garden so long hoses don't have to be run from the house. These hydrants have hose-bib connections just like the through-the-wall hydrants and can contaminate the water supply just as easily; therefore, they are an area of concern.

You can install screw-on vacuum breakers on yard hydrants, but there's still the potential problem with freezing (see the sidebar on the facing page). You can manually drain the hydrant the same way you do the through-the-wall hydrant; however, this is rather awkward to do on a yard hydrant, because you have to wait several minutes for the large amount of water in the vertical hydrant column to drain. If you want, manually reset the vacuum breaker to the closed position. To deal with this problem, manufacturers have developed new yard hydrants that are anti-siphon and drain automatically. Unfortunately, these cost several hundred dollars.

Laundry tub faucet with hose bib

A laundry tub faucet is another hose-bib connection that typically gets overlooked by both city/county inspectors and home inspectors alike. Such a faucet with a large tub underneath can easily become a cross-connection candidate. All the owner has to do is place a short piece of hose on the bib and leave the hose end lying in the bottom of a laundry tub. Whatever is in the tub, from ink dye to toxic chemicals, can very easily be sucked into the water-supply system. Similarly, the owner might attach a long garden hose to the faucet hose bib and start spraying the garden with

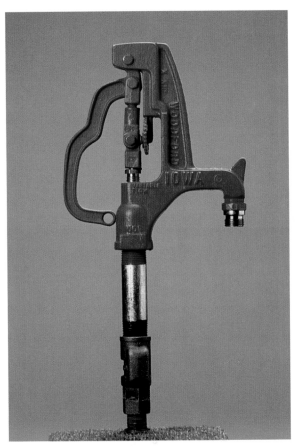

A yard hydrant with hose-bib threads at the spout is a possible cross-connection point. (Photo courtesy Woodford Manufacturing.)

fertilizer or the lawn around the house with pesticides.

Therefore, the laundry tub faucet has the same potential for a cross-connection as a common through-the-wall hydrant. For some reason, codes have never addressed this problem. Laundry tub faucets with hose bibs are not required to have a backflow preventer or check valves on the water-pressure line leading to the tub. When inspecting the house, simply tell the owner of the possible problem that he or she could create.

Laundry Tub Faucet Cross-Connection

Laundry faucet with hose-bib connection →

Short piece of hose →

Dye or toxic chemicals

If a short piece of hose from the laundry faucet is left lying in a batch of dye or toxic chemicals and a backflow condition occurs, the contaminants will be siphoned into the house's water lines.

Bath tubs with fill spout inside the tub

On some old-fashioned bath tubs, the fill spout is located inside the tub. The problem here, of course, is that you do not have the required 1-in. gap between the spout and the overflow water. If the spout can be under water, then it can siphon whatever surrounds it back into the water lines. Because the overflow drain of the tub is below the spout, most people think there's no problem with this setup, but you cannot assume the drain is going to work. Drains have a habit of clogging up and the tub drain, being the lowest, is always the first to start having the sewage back up into it

when the sewer line clogs or the septic system stops draining.

To put this in the proper perspective, no one is saying that you should rip out the tub and replace it. All you are doing is listing an area of concern for the new owners. They need to know that the possibility of a cross-connection exists. It will be up to them to weigh the pros and cons and decide what to do—the same as with a yard hydrant or any other possible cross-connection point.

Dog-wash stations

Because most dog-wash stations are homemade, they invariably don't have a vacuum breaker or a check valve. A dog-wash station is basically a raised platform tub/shower, which makes it much easier to create a cross-connection due to the short distance from tub to shower head. After the dog is sprayed, the shower head is commonly laid back down into the tub of water. The sprayer head lying in the tub of water makes the cross-connection; all is needed now is something to create a backflow. This, of course, can come with a water line break. All the water in the tub, perhaps a toxic flea/tick bath, will flow from the tub directly into the building's water lines. If the house does not have a backflow preventer, the contaminated water could then flow out into the well or city water lines. To prevent this possible problem, suggest a vacuum breaker where the rigid pipe changes to flex pipe.

Water-conditioning systems

The problem with water-conditioning systems is that the high-pressure discharge line that drains away the backwash water cannot be plumbed directly into the house drain lines, which is invariably where inexperienced installers put it. Typically, the installer drills a hole in the sewer line and inserts the discharge hose or sticks the hose deep into a P-trap or deep into a floor drain. As in any other system drain, the possibility of a cross-connection and thus contamination of the drinking water exists if the open end of the high-

The high-pressure discharge pipe for a water conditioner is not allowed to go straight into a trap—it must extend above the trap in such a way that it has a 1-in. gap above the spillover point.

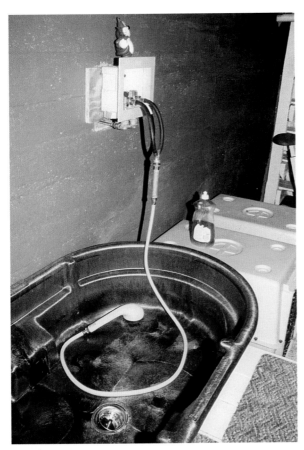

A dog-wash station without a vacuum breaker on the water line is a cross-connection problem waiting to happen.

pressure discharge line can be immersed in any type of drain or sewer water.

There must be a 1-in. gap (minimum) between the end of the discharge pipe and the overflow point. There are several ways to accomplish this. For example, you can insert the discharge pipe into a drainpipe as long as the overflow point of the drainpipe is below the end of the discharge pipe. But you just can't stick the discharge pipe into a trap and let it drain. A good solution is to install a T fitting above the drain trap and then attach a short piece of pipe above that. Clamp the discharge pipe to the short pipe. If the sewage backs up, it will flow out the T and not go up into the discharge pipe (see the photo at right).

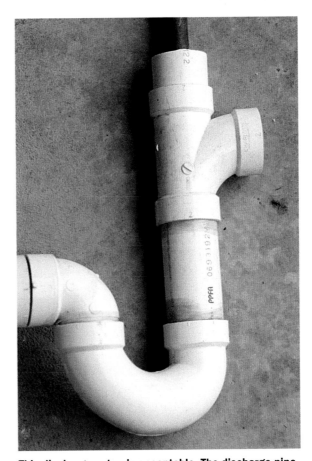

This discharge setup is acceptable. The discharge pipe terminates in the 2-in. drainpipe about 1 in. down. The spillover point is via the T fitting and is 3 in. to 4 in. below the discharge pipe opening.

Spring-fed water source

The idea of having pure spring water fed into a house is an appealing one, but it's not without its potential drawbacks. Springs are relatively easy to contaminate, as a new neighbor of mine and his family discovered a few years ago. The couple's baby had been sick since the day they moved in. The doctor said the problem was the water, and I thought the most likely spot of contamination was at the spring head. The spring appeared to be in good shape, but I found out that the water my neighbors were getting into the house was not coming from the spring.

I verified this by putting a plastic bag over the outgoing water pipe at the spring head. The water flowing into the house did not diminish, which proved that the water flowing into the house was coming from another source. The other source turned out to be a creek that the pipe had to cross

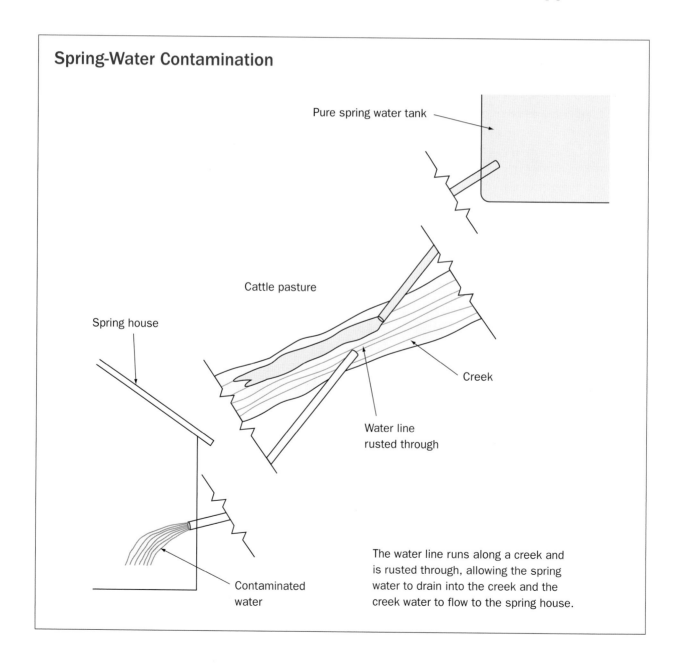

Spring-Water Contamination

Pure spring water tank

Cattle pasture

Spring house

Creek

Water line rusted through

Contaminated water

The water line runs along a creek and is rusted through, allowing the spring water to drain into the creek and the creek water to flow to the spring house.

as it went down the mountain. The pipe had rusted out, and the water flowing into the house was contaminated creek water (the creek was in a cow pasture), not pure spring water. The possibility of contamination is one of the reasons some areas don't allow spring water to be used as potable water.

Well-seal problems

There are a number of potential cross-connection problems with well heads and well seals. One of the most common is when the top of the well casing has been cut off below ground level and buried. The inspector should always write this up as an area of concern, because it is almost impossible to get a good seal in a steel well casing underground. Most well drillers do not cut the last section of casing off with a pipe cutter, which would give a nice clean cut; instead, they use a torch and burn it off. This puts a lot of slag on the inner side of the casing, which the well seal cannot make watertight because of the irregular surface. Thus surface water can seep into the well and cause contamination.

Another potential problem occurs when the well seal is below ground level in a pit. This is an extremely common way for the well water to get contaminated. In areas where the pipes might freeze and there is no room in the house for the pump and water-pressure tank, a concrete tank is typically sunk over the well casing, with the water pump and water-pressure tank sitting immediately next to the casing. The problem here is that sometimes water seeps into the tank through cracks in the walls or via the two overhead lids if surface water flows over the tank, resulting in the top of the casing being covered by water. If the well seal is covered by water, then water invariably gets into the well via the seal or through the air vent.

Hand-held shower sprayers

The problem with hand-held shower sprayers is that the flexible pipe that connects to the sprayer is long enough for the sprayer to be completely immersed in the tub water. If any dyes or chemicals are in the tub (as they might be if the owners were doing some tie-dying or mixing some homemade insecticide), the contaminated water can siphon back into the house. Most commercial hand-held sprayers have vacuum breakers, but most residential ones do not. (They

The well casing for this submersible pump is cut off 3 ft. below ground level. This installation is against code in many areas because of the possibility of water filling the hole and being sucked into the well. The vertical pipe is the well vent. Note the wire splice—it will also be under water as the hole fills.

An area of concern is a hand-held sprayer that can be submerged in the tub water. If the flexible hose connects directly to the shower arm, there is probably no vacuum breaker, creating the possibility of backflow.

A vacuum breaker attached to the shower-head arm prevents contaminated water from siphoning back into the house water lines.

are, however, available and are easily installed.) If no vacuum breaker is on the system, the inspector should write it up as an area of concern.

To determine if the hand-held shower system has a vacuum breaker, look for a small, barrel-like fitting about 1 in. to 1½ in. long that is attached to the chrome shower-head arm coming out of the wall. If the hose is attached directly to the arm itself, it probably does not have one.

Whirlpools with integrated sprayers may or may not have any type of backflow protection. Some come with it, some come without it and get installed that way, others come without it and the backflow protection is installed on site. One of two types of protection can be installed: a

vacuum breaker or a check valve. There is no way of knowing if a check valve is installed on the system—it will be hidden under the skirt. If a vacuum breaker is installed, it should be visible. However, if it is installed on any part of the hose or sprayer head that can be immersed under water, write it up. The vacuum breaker should not be under water. If you can't see any backflow protection, simply write it up as "none visible."

Some lavatory and kitchen faucets come with a pull-out sprayer on a hose that is long enough to be immersed in the sink basin. These normally have some type of vacuum breaker or check valve built into the purchased assembly, so there is rarely anything to write up here.

Index